D1240963

Japanese Sentence Patterns for
Effective Communication

Japanese Sentence Patterns for Effective Communication

A Self-Study Course and Reference

Taeko Kamiya

KODANSHA USA

Published by Kodansha USA Publishing, LLC
451 Park Avenue South, New York, NY 10016

Distributed in the United Kingdom and continental Europe
by Kodansha Europe Ltd.

First published in Japan in 2005 by Kodansha International
First US edition 2012 by Kodansha USA,
an imprint of Kodansha USA Publishing, LLC

25 24 23 22 21 20   10 9 8 7 6 5

The Library of the Congress has cataloged the earlier printing as follows:
Library of Congress Cataloging-in-Publication Data

Kamiya, Taeko
   Japanese sentence patterns for effective communication : a self-study
      course and reference / Taeko Kamiya.
   p. cm.
   Includes index.
   ISBN-13: 978-4-7700-2983-6 (pbk.)
   ISBN-10: 4-7700-2983-7 (pbk.)
   1. Japanese language--Conversation and phrase books--English.
PL539.K25 2006
495.6'83421--dc22
                        2005050427

kodanshausa.com

CONTENTS

PREFACE

As a student of Japanese, aren't there times when you stop and think, or ask yourself, "How can I say this?" or "What is the proper way to put that in Japanese?" You might want to say, "My brother is a pilot" or "I went shopping with a friend," or you might want to ask a question like "What time will the party start?" or "May I borrow your dictionary?" You might have learned how to say these things in Japanese before, but have forgotten; or, being a total beginner, maybe you have never learned them at all, but wish to. In any case, this book will help you to express yourself in Japanese.

This volume contains 142 basic expressions, or sentence patterns, that are divided into twelve chapters according to their linguistic function. Chapter 1, for instance, presents some expressions used to identify and describe people and things; Chapter 7 gives expressions related to making requests and suggestions; and Chapter 11 deals with conditional, passive, causative, and causative-passive forms.

The basic expressions appear in English and represent ideas or patterns to be expressed in Japanese. They are numbered and arranged from easiest to most difficult. Each has a Japanese translation with key words in bold type, highlighting the pattern to be learned. The pattern is then explained and illustrated with example sentences. Finally, a practice section is given for every pattern, to allow you to speak Japanese and test your understanding of the material introduced.

You can use this book to refresh your knowledge of what you have learned in the past, or to acquaint yourself with new expressions. Or you can use it as an introductory textbook if you are studying on your own. The list of basic expressions following the table of contents is meant to help you quickly locate expressions listed in the book, but you can also use it as a learning tool. That is, by covering the Japanese or English half, you can practice repeating the equivalent sentences.

I hope this book will prove helpful and satisfy your needs, whatever they may be. I wish to thank my editors at Kodansha International, Michael Staley and Shigeyoshi Suzuki, for making its publication possible.

Taeko Kamiya

Pacific Grove, CA
2005

List of Basic Expressions

1 Identifying and Describing People and Things

1 (a) (As for myself,) I am John Harris. (INTRO-
       DUCING ONESELF)

   (b) I am (the one whose name is) John Har-
       ris.

2   Mr. Oda is a teacher of Japanese.

3 (a) This is my dictionary.

   (b) This dictionary is mine.

4 (a) Is Ms. Takagi a lawyer?

   (b) Is this Japanese or Chinese?

5 (a) Who is that person?

   (b) What is that?

(a) 私はジョン・ハリスだ / です。
Watashi wa Jon Harisu da / desu.

(b) 私がジョン・ハリスだ / です。
Watashi ga Jon Harisu da / desu.

小田さんは日本語の先生だ / です。
Oda-san wa Nihongo no sensei da / desu.

(a) これは私の辞書だ / です。
Kore wa watashi no jisho da / desu.

(b) この辞書は私のだ / です。
Kono jisho wa watashi no da / desu.

(a) 高木さんは弁護士ですか。
Takagi-san wa bengoshi desu ka.

(b) これは日本語ですか、中国語ですか。
Kore wa Nihongo desu ka, Chūgokugo desu ka.

(a) あの人はだれですか。
Ano hito wa dare desu ka.

(b) あれは何ですか。
Are wa nan desu ka.

私は銀行員ではない / ではありません。
Watashi wa ginkōin de wa nai / de wa arimasen.

(a) 私の父は医者だ / です。
Watashi no chichi wa isha da / desu.

(b) 佐田さんのお父さんも医者だ / です。
Sada-san no o-tō-san mo isha da / desu.

小川さんも槇さんも私の友達だ / です。
Ogawa-san mo Maki-san mo watashi no tomodachi da / desu.

ロスさんは英語の先生だった / でした。
Rosu-san wa Eigo no sensei datta / deshita.

ディナーはフランス料理ではなかった / ではありませんでした。
Dinā wa Furansu ryōri de wa nakatta / de wa arimasen deshita.

(a) いいワインだ / ですね。
Ii wain da / desu ne.

(b) きれいな絵だ / ですね。
Kireina e da / desu ne.

(a) この車は新しい / 新しいです。
Kono kuruma wa atarashii / atarashii desu.

(b) あの画家は有名だ / 有名です。
Ano gaka wa yūmei da / yūmei desu.

(a) このパイはおいしくない / おいしくありません。
Kono pai wa oishiku nai / oishiku arimasen.

(b) その書類は必要ではない / 必要ではありません。
Sono shorui wa hitsuyō de wa nai / hitsuyō de wa arimasen.

P. 28

14 (a) The picnic was fun.

(b) The banquet was gorgeous.

P. 29

15 (a) The lecture was not long.

(b) He wasn't honest.

P. 31

16 This is an apartment and that is a hotel.

P. 33

17 (a) This coat is soft and light.

(b) The clerk is kind and polite.

P. 35

18 (a) This steak is delicious and, what's more, it's inexpensive.

(b) The room is clean and, what's more, it's sunny.

P. 36

19 Rabbits have red eyes.

P. 38

20 (a) Exams are sometimes difficult and sometimes easy.

(b) This street is sometimes quiet and sometimes lively.

(a) ピクニックは楽しかった / 楽しかったです。
Pikunikku wa tanoshikatta / tanoshikatta desu.

(b) 宴会は豪華だった / 豪華でした。
Enkai wa gōka datta / gōka deshita.

(a) 講義は長くなかった / 長くありませんでした。
Kōgi wa nagaku nakatta / nagaku arimasen deshita.

(b) あの人は正直ではなかった / 正直ではありませんでした。
Ano hito wa shōjiki de wa nakatta / shōjiki de wa arimasen deshita.

これはアパートで、それはホテルだ / です。
Kore wa apāto de, sore wa hoteru da / desu.

(a) このコートは柔らかくて軽い / 軽いです。
Kono kōto wa yawarakakute karui / karui desu.

(b) 店員は親切で丁寧だ / 丁寧です。
Ten'in wa shinsetsu de teinei da / teinei desu.

(a) このステーキはおいしいし、安い / 安いです。
Kono sutēki wa oishii shi, yasui / yasui desu.

(b) 部屋は清潔だし、明るい / 明るいです。
Heya wa seiketsu da shi, akarui / akarui desu.

うさぎは目が赤い / 赤いです。
Usagi wa me ga akai / akai desu.

(a) 試験は難しかったり、やさしかったりする / します。
Shiken wa muzukashikattari, yasashikattari suru / shimasu.

(b) この通りは静かだったり、にぎやかだったりする / します。
Kono tōri wa shizuka dattari, nigiyaka dattari suru / shimasu.

2 Describing the Existence of Animate and Inanimate Things

P. 40

21 (a) There is a TV set.

(b) There are boys.

P. 42

22 (a) There isn't any food.

(b) There is no interpreter.

P. 44

23 (a) There was an earthquake.

(b) There was a black bear.

P. 45

24 (a) There was no shortcut.

(b) There were no passengers.

P. 47

25 (a) There are stamps and envelopes.

(b) There are cameramen and reporters (and others).

P. 48

26 (a) There are lots of apples.

(a) テレビがある / あります。
Terebi ga aru / arimasu.

(b) 男の子がいる / います。
Otoko no ko ga iru / imasu.

(a) 食べ物が / はない / ありません。
Tabemono ga / wa nai / arimasen.

(b) 通訳が / はいない / いません。
Tsūyaku ga / wa iniai / imasen.

(a) 地震があった / ありました。
Jishin ga atta / arimashita.

(b) 黒い熊がいた / いました。
Kuroi kuma ga ita / imashita.

(a) 近道が / はなかった / ありませんでした。
Chikamichi ga / wa nakatta / arimasen deshita.

(b) 乗客が / はいなかった / いませんでした。
Jōkyaku ga / wa inakatta / imasen deshita.

(a) 切手と封筒がある / あります。
Kitte to fūtō ga aru / arimasu.

(b) カメラマンやレポーターがいる / います。
Kameraman ya repōtā ga iru / imasu.

(a) りんごがたくさんある / あります。
Ringo ga takusan aru / arimasu.

(b) There are five actors.

P. 50

27 (a) There is a bookcase in this room.

(b) There are boys under the tree.

P. 53

28 (a) What is on the desk?

(b) Who is in the reception room?

P. 55

29 (a) How many books are there?

(b) How many foreign students are there?

P. 58

30 (a) Is anything there?

No, there is nothing.

(b) Is anybody there?

No, there is nobody.

P. 60

31 (a) The document is on the table.

(b) The section chief is in the president's room.

(b) 俳優が5人いる / います。
Haiyū ga go-nin iru / imasu.

(a) この部屋に本箱がある / あります。
Kono heya ni honbako ga aru / arimasu.

(b) 木の下に男の子がいる / います。
Ki no shita ni otoko no ko ga iru / imasu.

(a) 机の上に何がありますか。
Tsukue no ue ni nani ga arimasu ka.

(b) 応接室にだれがいますか。
Ōsetsushitsu ni dare ga imasu ka.

(a) 本は何冊ありますか。
Hon wa nan-satsu arimasu ka.

(b) 留学生は何人いますか。
Ryūgakusei wa nan-nin imasu ka.

(a) 何かありますか。
Nani ka arimasu ka.

いいえ、何もありせん。
Iie, nani mo arimasen.

(b) だれかいますか。
Dare ka imasu ka.

いいえ、だれもいません。
Iie, dare mo imasen.

(a) 書類は机の上にある / あります。
Shorui wa tsukue no ue ni aru / arimasu.

(b) 課長は社長の部屋にいる / います。
Kachō wa shachō no heya ni iru / imasu.

3 Making Comparisons

(a) エレベーターはどこにありますか。
Erebētā wa doko ni arimasu ka.

(b) 木村さんはどこにいますか。
Kimura-san wa doko ni imasu ka.

(a) 本田さんには白髪がある / あります。
Honda-san ni wa shiraga ga aru / arimasu.

(b) リンダ (さん) には子供がある / いる / あります / います。
Rinda(-san) ni wa kodomo ga aru / iru / arimasu / imasu.

今日のほうが昨日より寒い / 寒いです。
Kyō no hō ga kinō yori samui / samui desu.

富士山は日本で一番美しい山だ / です。
Fuji-san wa Nihon de ichiban utsukushii yama da / desu.

このパイとそのパイと、どちらが甘いですか。
Kono pai to sono pai to, dochira ga amai desu ka.

そのパイのほうが甘いですよ。
Sono pai no hō ga amai desu yo.

この3つの中で、どれが一番丈夫ですか。
Kono mittsu no naka de, dore ga ichiban jōbu desu ka.

この赤いのが一番丈夫でしょう。
Kono akai no ga ichiban jōbu deshō.

4 Describing Actions in the Present, Future, and Past

この画家はピカソ (と同じ) くらい有名だ / 有名です。
Kono gaka wa Pikaso (to onaji) kurai yūmei da / yūmei desu.

このかばんはそのかばんほど重くない / 重くありません。
Kono kaban wa sono kaban hodo omoku nai / omoku arimasen.

彼は毎朝6時に起きる / 起きます。
Kare wa maiasa roku-ji ni okiru / okimasu.

食堂で朝ご飯を食べる / 食べます。
Shokudō de asagohan o taberu / tabemasu.

酒井さんはコーヒーは飲まない / 飲みません。
Sakai-san wa kōhī wa nomanai / nomimasen.

チャールズ (さん) は毎日自転車で学校へ / に来る / 来ます。
Chāruzu(-san) wa mainichi jitensha de gakkō e / ni kuru / kimasu.

朝8時に家を出る / 出ます。
Asa hachi-ji ni uchi o deru / demasu.

ジョン (さん) は日本の会社に入る / 入ります。
Jon(-san) wa Nihon no kaisha ni hairu / hairimasu.

今出掛けるところだ / です。
Ima dekakeru tokoro da / desu.

先月友達と旅行した / 旅行しました。
Sengetsu tomodachi to ryokō shita / ryokō shimashita.

(a) パーティーは7時から始まった / 始まりました。
Pātī wa shichi-ji kara hajimatta / hajimarimashita.

(b) 動物園まで歩いた / 歩きました。
Dōbutsuen made aruita / arukimashita.

父は今起きたところだ / です。
Chichi wa ima okita tokoro da / desu.

その子は電気をつけたまま寝る / 寝ます。
Sono ko wa denki o tsuketa mama neru / nemasu.

音楽を聞きながら勉強する / 勉強します。
Ongaku o kikinagara benkyō suru / benkyō shimasu.

桜の花は3月に咲き始める / 咲き始めます。
Sakura no hana wa san-gatsu ni sakihajimeru / saki hajimemasu.

彼はもうすぐ論文を書き終わる / 書き終わります。
Kare wa mō sugu ronbun o kakiowaru / kakiowarimasu.

今朝、朝ご飯を食べなかった / 食べませんでした。
Kesa, asagohan o tabenakatta / tabemasen deshita.

昨日は公園へ行った / 行きましたが、今日は行かなかった / 行きませんでした。
Kinō wa kōen e itta / ikimashita ga, kyō wa ikanakatta / ikimasen deshita.

5 Actions: in Progress, Completed, Successive, Simultaneous, and Miscellaneous

今、朝ご飯を食べている / 食べています。
Ima, asagohan o tabete iru / tabete imasu.

鳥が空を飛んでいる / 飛んでいます。
Tori ga sora o tonde iru / imasu.

子供達はテレビを見てばかりいる / 見てばかりいます。
Kodomo-tachi wa terebi o mite bakari iru / mite bakari imasu.

両親はボストンに住んでいる / 住んでいます。
Ryōshin wa Bosuton ni sunde iru / sunde imasu.

会議室のドアが開いている / 開いています。
Kaigishitsu no doa ga aite iru / aite imasu.

廊下の電気がつけてある / つけてあります。
Rōka no denki ga tsukete aru / tsukete arimasu.

明日のピクニックのために飲み物を買っておいた / 買っておきました。
Ashita no pikunikku no tame ni nomimono o katte oita / katte oki-mashita.

私達はもうプロジェクトを仕上げてしまった / 仕上げてしまいました。
Watashi-tachi wa mō purojekuto o shiagete shimatta / shiagete shi-maimashita.

初めて刺身を食べてみた / 食べてみました。
Hajimete sashimi o tabete mita / tabete mimashita.

犬が走っていく / 走っていきます。
Inu ga hashitte iku / hashitte ikimasu.

空が晴れてきた / 晴れてきました。
Sora ga harete kita / harete kimashita.

彼はコーヒーを飲んで8時前に家を出る / 出ます。
Kare wa kōhī o nonde hachi-ji mae ni uchi o deru / demasu.

晩ご飯を食べてから散歩した / 散歩しました。
Bangohan o tabete kara sanpo shita / sanpo shimashita.

彼はいつも寝る前にシャワーを浴びる / 浴びます。
Kare wa itsumo neru mae ni shawā o abiru / abimasu.

彼女は新聞を読む時(に)めがねをかける / かけます。
Kanojo wa shinbun o yomu toki (ni) megane o kakeru / kakemasu.

野田さんが来た時 (に) 私は手紙を書いていた / 書いていました。
Noda-san ga kita toki (ni) watashi wa tegami o kaite ita / kaite imashita.

私が友達と話している間子供は外で遊んでいた / 遊んでいました。
Watashi ga tomodachi to hanashite iru aida kodomo wa soto de asonde ita / iasonde mashita.

6   Stating Purpose, Cause, and Reason

彼が来るまでロビーで雑誌を読んでいた / 読んでいました。
Kare ga kuru made robī de zasshi o yonde ita / yonde imashita.

プロジェクトが完成するまでに二か月かかる / かかります。
Purojekuto ga kansei suru made ni nikagetsu kakaru / kakarimasu.

私達は湖でモーターボートに乗ったり、魚を釣ったりする /
します。
*Watachi-tachi wa mizuumi de mōtābōto ni nottari, sakana o tsuttari
suru / shimasu.*

彼は英語を教えるばかりでなく小説も書く / 書きます。
*Kare wa Eigo o oshieru bakari de naku shōsetsu mo kaku / kaki-
masu.*

図書館へ本を返しに行った / 行きました。
Toshokan e hon o kaeshi ni itta / ikimashita.

森田さんは会社に行くのに地下鉄を使っている/使っています。
*Morita-san wa kaisha ni iku noni chikatetsu o tsukatte iru / tsu-
katte imasu.*

彼は旅行するためにアルバイトしている / アルバイトしています。
Kare wa ryōko suru tame ni arubaito shite iru / arubaito shite imasu.

7   Commands, Requests, Suggestions, Approval, Disapproval, Prohibition, and Obligation

雪で列車が止まった / 止まりました。
Yuki de ressha ga tomatta / tomarimashita.

熱が下がるように薬を飲む / 飲みます。
Netsu ga sagaru yō ni kusuri o nomu / nomimasu.

(a) 彼が釣りに行くから、私も行く / 行きます。
Kare ga tsuri ni iku kara, watashi mo iku / ikimasu.

(b) 食べすぎたから / ので眠くなった / 眠くなりました。
Tabesugita kara / node, nemuku natta / nemuku narimashita.

(a) 水が冷たいから / ので泳がない / 泳ぎません。
Mizu ga tsumetai kara oyoganai / oyogimasen.

(b) 花がきれいだったから / ので写真を撮った / 撮りました。
Hana ga kirei datta kara / node shashin o totta / torimashita.

どうして / なぜパーティーに行かないのですか。
Dōshite / naze pāti ni ikanai no desu ka.

明日試験があるのです。
Ashita shiken ga aru no desu.

もっと練習しなさい。
Motto renshū shinasai.

どうぞこちらでお待ちください。
Dōzo kochira de o-machi kudasai.

ドアを閉めてください。
Doa o shimete kudasai.

この通りに車を止めないでください。
Kono tōri ni kuruma o tomenai de kudasai.

辞書を貸してくださいませんか。
Jisho o kashite kudasaimasen ka.

ここに雑誌を置かないでくださいませんか。
Koko ni zasshi o okanai de kudasaimasen ka.

竹田さんに来る / 来ないように言ってください。
Takeda-san ni kuru / konai yō ni itte kudasi.

パレードを見に行こう / 行きましょう。
Parēdo o mi ni ikō / ikimashō.

新しい車は買わないでおこう / 買わないでおきましょう。
Atarashii kuruma wa kawanai de okō / kawanai de okimashō.

サンドイッチでも食べようか / 食べましょうか。
Sandoitchi demo tabeyō ka / tabemashō ka.

先生に聞いたらどう？
Sensei ni kiitara dō?

P. 170

96   You had better eat more vegetables.

P. 171

97   You had better not drink too much coffee.

P. 173

98 (a) It is all right if you write in pencil.

      (b) It is all right if the price is high.

P. 175

99   You must not watch TV in this room.

P. 176

100 (a) I have to get up early every morning.

      (b) The office must be spacious.

      (c) Schools must be safe.

P. 178

101 (a) I don't have to do homework tonight.

      (b) The report doesn't have to be detailed.

      (c) The ceremony doesn't have to be gorgeous.

もっと野菜を食べたほうがいい / いいです。
Motto yasai o tabeta hō ga ii / ii desu.

コーヒーを飲みすぎないほうがいい / いいです。
Kōhī o nomisuginai hō ga ii / ii desu.

(a) 鉛筆で書いてもいい / いいです。
Enpitsu de kaite mo ii / ii desu.

(b) 値段は高くてもいい / いいです。
Nedan wa takaute mo ii / ii desu.

この部屋でテレビを見てはいけない / いけません。
Kono heya de terebi o mite wa ikenai / ikemasen.

(a) 毎朝早く起きなければならない / なりません。
Maiasa hayaku okinakereba naranai / narimasn.

(b) オフィスは広くなければならない / なりません。
Ofisu wa hiroku nakereba naranai / narimasen.

(c) 学校は安全でなければならない / なりません。
Gakkō wa anzen de nakereba naranai / narimasen.

(a) 今晩宿題をしなくてもいい / いいです。
Konban shukudai o shinakute mo ii / ii desu.

(b) レポートは詳しくなくてもいい / いいです。
Repōto wa kuwashiku nakute mo ii / ii desu.

(c) 式は豪華でなくてもいい / いいです。
Shiki wa gōka de nakute mo ii / ii desu.

8 Expressing Ability, Preference, Desire, Intention, Resolution, and Experience

P. 181

102   Mr. Hill can speak Chinese.

P. 183

103   I have reached the point where I can read kanji.

P. 185

104 (a) I can see a lake in the distance. (IMPLYING: A lake can be seen in the distance.)

(b) I can hear music. (IMPLYING: Music can be heard.)

P. 187

105 (a) Mr. Harris is good at golf.

(b) Jim is good at memorizing words.

P. 189

106 (a) Ken likes jazz.

(b) Bill doesn't like to listen to music.

P. 191

107 (a) I want a stereo.

(b) My son wants a bicycle.

ヒルさんは中国語を話すことができる / できます。
Hiru-san wa Chūgokugo o hanasu koto ga dekiru / dekimasu.

漢字が読めるようになった / なりました。
Kanji ga yomeru yō ni natta / narimashita.

(a) 遠くに湖が見える / 見えます。
Tōku ni mizuumi ga mieru / miemasu.

(b) 音楽が聞こえる / 聞こえます。
Ongaku ga kikoeru / kikoemasu.

(a) ハリスさんはゴルフが上手だ / 上手です。
Harisu-san wa gorufu ga jōzu da / jōzu desu.

(b) ジム (さん) は言葉を覚えるのが早い / 早いです。
Jimu(-san) wa kotoba o oboeru no ga hayai / hayai desu.

(a) ケン (さん) はジャズが好きだ / 好きです。
Ken(-san) wa jazu ga suki da / suki desu.

(b) ビル (さん) は音楽を聞くのが嫌いだ / 嫌いです。
Biru(-san) wa ongaku o kiku no ga kirai da / kirai desu.

(a) 私はステレオが欲しい / 欲しいです。
Watashi wa sutereo ga hoshii / hoshii desu.

(b) 息子は自転車を欲しがっている / 欲しがっています。
Musuko wa jitensha o hoshigatte iru / hoshigatte imasu.

P. 192

108   I want him to write the report.

P. 194

109 (a) I want to eat a steak now.

(b) My wife wants to go to the opera.

P. 196

110   He intends to become a doctor.

P. 197

111   I think I'll teach English to Japanese students.

P. 199

112   I decided to work in Japan.

P. 200

113   It will be arranged that Mr. Oda will take charge of the project.

P. 202

114   There are times when I do homework in the train.

P. 204

115   I have been to China.

私は彼にレポートを書いてほしい / 書いてほしいです。
Watashi wa kare ni repōto o kaite hoshii / kaite hoshii desu.

(a) 私は今ステーキを / が食べたい / 食べたいです。
Watashi wa ima sutēki o / ga tabetai / tabetai desu.

(b) 家内はオペラに行きたがっている / 行きたがっています。
Kanai wa opera ni ikitagatte iru / ikitagatte imasu.

彼は医者になるつもりだ / です。
Kare wa isha ni naru tsumori da / desu.

日本の学生に英語を教えようと思う / 思います。
Nihon no gakusei ni Eigo o oshieyō to omou / omoimasu.

私は日本で働くことにした / しました。
Watashi wa Nihon de hataraku koto ni shita / shimashita.

小田さんがプロジェクトを担当することになる / なります。
Oda-san ga purojekuto o tantō suru koto ni naru / narimasu.

電車の中で宿題をすることがある / あります。
Densha no naka de shukudai o suru koto ga aru / arimasu.

私は中国へ行ったことがある / あります。
Watashi wa Chūgoku e itta koto ga aru / arimasu.

9 Describing the Actions of Giving and Receiving

10 Expressing Conjecture and Hearsay, and Quoting People

私は幸子 (さん) にプレゼントをあげる / あげます。
Watashi wa Sachiko(-san) ni purezento o ageru / agemasu.

私は時々リタさんに辞書を貸してあげる / 貸してあげます。
Watashi wa tokidoki Rita-san ni jisho o kashite ageru / kashite age-masu.

私は友達に / から葉書をもらった / もらいました。
Watashi wa tomodachi ni / kara hagaki o moratta / moraimashita.

原さんにゴルフを教えてもらう / 教えてもらいます。
Hara-san ni gorufu o oshiete morau / oshiete moraimasu.

母が (私に) この指輪をくれた / くれました。
Haha ga (watashi ni) kono yubiwa o kureta / kuremashita.

久保さんが (私達に) すき焼きを作ってくれた / 作ってくれました。
Kubo-san ga (watashi-tachi ni) sukiyaki o tsukutte kureta / tsukutte kuremashita.

(a) ジョンソンさんは今日来るだろう / でしょう。
Jonson-san wa kyō kuru darō / deshō.

(b) あのホテルは高いだろう / でしょう。
Ano hoteru wa takai darō / deshō.

(c) ベン (さん) はダンスが上手だろう / でしょう。
Ben(-san) wa dansu ga jōzu darō / deshō.

P. 219

123 (a) It might rain tomorrow.

(b) The movie might be boring.

(c) He might be bad at singing.

P. 221

124 (a) There is no doubt that he will succeed.

(b) This watch must be expensive.

(c) The ceremony must have been gorgeous.

P. 223

125 (a) Sales will increase, I'm sure.

(b) I'm quite sure that the meeting was short.

(c) That inn is sure to be quiet.

P. 225

126 (a) It looks like it will snow.

(b) This cake looks delicious.

(c) That child looks healthy.

(a) 明日雨が降るかもしれない / かもしれません。
Ashita ame ga furu kamoshirenai / kamoshiremasen.

(b) 映画はつまらないかもしれない / かもしれません。
Eiga wa tsumaranai kamoshirenai / kamoshiremasen.

(c) 彼は歌が下手かもしれない / かもしれません。
Kare wa uta ga heta kamoshirenai / kamoshiremasen.

(a) 彼は成功するに違いない / 違いありません。
Kare wa seikō suru ni chigainai / chigaiarimasen.

(b) この時計は高いに違いない / 違いありません。
Kono tokei wa takai ni chigainai / chigaiarimasen.

(c) 式は豪華だったに違いない / 違いありません。
Shiki wa gōka datta ni chigainai / chigaiarimasen.

(a) 売り上げは増えるはずだ / です。
Uriage wa fueru hazu da / desu.

(b) 会議は短かったはずだ / です。
Kaigi wa mijikakatta hazu da / desu.

(c) あの旅館は静かなはずだ / です。
Ano ryokan wa shizukana hazu da / desu.

(a) 雪が降りそうだ / そうです。
Yuki ga furi sō da / sō desu.

(b) このケーキはおいしそうだ / そうです。
Kono kēki wa oishi sō da / sō desu.

(c) あの子は元気そうだ / そうです。
Ano ko wa genki sō da / sō desu.

127 (a) It seems that Mr. Ross will return to America.

(b) It seems that the game was boring.

(c) That singer seems to be famous.

128 (a) It seems that a house will be built over there.

(b) Mr. Ono's illness seems to be serious.

(c) It seems that the negotiations were difficult.

129 I heard that there was a fire in Ginza.

130 (a) Helen said, "I'll come at 9 o'clock."

(b) Sam said that his trip was enjoyable.

11 Using Conditional, Passive, Causative, and Causative-Passive Forms

131 (a) When spring comes, the flowers bloom.

(a) ロスさんはアメリカに帰るらしい / らしいです。
   Rosu-san wa Amerika ni kaeru rashii / rashii desu.

(b) 試合はつまらなかったらしい / らしいです。
   Shiai wa tsumaranakatta rashii / rashii desu.

(c) あの歌手は有名らしい / らしいです。
   Ano kashu wa yūmei rashii / rashii desu.

(a) あそこに家が建つようだ / ようです。
   Asoko ni uchi ga tatsu yō da / yō desu.

(b) 小野さんの病気は重いようだ / ようです。
   Ono-san no byōki wa omoi yō da / yō desu.

(c) 交渉は困難だったようだ / ようです。
   Kōshō wa kannan datta yo da / yō desu.

銀座で火事があったそうだ / そうです。
Ginza de kaji ga atta sō da / sō desu.

(a) ヘレンは (さん)「9時に来ます」と言った / 言いました。
   Heren(-san) wa "Ku-ji ni kimasu" to itta / iimashita.

(b) サム (さん) は旅行は楽しかったと言った / 言いました。
   Samu(-san) wa ryokō wa tanoshikatta to itta / iimashita.

(a) 春が来ると、花が咲く / 咲きます。
   Haru ga kuru to, hana ga saku / sakimasu.

(b) If the walls are white, the room will be bright.

(c) If you are bad at Japanese, you can't work here.

P. 237

132 (a) If you exercise regularly, you'll get thin.

(b) If it is cheaper, I intend to buy it.

(c) If the waves are calm, let's (go for a) swim.

P. 240

133 (a) If you are going to buy stocks, now is a good time.

(b) If it's that interesting, let's go to see it.

(c) If you like Japanese food, I'll cook some for you.

P. 242

134 (a) He plays golf even if it rains.

(b) I want to continue studying even if it is difficult.

(c) Even though she is rich, she doesn't spend money.

(b) 壁が白いと、部屋が明るい / 明るいです。
Kabe ga shiroi to, heya ga akarui / akarui desu.

(c) 日本語が下手だと、ここでは働けない / 働けません。
Nihongo ga heta da to, koko de wa hatarakenai / hatarakemasen.

(a) きちんと運動すれば / 運動したらやせる / やせます。
Kichin to undō sureba / undō shitara yaseru / yasemasu yo.

(b) もっと安ければ / 安かったら買うつもりだ / です。
Motto yasukereba / yasukattara kau tsumori da / desu.

(c) 波が静かなら（ば）/ 静かだったら泳ごう / 泳ぎましょう。
Nami ga shizuka nara(ba) / shizuka dattara oyogō / oyogimashō.

(a) 株を買う（の）なら、今がいい時期だ / です。
Kabu o kau (no) nara, ima ga ii jiki da / desu.

(b) そんなにおもしろい（の）なら、見に行こう / 行きましょう。
Sonna ni omoshiroi (no) nara, mi ni ikō / ikimashō.

(c) 日本食が好きなら、作ってあげる / 作ってあげます。
Nihonshoku ga suki nara, tsukutte ageru / tsukutte agemasu.

(a) 彼は雨が降ってもゴルフをする / します。
Kare wa ame ga futte mo gorufu o suru / shimasu.

(b) 難しくても勉強を続けたい / 続けたいです。
Muzukashikute mo benkyō o tsuzuketai / tsuzuketai desu.

(c) 彼女は裕福でも、お金を使わない / 使いません。
Kanojo wa yūfuku demo, o-kane o tsukawanai / tsukaimasen.

12   Making Relative Clauses

私はセールスマンにだまされた / だまされました。
Watashi wa sērusuman ni damasareta / damasaremashita.

勝は泥棒に自転車を盗まれた / 盗まれました。
Masaru wa dorobō ni jitensha o nusumareta / nusumaremashita.

私は友達に夜遅く家に来られた / 来られました。
Watashi wa tomodachi ni yoru osoku uchi ni korareta / korare-mashita.

佐々木さんは私にレポートを書かせた / 書かせました。
Sasaki-san wa watashi ni repōto o kakaseta / kakasemashita.

私は父に駅まで歩かせられた / 歩かせられました。
Watashi wa chichi ni eki made arukaserareta / arukaseraremashita.

先生と話している学生はジョン・ミラーさんだ / です。
Sensei to hanashite iru gakusei wa Jon Mirā-san da / desu.

彼が / の書く小説はいつもよく売れる / 売れます。
Kare ga / no kaku shōsetsu wa itsumo yoku ureru / uremasu.

高かったコンピューターが安くなった / 安くなりました。
Takakatta konypūtā ga yasuku natta / yasuku narimashita.

1

Identifying and Describing People and Things

1

(a) (As for myself,) I am John Harris. (INTRODUCING ONE-SELF)

(b) I am (the one whose name is) John Harris.

(a) 私はジョン・ハリスだ / です。
*Watashi **wa** Jon Harisu **da** / **desu**.*

(b) 私がジョン・ハリスだ / です。
*Watashi **ga** Jon Harisu **da** / **desu**.*

In the Japanese sentence (a) above, *watashi* ("I") is followed by the particle *wa* ("as for"), which marks it as the topic of the sentence, while in (b) it is followed by the particle *ga*, which marks it as the subject of the sentence. The "topic," usually coming at the beginning of the sentence, establishes what the sentence is about. It must be someone or something that both the speaker and the listener can see or hear, or identify from previous conversation or shared knowledge. The "subject," on the other hand, is the doer of the action or the person or thing in the state expressed by the sentence. It must be someone or something that is newly introduced into the conversation or discourse, or is emphasized.

"I am John Harris" is an equally good translation for both Japanese sentences (a) and (b). However, the meaning of the sentence is different depending on which particle follows *watashi*. The sentence with *wa* is not emphatic; the one with *ga* is. Thus, *wa* would be used if John was introducing himself to someone, while *ga* would be more appropriate if he was answering the question "Who is John Harris?" or was otherwise stating with emphasis that he, as opposed to anyone else, was John Harris.

(The difference between, and usage of, *wa* and *ga* is complicated. Sometimes the topic and subject are the same, as in (a), where no emphasis is involved; often a sentence has both a topic and a subject (→ Pattern 19), in which case the two have distinct functions; and in certain cases the subject is not marked by *ga*, but by *wa*. These points will be dealt with later on.)

Personal pronouns ("I," "you," etc.) in Japanese have a variety of forms, and the speaker selects which to use depending on his/her gender and desired speech style (formal, plain, rough, etc.) The following chart shows the most commonly used first- and second-person (singular) pronouns.

	first person ("I")	second person ("you")
very formal	私 *watakushi*	———
polite	私 / わたし *watashi*	あなた *anata*
plain	僕 *boku* (used by men)	君 *kimi* (used by men)
rough	おれ *ore* (used by men)	お前 *omae* (used by men)

The third-person (singular) pronouns are *kare* ("he") and *kanojo* ("she"). These may be used in almost any situation, formal or informal, but they should not be used in reference to social superiors or young children. *Ano hito* ("that person") is another pronoun that can be used to mean "he" or "she," but it sometimes carries a negative nuance.

For the plural forms of personal pronouns, add the suffix -*tachi* or -*ra*: *watashi-tachi* (or *watashira*), *boku-tachi* (or *bukura*), *kimi-tachi* (or *kimira*), *karera* (or, less frequently, *kare-tachi*), *kanojo-tachi* (or *kanojora*), etc. In the case of *anata*, the suffix -*gata* may be used instead of -*tachi* for politeness: *anata-gata*. The suffixes -*tachi* and -*gata* may also be added to certain nouns: *gakusei-tachi* ("students"), *sensei-gata* ("teachers"), etc., although in most cases a suffix is not required to make a noun plural in Japanese.

The copula *da* or *desu* at the end of a sentence is equivalent to the English "am," "is," or "are." *Da* is an example of the plain style of speech used among family and friends, while *desu* is polite and is used among adults who are not close friends.

Examples

1. I am an American.
   私はアメリカ人です。
   Watashi wa Amerikajin desu.

2. She is a nurse.
   彼女は看護師だ。
   Kanojo wa kangoshi da.

3. Tom is a student.
   トムは学生です。
   Tomu wa gakusei desu.

4. He (newly introduced) is the person in charge.
   あの人が担当者です。
   Ano hito ga tantōsha desu.

5. Sarah (not Linda) is a dietician.
   サラが栄養士だ。
   Sara ga eiyōshi da.

Practice

singer	歌手	*kashu*
engineer	エンジニア	*enjinia*
company employee	会社員	*kaishain*
architect	建築家	*kenchikuka*

Say the following in Japanese:

1. She is a singer.

2. I (not Bill) am an engineer.

3. Anne is a company employee.

4. He (newly introduced) is an architect.

/Answers/

1. 彼女は歌手だ / です。
   Kanojo wa kashu da / desu.

2. 私がエンジニアだ / です。
   Watashi ga enjinia da / desu.

3. アンは会社員だ / です。
   An wa kaishain da / desu.

4. あの人が建築家だ / です。
   Ano hito ga kenchikuka da / desu.

2

Mr. Oda is a teacher of Japanese.

小田さんは日本語の先生だ / です。
*Oda-**san** wa Nihongo **no** sensei da / desu.*

-*San* is an honorific suffix that is applied to a person's family name or given name, or to certain occupational titles. It corresponds roughly to the English "Mr.," "Ms.," "Miss," or "Mrs." but is less formal. In most cases, Japanese prefer to address one another by family name plus by -*san*.* In Japanese the family name precedes the given name, but foreign names pronounced or written in Japanese do not need to be reversed to follow this order. One should never use -*san* with one's own name, or when referring to any member of one's family (→ Pattern 7).

---

* In casual conversation among friends, one may address or refer to another by given name alone, without -*san*. But the acceptability of this depends on the relationship of the speaker and listener. Male speakers almost never address or refer to Japanese females by given name alone, but female speakers sometimes do—or they use -*chan* instead of -*san*. Throughout this book, -*san* is given in parentheses where it conceivably can be omitted, and it is dropped altogether where it is natural to do so—after certain given names, for example.

A noun followed by the particle *no* (*Nihongo* in the above example) forms a phrase that modifies the noun that follows it. *No* can be variously translated as "'s" (possessive), "of," "for," or can be used to express apposition (Example 4). This particle can also be used with pronouns: *watashi no* ("my"), *anata no* ("your"), *kare no* ("his"), *kanojo no* ("her"), *karera no* ("their"), etc. However, pronoun forms in general are often avoided in Japanese since they tend to sound wordy.

Examples

1. Mr. Brown is my boss.
   ブラウンさんは私のボスです。
   Buraun-san wa watashi no bosu desu.

2. Linda is a school nurse. / Linda is a nurse for the school.
   リンダは学校の看護師だ。
   Rinda wa gakkō no kangoshi da.

3. Ms. Akiko Kubo is secretary to a lawyer.
   久保秋子さんは弁護士の秘書です。
   Kubo Akiko-san wa bengoshi no hisho desu.

4. My friend Nobuko is a clerk at a department store.
   友達の信子さんはデパートの店員です。
   Tomodachi no Nobuko-san wa depāto no ten'in desu.

Practice

music	音楽	*ongaku*	coach	コーチ	*kōchi*
writer	作家	*sakka*	assistant	助手	*joshu*
baseball	野球	*yakyū*			

Say the following in Japanese:

1. Miss Tanaka is a music teacher.
2. He is Mr. Izumi, a writer.
3. Mr. Sam Adams is our baseball coach.
4. She is Mr. Benson's assistant.

/Answers/

1. 田中さんは音楽の先生だ / です。
   Tanaka-san wa ongaku no sensei da / desu.

2. あの人は作家の泉さんだ / です。
   Ano hito wa sakka no Izumi-san da / desu.

3. サム・アダムスさんは私達の野球のコーチだ / です。
   Samu Adamusu-san wa watashi-tachi no yakyū no kōchi da / desu.

4. 彼女はベンソンさんの助手だ / です。
   Kanojo wa Benson-san no joshu da / desu.

3

(a) This is my dictionary.
(b) This dictionary is mine.

(a) **これ**は私の辞書だ / です。
   ***Kore** wa watashi no jisho da / desu.*

(b) **この**辞書は私のだ / です。
   ***Kono** jisho wa watashi no da / desu.*

The Japanese demonstrative pronouns *kore*, *sore*, and *are* are equivalent to the English "this" (or "these"), "that" (or "those"), and "that over there" (or "those over there"). *Kore* indicates a thing near the speaker, *sore* a thing near the listener, and *are* a thing some distance away from both. These pronouns have the polite forms *kochira*, *sochira*, and *achira*, respectively, which may be used to refer to people (Example 3) as well as things.

When *kore*, *sore*, or *are* is used to modify a noun, it takes the form *kono*, *sono*, or *ano* (Example 4), and the polite *kochira*, *sochira*, or *achira* takes the form *kochira no*, *sochira no*, or *achira no* (Example 5).

As noted above (→ Pattern 2), the particle *no* following a noun can function as a possessive (Examples 1, 2, 4, 5).

Examples

1. This is the section chief's coat.
   これは課長のコートです。
   Kore wa kachō no kōto desu.

2. That over there is Mr. Johnson's car.
   あちらがジョンソンさんの車です。
   Achira ga Jonson-san no kuruma desu.

3. This is Professor Hara.
   こちらは原先生です。
   Kochira wa Hara-sensei desu.

4. These magazines are Bill's.
   この雑誌はビルのだ。
   Kono zasshi wa Biru no da.

5. That umbrella is Ms. Kimura's.
   そちらの傘は木村さんのです。
   Sochira no kasa wa Kimura-san no desu.

hat	帽子	*bōshi*
bag	かばん	*kaban*
accountant	計理士	*keirishi*
cell phone	携帯 (電話)	*keitai (denwa)*
building	ビル	*biru*
post office	郵便局	*yūbinkyoku*

Say the following in Japanese:

1. This is Ms. Mori's hat.

2. That bag is Mr. Sada's.

3. This is Mr. Oka, the accountant.

4. This cell phone is mine.

5. That building over there is the Meguro post office.

---

1. これは森さんの帽子だ / です。
   Kore wa Mori-san no bōshi da / desu.

2. そのかばんは佐田さんのだ / です。
   Sono kaban wa Sada-san no da / desu.

3. こちらは計理士の岡さんだ / です。
   Kochira wa keirishi no Oka-san da / desu.

4. この携帯は私のだ / です。
   Kono keitai wa watashi no da / desu.

5. あのビルが目黒の郵便局だ / です。
   Ano biru ga Meguro no yūbinkyoku da / desu.

(a) Is Ms. Takagi a lawyer?

(b) Is this Japanese or Chinese?

(a) 高木さんは弁護士です**か**。

*Takagi-san wa bengoshi desu **ka**.*

(b) これは日本語ですか、中国語です**か**。

*Kore wa Nihongo desu ka, Chūgokugo desu **ka**.*

The particle *ka* at the end of a sentence turns the sentence into a question. To form alternate questions, simply tack on additional questions, omitting the topic (which does not need to be repeated; Examples 3, 4).

Examples

1. Is Ms. Narita a reporter for a newspaper (company)?

   成田さんは新聞社のレポーターですか。

   Narita-san wa shinbunsha no repōtā desu ka.

2. Is that the section chief's desk?

   それは課長の机ですか。

   Sore wa kachō no tsukue desu ka.

3. Is Mr. Mikami an engineer or an architect?

   三上さんはエンジニアですか、建築家ですか。

   Mikami-san wa enjinia desu ka, kenchikuka desu ka.

4. Is this book yours or Bill's? / Is this book yours? Bill's?

   この本はあなたのですか、ビルのですか。

   Kono hon wa anata no desu ka, Biru no desu ka.

art museum	美術館	*bijutsukan*
middle school	中学	*chūgaku*
high school	高校	*kōkō*

Say the following in Japanese:

1. Is that over there an art museum?
2. Is this your bag or Mr. Hara's (bag)?
3. Is Mr. Yagi a middle school teacher or a high school teacher?

Answers

1. あれは美術館ですか。
   Are wa bijutsukan desu ka.

2. これはあなたのかばんですか、原さんの（かばん）ですか。
   Kore wa anata no kaban desuka, Hara-san no (kaban) desu ka.

3. 八木さんは中学の先生ですか、高校の先生ですか。
   Yagi-san wa chūgaku no sensei desu ka, kōkō no sensei desu ka.

5

(a) Who is that person?

(b) What is that?

(a) あの人は**だれ**ですか。
   *Ano hito wa **dare** desu ka.*

(b) あれは**何**ですか。
   *Are wa **nan** desu ka.*

The interrogatives *dare* ("who") and *nan* or *nani* ("what") are placed after the topic (marked by the particle *wa*) to form who- and what-questions.

Examples

1. Who is the prime minister of Japan?
   日本の首相はだれですか。
   Nihon no shushō wa dare desu ka.

2. Who is in charge of this class?
   このクラスの受け持ちはだれですか。
   Kono kurasu no ukemochi wa dare desu ka.

3. What is that tower over there?
   あの塔は何ですか。
   Ano tō wa nan desu ka.

4. What are these boxes?
   この箱は何ですか。
   Kono hako wa nan desu ka.

Practice

manager	マネージャー	*manējā*
noise	音	*oto*
name	名前	*namae*
hot spring	温泉	*onsen*

Say the following in Japanese:

1. Who is the manager of this store?
2. What is that noise?
3. What is the name of that hot spring?

6

I am not a bank employee.

私は銀行員**ではない / ではありません**。
*Watashi wa ginkōin **de wa nai** / **de wa arimasen**.*

In negative sentences, the copula *da* changes to *de wa nai*, and *desu* to *de wa arimasen*. In colloquial speech, *ja nai* or *ja arimasen* can be used in place of *de wa nai* or *de wa arimasen*.

Examples

1. Mr. Nelson is not a diplomat.

   ネルソンさんは外交官ではありません。
   Neruson-san wa gaikōkan de wa arimasen.

2. We are not Professor Sano's students.

   私達は佐野先生の学生じゃありません。
   Watashi-tachi wa Sano-sensei no gakusei ja arimasen.

3. This is not Tokyo Station.

   これは東京駅ではありません。
   Kore wa Tōkyō eki de wa arimasen.

4. That pencil is not Jeff's.

その鉛筆はジェフのじゃない。

Sono enpitsu wa Jefu no ja nai.

5. That building over there isn't a hospital.

あのビルは病院ではない。

Ano biru wa byōin de wa nai.

Practice

journalist	ジャーナリスト	*jānarisuto*
kindergarten	幼稚園	*yōchien*
photographer	写真家	*shashinka*
school	学校	*gakkō*
dormitory	寮	*ryō*

Say the following in Japanese:

1. Ms. Noda is not a journalist.
2. She is not a kindergarten teacher.
3. My friend Dan isn't a photographer.
4. That (over there) is not the school dormitory.

Answers

1. 野田さんはジャーナリストではない / ではありません。
   Noda-san wa jānarisuto de wa nai / de wa arimasen.

2. 彼女は幼稚園の先生じゃない / じゃありません。
   Kanojo wa yōchien no sensei ja nai / ja arimasen.

3. 友達のダン（さん）は写真家ではない / ではありません。
   Tomodachi no Dan(-san) wa shashinka de wa nai / de wa arimsen.

4. あれは学校の寮ではない / ではありません。
   Are wa gakkō no ryō de wa nai / de wa arimasen.

7

(a) My father is a doctor.

(b) Ms. Sada's father also is a doctor.

(a) 私の**父**は医者だ / です。
*Watashi no **chichi** wa isha da / desu.*

(b) 佐田さんの**お父さんも**医者だ / です。
*Sada-san no **o-tō-san mo** isha da / desu.*

The terms used to address or refer to one's own family members are different from those used to address or refer to those of someone else. Referring to one's own father, one uses the humble form *chichi*; referring to someone else's, one uses the honorific form *o-tō-san*. But, when one addresses one's own father, one should use *o-tō-san*. The chart below shows how to refer to and address one's own family members, and someone else's.

	third-person reference		direct address	
	one's own	someone else's	one's own	someone else's
father	父 *chichi*	お父さん *o-tō-san*	お父さん *o-tō-san*	お父様 *o-tō-sama*****
mother	母 *haha*	お母さん *o-kā-san*	お母さん *o-kā-san*	お母様 *o-kā-sama*
older brother	兄 *ani*	お兄さん *o-nī-san*	お兄さん *o-nī-san*	given name + *san / sama* お兄さん *o-nī-san* お兄様 *o-nī-sama*
younger brother	弟 *otōto*	弟さん *otōto-san*	given name	given name + *san / sama* 弟さん *otōto-san* 弟様 *otōto-sama*

older sister	姉 *ane*	お姉さん *o-nē-san*	お姉さん *o-nē-san*	given name + *san / sama* お姉さん *o-nē-san* お姉様 *o-nē-sama*
younger sister	妹 *imōto*	妹さん *imōto-san*	given name	given name + *san / sama* 妹さん *imōto-san* 妹様 *imōto-sama*
child	子供 *kodomo* (うちの) 子 *(uchi no) ko*	子供さん *kodomo-san* お子さん *oko-san* お子様 *oko-sama*	given name	given name + *chan / kun*
son	息子 *musuko*	息子さん *musuko-san*	given name	given name + *san / kun*
daughter	娘 *musume*	娘さん *musume-san* お嬢さん *o-jō-san* お嬢様 *o-jō-sama*	given name	given name + *san / chan* お嬢さん *o-jō-san* お嬢様 *o-jō-sama*
grandfather	祖父 *sofu*	おじいさん *o-jī-san*	おじいさん *o-jī-san*	おじいさん *o-jī-san* おじい様 *o-jī-sama*
grandmother	祖母 *sobo*	おばあさん *o-bā-san*	おばあさん *o-bā-san*	おばあさん *o-bā-san* おばあ様 *o-bā-sama*
husband	主人 *shujin*	ご主人 (様) *go-shujin(-sama)*	あなた *anata*	family name + *san*
wife	家内 *kanai* 妻 *tsuma*	奥さん *oku-san* 奥様 *oku-sama*	お前 *o-mae* given name	奥さん *oku-san* 奥様 *oku-sama*

* -*Sama* is more polite than -*san*.

The particle *mo* following a noun, as in (b) above, replaces the topic-marker *wa*. It means "also," "too," or, in negative sentences, "either" (Examples 3, 4).

1. My older brother is a civil servant. The section chief's older brother is also a civil servant.

私の兄は公務員です。課長のお兄さんも公務員です。

Watashi no ani wa kōmuin desu. Kachō no o-nī-san mo kōmuin desu.

2. My son is a college student. Professor Takagi's son is also a college student.

息子は大学生です。高木先生の息子さんも大学生です。

Musuko wa daigakusei desu. Takagi-sensei no musuko-san mo daigakusei desu.

3. My wife isn't a secretary. Mr. Hill's wife isn't, either.

家内は秘書じゃない。ヒルさんの奥さんも秘書じゃない。

Kanai wa hisho ja nai. Hiru-san no oku-san mo hisho ja nai.

4. My grandfather isn't a politician. My friend's grandfather isn't, either.

祖父は政治家ではない。友達のおじいさんも政治家ではない。

Sofu wa seijika de wa nai. Tomodachi no o-jī-san mo seijika de wa nai.

Practice

history	歴史	*rekishi*
salesman	セールスマン	*sērusuman*
dentist	歯医者	*haisha*

Say the following in Japanese:

1. My mother is a history teacher. Miss Hayashi's mother is also a history teacher.

2. My husband is a car salesman. Ms. Oka's husband is also a car salesman.

3. My daughter isn't a dentist. Ms. Yano's daughter isn't, either.

---

1. 母は歴史の先生だ / です。林さんのお母さんも歴史の先生だ / です。
   Haha wa rekishi no sensei da / desu. Hayashi-san no o-kā-san mo rekishi no sensei da / desu.

2. 主人は車のセールスマンだ / です。岡さんのご主人も車のセールスマンだ / です。
   Shujin wa kuruma no sērusuman da / desu. Oka-san no go-shujin mo kuruma no sērusuman da / desu.

3. 娘は歯医者じゃない / じゃありません。矢野さんのお嬢さんも歯医者じゃない / じゃありません。
   Musume wa haisha ja nai / ja arimasen. Yano-san no o-jō-san mo haisha ja nai / ja arimasen.

8

Mr. Ogawa and Mr. Maki are both my friends.

小川さん**も**槇さん**も**私の友達だ / です。

*Ogawa-san **mo** Maki-san **mo** watashi no tomodachi da / desu.*

The particle *mo* can follow two different nouns in a sentence to indicate that the two nouns fall into a similar category. The phrase formed by the repeated use of *mo* is used as the subject of an affirmative sentence, where it means "both … and" (Examples 1, 2), or as the subject or predicate of a negative sentence, where it means "neither … nor" (Examples 3, 4).

1. This room and that room are both conference rooms.

   この部屋もその部屋も会議室です。

   Kono heya mo sono heya mo kaigishitsu desu.

2. Both he and she are graduates of Harvard.

   彼も彼女もハーバードの卒業生だ。

   Kare mo kanojo mo Hābādo no sotsugyōsei da.

3. Neither Jim nor Sam is a football player.

   ジムもサムもフットボールの選手じゃない。

   Jimu mo Samu mo futtobōru no senshu ja nai.

4. My younger sister is neither a pianist nor a singer.

   妹はピアニストでも歌手でもありません。

   Imōto wa pianisuto demo kashu demo arimasen.

Practice

pilot	パイロット	*pairotto*
hotel	ホテル	*hoteru*
apartment	アパート	*apāto*
textbook	教科書	*kyōkasho*
reference book	参考書	*sankōsho*

Say the following in Japanese:

1. My older brother and younger brother are both pilots.
2. Neither Mr. Ross nor Mr. Hill are bank employees.
3. This building is neither a hotel nor an apartment.
4. Neither this textbook nor that reference book is mine.

1. 兄も弟もパイロットだ / です。
   Ani mo otōto mo pairotto da / desu.

2. ロスさんもヒルさんも銀行員じゃない / じゃありません。
   Rosu-san mo Hiru-san mo ginkōin ja nai / ja arimasen.

3. このビルはホテルでもアパートでもない / でもありません。
   Kono biru wa hoteru demo apāto demo nai / demo arimasen.

4. この教科書もその参考書も私のじゃない / じゃありません。
   Kono kyōkasho mo sono sankōsho mo watashi no ja nai. / ja arimasen.

9

Ms. Ross was an English teacher.

ロスさんは英語の先生だった / でした。
*Rosu-san wa Eigo no sensei **datta** / **deshita**.*

To express the past tense, the copula *da* changes to *datta*, and *desu* to *deshita*.

Examples

1. My grandfather was the principal of an elementary school.
   祖父は小学校の校長でした。
   Sofu wa shōgakkō no kōchō deshita.

2. Mr. Brown was the governor of California.
   ブラウンさんはカリフォルニアの知事だった。
   Buraun-san wa Kariforunia no chiji datta.

3. This store was a camera shop.

   この店はカメラ屋だった。

   Kono mise wa kameraya datta.

4. This room and that room were both our classrooms.

   この部屋もその部屋も私達の教室でした。

   Kono heya mo sono heya mo watashi-tachi no kyōshitsu deshita.

Practice

Japanese literature	日本文学	*Nihon bungaku*
professor	教授	*kyōju*
scientist	科学者	*kagakusha*
restaurant	レストラン	*resutoran*
rich man/woman	金持ち	*kanemochi*
second home	別荘	*bessō*

Say the following in Japanese:

1. Mr. Atkins was a professor of Japanese literature.

2. Both my father and my older brother were scientists.

3. This restaurant was a rich man's second home.

Answers

1. アトキンズさんは日本文学の教授だった / でした。
   Atokinzu-san wa Nihon bungaku no kyōju datta / deshita.

2. 父も兄も科学者だった / でした。
   Chichi mo ani mo kagakusha datta / deshita.

3. このレストランは金持ちの別荘だった / でした。
   Kono resutoran wa kanemochi no bessō datta / deshita.

10

The dinner wasn't French cuisine.

ディナーはフランス料理**ではなかった / ではありませんでした**。

*Dinā wa Furansu ryōri **de wa nakatta** / **de wa arimasen deshita**.*

To express the negative past tense ("was not …"), *datta* changes to *de wa nakatta*, and *deshita* to *de wa arimasen deshita*. In colloquial speech, *ja* may be used in place of *de wa* in either of these negative forms.

The negative past form of a sentence that uses the particle *mo* repeatedly (→ Pattern 8) is *demo … demo nakatta* (plain style; Example 3) or *demo … demo arimasen deshita* (polite style).

Examples

1. That car wasn't Mr. Sakamoto's.

   あの車は坂本さんのじゃありませんでした。

   Ano kuruma wa Sakamoto-san no ja arimasen deshita.

2. That man wasn't Mr. Gibson of the American Embassy.

   あの男の人はアメリカ大使館のギブソンさんではありませんでした。

   Ano otoko no hito wa Amerika taishikan no Gibuson-san de wa arimasen deshita.

3. She was neither a writer nor a poet.

   彼女は作家でも詩人でもなかった。

   Kanojo wa sakka demo shijin demo nakatta.

Practice

movie theater	映画館	*eigakan*
foreigner	外国人	*gaikokujin*
student	学生	*gakusei*
present	プレゼント	*purezento*
watch	時計	*tokei*

Say the following in Japanese:

1. That was not a movie theater.

2. That foreigner was neither a teacher nor a student.

3. The present wasn't a watch.

/Answers/

1. あれは映画館ではなかった / ではありませんでした。
   Are wa eigakan de wa nakatta / de wa arimasen deshita.

2. あの外国人は先生でも学生でもなかった / でもありませんでした。
   Ano gaikokujin wa sensei demo gakusei demo nakatta / demo arimasen deshita.

3. プレゼントは時計じゃなかった / じゃありませんでした。
   Purezento wa tokei ja nakatta / ja arimasen deshita.

11

(a) It's good wine, isn't it?

(b) It's a pretty picture, isn't it?

(a) いいワインだ / ですね。
   Ii wain da / desu **ne**.

(b) きれいな絵だ / ですね。
   Kireina e da / desu **ne**.

In Japanese there are two types of adjectives: the *i*-adjective, which ends with *i*, and the *na*-adjective, which ends with *na*. Both are placed right before the nouns they modify.

The particle *ne* at the end of a sentence, as in (a) and (b) above, is a tag question: it asks, "isn't it?," "is it?," "isn't he?," or "is she?" etc., indicating the speaker's request for confirmation.

Examples

1. They're sweet oranges, aren't they?
   甘いオレンジですね。
   Amai orenji desu ne.

2. It's a cute dog, isn't it?
   かわいい犬ですね。
   Kawaii inu desu ne.

3. It's a quiet park, isn't it?
   静かな公園ですね。
   Shizukana kōen desu ne.

4. She's a kind person, isn't she?
   親切な人だね。
   Shinsetsuna hito da ne.

Practice

cold (of air)	寒い	*samui*
day	日	*hi*
interesting	おもしろい	*omoshiroi*
serious	まじめな	*majimena*
convenient	便利な	*benrina*

Say the following in Japanese:

1. It's a cold day, isn't it?
2. It's an interesting book, isn't it?
3. He's a serious student, isn't he?
4. It's a convenient bag, isn't it?

/Answers/

1. 寒い日だ / ですね。
   Samui hi da / desu ne.

2. おもしろい本だ / ですね。
   Omoshiroi hon da / desu ne.

3. まじめな学生だ / ですね。
   Majimena gakusei da / desu ne.

4. 便利なかばんだ / ですね。
   Benrina kaban da / desu ne.

12

(a) This car is new.

(b) That painter is famous.

(a) この車は**新しい** / **新しいです**。
*Kono kuruma wa **atarashii** / **atarashii desu**.*

(b) あの画家は**有名だ** / **有名です**。
*Ano gaka wa **yūmei da** / **yūmei desu**.*

I-adjectives used as predicates behave like verbs. When *atarashii* is used as a predicate, for example, it means "is new," not just "new." Therefore, the copula *da* ("is") does not follow it. (The copula *desu* may, however, be added for politeness.) On the other hand, *na*-adjectives used as predicates behave like nouns. When *yūmeina* is used as a predicate, the stem form (the form without *na*) must be followed by the copula *da* or *desu*.

1. This work is difficult.

   この仕事は難しい。

   Kono shigoto wa muzukashii.

2. Our new office is large.

   私達の新しい事務所は広いです。

   Watashi-tachi no atarashii jimusho wa hiroi desu.

3. That mountain is dangerous.

   あの山は危険だ。

   Ano yama wa kiken da.

4. My father and mother are both healthy.

   父も母も元気です。

   Chichi mo haha mo genki desu.

Practice

young	若い	*wakai*
cold (to the touch)	冷たい	*tsumetai*
coffee	コーヒー	*kōhī*
accurate	正確な	*seikakuna*

Say the following in Japanese:

1. Jim and Sarah are both young.
2. This coffee is cold, isn't it?
3. This watch is accurate.

1. ジム (さん) もサラ (さん) も若い / 若いです。
   Jimu(-san) mo Sara(-san) mo wakai / wakai desu.

2. このコーヒーは冷たい / 冷たいですね。
   Kono kōhī wa tsumetai / tsumetai desu ne.

3. この時計は正確だ / 正確です。
   Kono tokei wa seikaku da / seikaku desu.

13

> (a) This pie is not delicious.
>
> (b) Those papers are not necessary.

(a) このパイは**おいしくない** / **おいしくありません**。
   *Kono pai wa oishi**ku nai** / oishi**ku arimasen**.*

(b) その書類は必要**ではない** / 必要**ではありません**。
   *Sono shorui wa hitsuyō **de wa nai** / hitsuyō **de wa arimasen**.*

The negative form of an *i*-adjective is the stem form (the form without *i*) followed by *ku nai*. The negative form of a *na*-adjective is the stem (the form without *na*) followed by *de wa nai* or *ja nai*. In Japanese the negative form may be used both attributively (before a noun, to modify it) or predicatively (as a predicate). If it is used predicatively, *desu* may be added for politeness, or *arimasen* may replace *nai* for the same effect.

Examples

1. Bill's grades are not good.

   ビル (さん) の成績はよくない (です) 。
   Biru(-san) no seiseki wa yoku nai (desu).

2. The subway station isn't far.

地下鉄の駅は遠くありません。

Chikatetsu no eki wa tōku arimasen.

3. They are not happy.

あの人たちは幸せではない。

Ano hito-tachi wa shiawase de wa nai.

4. The procedures are not simple.

手続きは簡単ではありません。

Tetsuzuki wa kantan de wa arimasen.

Practice

cheap	安い	*yasui*		work	仕事	*shigoto*
company	会社	*kaisha*		complicated	複雑な	*fukuzatsuna*
bright	明るい	*akarui*				

Say the following in Japanese:

1. That restaurant isn't cheap, is it?
2. The company conference room isn't bright.
3. This work is not complicated.

Answers

1. あのレストランは安くない (です) ね。
   Ano resutoran wa yasuku nai (desu) ne.

2. 会社の会議室は明るくない / 明るくありません。
   Kaisha no kaigishitsu wa akaruku nai / akaruku arimasen.

3. この仕事は複雑ではない / 複雑ではありません。
   Kono shigoto wa fukuzatsu de wa nai / fukuzatsu de wa arimasen.

(a) The picnic was fun.

(b) The banquet was gorgeous.

(a) ピクニックは楽し**かった** / 楽し**かった**です。
   *Pikunikku wa tanoshi**katta** / tanoshi**katta** desu.*

(b) 宴会は豪華**だった** / 豪華**でした**。
   *Enkai wa gōka **datta** / gōka **deshita**.*

For the past tense of an *i*-adjective, the final *i* changes to *katta*, which may be followed by *desu* for politeness. For the past tense of a *na*-adjective, the copula *da* changes to *datta*, or *desu* to *deshita*.

Examples

1. The package was heavy.

   小包は重かったです。
   Kozutsumi wa omokatta desu.

2. The mountain road was narrow.

   山道は狭かった。
   Yamamichi wa semakatta.

3. That city was lively.

   その町はにぎやかでした。
   Sono machi wa nigiyaka deshita.

4. My secretary was competent.

   私の秘書は有能だった。
   Watashi no hisho wa yūnō datta.

clerk	店員	*ten'in*		mountain	山	*yama*
polite	丁寧な	*teineina*		steep	険しい	*kewashii*
stubborn	頑固な	*gankona*				

Say the following in Japanese:

1. The store clerk was polite.

2. My grandfather was stubborn.

3. The mountain was steep.

Answers

1. 店員は丁寧だった / 丁寧でした。
   Ten'in wa teinei datta / teinei deshita.

2. 祖父は頑固だった / 頑固でした。
   Sofu wa ganko datta /ganko deshita.

3. 山は険しかった / 険しかったです。
   Yama wa kewashikatta / kewashikatta desu.

15

(a) The lecture was not long.

(b) He wasn't honest.

(a) 講義は長く**なかった** / 長く**ありませんでした**。
   *Kōgi wa naga**ku nakatta** / nagaku **arimasen deshita**.*

(b) あの人は正直**ではなかった** / 正直**ではありません**
   でした。
   *Ano hito wa shōjiki **de wa nakatta** / shōjiki **de wa arimasen deshita**.*

For the negative past tense, the *nai* of the negative form of an *i*-adjective changes to *nakatta* (*desu* may follow for politeness), or *arimasen* changes to *arimasen deshita*. For *na*-adjectives, the negative copula *de wa nai* changes to *de wa nakatta*, or *de wa arimasen* to *de wa arimasen deshita*.

Examples

1. The earthquake was not big.

   地震は大きくなかった（です）。
   Jishin wa ōkiku nakatta (desu).

2. The exam wasn't easy.

   試験はやさしくありませんでした。
   Shiken wa yasashiku arimasen deshita.

3. Her dress wasn't showy.

   彼女のドレスは派手じゃなかった。
   Kanojo no doresu wa hade ja nakatta.

4. Their life was not luxurious.

   彼らの生活はぜいたくではありませんでした。
   Kare-ra no seikatsu wa zeitaku de wa arimasen deshita.

Practice

game	試合	*shiai*
clean	きれいな	*kireina*
handbag	ハンドバッグ	*handobaggu*
expensive	高い	*takai*

Say the following in Japanese:

1. The game was not interesting.

2. That city's streets were not clean.

3. This handbag wasn't expensive.

---

1. 試合はおもしろくなかった（です）。
   Shiai wa omoshiroku nakatta (desu).

2. その町の道はきれいではなかった / きれいではありませんでした。
   Sono machi no michi wa kirei de wa nakatta / kirei de wa arimasen deshita.

3. このハンドバッグは高くなかった / 高くありませんでした。
   Kono handobaggu wa takaku nakatta / takaku arimasen deshita.

16

This is an apartment and that is a hotel.

これはアパート**で**、それはホテルだ / です。

*Kore wa apāto **de**, sore wa hoteru da / desu.*

De is the conjunctive form of the copula *da* or *desu* and is used to link two sentences. It means "and."

NOTE: The tense of a sentence ending with a noun followed by a copula is determined by the final form of a copula.

Examples

1. This scarf is silk and that one is nylon.

   このスカーフは絹で、そのスカーフはナイロンです。

   Kono sukāfu wa kinu de, sono sukāfu wa nairon desu.

2. He was a journalist and she was a photographer.

彼はジャーナリストで、彼女は写真家だった。

Kare wa jānarisuto de, kanojo wa shashinka datta.

3. This is my report and that is Ms. Hayashi's.

これが僕のレポートで、それは林さんのだ。

Kore ga boku no repōto de, sore wa Hayashi-san no da.

Practice

temple	お寺	*o-tera*
shrine	神社	*jinja*
receptionist	受付	*uketsuke*
small	小さい	*chiisai*
big	大きい	*ōkii*
section chief	課長	*kachō*

Say the following in Japanese:

1 This is a temple and that is a shrine.

2. Mr. Sasaki was a dentist and his wife was a receptionist.

3. This small car is mine and that big one is the section chief's.

Answers

1. これはお寺で、それは神社だ / です。
Kore wa o-tera de, sore wa jinja da / desu.

2. 佐々木さんは歯医者 (さん) で、奥さんは受付だった / でした。
Sasaki-san wa haisha(-san) de, oku-san wa uketsuke datta / deshita.

3. この小さい車が私ので、その大きい車は課長のだ / です。
Kono chiisai kuruma ga watashi no de, sono ōkii kuruma wa kachō no da / desu.

> (a) This coat is soft and light.
>
> (b) The clerk is kind and polite.

(a) このコートは柔らかくて軽い / 軽いです。
   Kono kōto wa yawarakakute karui / karui desu.

(b) 店員は親切で丁寧だ / 丁寧です。
   *Ten'in wa shinsetsu **de** teinei da / teinei desu.*

The *te* (or *de*) form of an *i*- or a *na*-adjective—obtained by replacing the *nai* of the negative form of an *i*-adjective with *te*, or, with *na*-adjectives, by adding *de* to the stem (→ Appendix 3)—is used to link adjectives (Examples 1, 3) or sentences (Examples 2, 4). It means "and."

NOTE: The tense of a sentence ending with an adjective is determined by the final form of the adjective or, in the case of *na*-adjectives, by the final form of the copula.

Examples

1. The new secretary is young and kind.
   新しい秘書は若くて優しいです。
   Atarashii hisho wa wakakute yasashii desu.

2. The wind was strong and the waves were high.
   風が強くて、波は高かった。
   Kaze ga tsuyokute, nami wa takakatta.

3. This structure is modern and magnificent.
   この建物はモダンで立派だ。
   Kono tatemono wa modan de rippa da.

4. His parents were rich and her parents were poor.

彼の両親は裕福で、彼女の両親は貧乏でした。

Kare no ryōshin wa yūfuku de, kanojo no ryōshin wa binbō deshita.

Practice

old	古い	*furui*
dirty	汚い	*kitanai*
room	部屋	*heya*
dark	暗い	*kurai*
careful	慎重な	*shinchōna*
strict	厳格な	*genkakuna*
generous/lenient	寛大な	*kandaina*

Say the following in Japanese:

1. The dormitory is old and dirty.

2. This room is bright and that one is dark.

3. Mr. Kida was serious and careful.

4. Professor Kishi is strict and Professor Sano is lenient.

Answers

1. 寮は古くて汚い / 汚いです。
   Ryō wa furukute kitanai / kitanai desu.

2. この部屋は明るくて、その部屋は暗い / 暗いです。
   Kono heya wa akarukute, sono heya wa kurai / kurai desu.

3. 木田さんはまじめで慎重だった / 慎重でした。
   Kida-san wa majime de shinchō datta / shinchō deshita.

4. 岸先生は厳格で、佐野先生は寛大だ / 寛大です。
   Kishi-sensei wa genkaku de, Sano-sensei wa kandai da / kandai desu.

18

> (a) This steak is delicious and, what's more, it's inexpensive.
>
> (b) The room is clean and, what's more, it's sunny.

(a) このステーキはおいしい**し**、安い / 安いです。
*Kono sutēki wa oishii **shi**, yasui / yasui desu.*

(b) 部屋は清潔だ**し**、明るい / 明るいです。
*Heya wa seiketsu da **shi**, akarui / akarui desu.*

The particle *shi* is used as a conjunction to link two or more states expressed by *i-* or *na*-adjectival predicates. It means "and moreover."

Examples

1. That movie is interesting and, what's more, it's educational.
   その映画は面白いし、教育的です。
   Sono eiga wa omoshiroi shi, kyōikuteki desu.

2. This tool is convenient, and it's light.
   この器具は便利だし、軽い。
   Kono kigu wa benri da shi, karui.

3. He was competent and he was also wise.
   彼は有能だったし、賢明だった。
   Kare wa yūnō datta shi, kenmei datta.

talk	話	*hanashi*
boring	つまらない	*tsumaranai*
fruit	果物	*kudamono*
fresh	新鮮な	*shinsenna*

Say the following in Japanese:

1. The section chief's talk was long and, what's more, it was boring.

2. These fruits are fresh, and they're inexpensive.

3. The nurses at the hospital were young, and also kind.

---

1. 課長の話は長いし、つまらなかった / つまらなかったです。
   Kachō no hanashi wa nagai shi, tsumaranakatta / tsumaranakatta desu.

2. この果物は新鮮だし、安い / 安いです。
   Kono kudamono wa shinsen da shi, yasui / yasui desu.

3. 病院の看護師さんは若かったし、親切だった / 親切でした。
   Byōin no kangoshi-san wa wakakatta shi, shinsetsu datta / shinsetsu deshita.

19

Rabbits have red eyes.

うさぎ**は**目**が**赤い / 赤いです。
*Usagi **wa** me **ga** akai / akai desu.*

In the sentence above, the noun marked by the particle *wa* is the topic, and the noun marked by the particle *ga* is the subject. The adjective at the end of the sentence is used as a predicate and, together with the subject, expresses something about the topic's attributes or state of being.

1. This car has a good engine.

   この車はエンジンがいい。

   Kono kuruma wa enjin ga ii.

2. I have a headache.

   私は頭が痛いです。

   Watashi wa atama ga itai desu.

3. That peninsula has a mild climate.

   その半島は気候が温暖です。

   Sono hantō wa kikō ga ondan desu.

4. His novels have complicated plots.

   彼の小説は筋が複雑だ。

   Kare no shōsetsu wa suji ga fukuzatsu da.

Practice

product	製品	*seihin*
quality	質	*shitsu*
house	家	*ie / uchi*
large/spacious	広い	*hiroi*
kitchen	台所	*daidokoro*
color	色	*iro*
bright	鮮やかな	*azayakana*

Say the following in Japanese:

1. This company's products are of good quality.

2. Her house has a large kitchen.

3. That picture has bright colors, doesn't it?

1. この会社の製品は質がいい / いいです。
   Kono kaisha no seihin wa shitsu ga ii / ii desu.

2. 彼女の家は台所が広い / 広いです。
   Kanojo no ie wa daidokoro ga hiroi / hiroi desu.

3. その絵は色が鮮やかだ / 鮮やかですね。
   Sono e wa iro ga azayaka da / azayaka desu ne.

20

> (a) Exams are sometimes difficult and sometimes easy.
>
> (b) This street is sometimes quiet and sometimes lively.

(a) 試験は難しかっ**たり**、やさしかっ**たりする** / **します**。

*Shiken wa muzukashikat**tari**, yasashikat**tari suru** / **shimasu**.*

(b) この通りは静かだっ**たり**、にぎやかだっ**たりする** / **します**。

*Kono tōri wa shizuka dat**tari**, nigiyaka dat**tari suru** / **shimasu**.*

The repeated use of the *tari* form of an *i*- or a *na*-adjective, followed by the verb *suru*, expresses alternative states in no particular sequence. It corresponds to the English "sometimes … and sometimes …". To obtain the *tari* form, add *kattari* to the stem of an *i*-adjective, or *dattari* to the stem of a *na*-adjective.

1. Steaks at this restaurant are sometimes tender and sometimes tough.

このレストランのステーキは軟らかかったり、硬かったりする。

Kono resutoran no sutēki wa yawarakakattari, katakattari suru.

2. His attitude is sometimes careful and sometimes bold.

彼の態度は慎重だったり、大胆だったりします。

Kare no taido wa shichō dattari, daitan dattari shimasu.

Practice

busy	忙しい	*isogashii*
free (not busy)	ひまな	*himana*
problem	問題	*mondai*
easy	簡単な	*kantanna*

Say the following in Japanese:

1. My father is sometimes busy and sometimes not busy.
2. The problems are sometimes simple and sometimes complicated.

Answers

1. 父は忙しかったり、ひまだったりする / します。
   Chichi wa isogashikattari, hima dattari suru / shimasu.

2. 問題は簡単だったり、複雑だったりする/ します。
   Mondai wa kantan dattari, fukuzatsu dattari suru / shimasu.

2 Describing the Existence of Animate and Inanimate Things

21

> (a) There is a TV set.
>
> (b) There are boys.

(a) テレビが**ある** / **あります**。
   *Terebi ga **aru** / **arimasu**.*

(b) 男の子が**いる** / **います**。
   *Otoko no ko ga **iru** / **imasu**.*

Two different verbs are used to express the idea that someone or something exists. *Aru* ("there is") is used for inanimate objects such as books, plants, buildings, etc., while *iru* ("there is") is used for animate objects such as people, animals, and insects. The polite forms of these verbs are *arimasu* and *imasu*, respectively.

When the particle *mo* ("also") is used in a sentence about the existence of someone or something, it replaces the subject-marker *ga* (Example 3).

Examples

1. There is a police box.
   交番があります。
   Kōban ga arimasu.

2. There is a policeman.
   警官がいます。
   Keikan ga imasu.

3. There are white birds. There are also blue birds.

白い鳥がいる。青い鳥もいる。

Shiroi tori ga iru. Aoi tori mo iru.

Practice

newspaper	新聞	*shinbun*
magazine	雑誌	*zasshi*
theater	劇場	*gekijō*

Say the following in Japanese:

1. There are old newspapers. There are also old magazines.

2. There is a big dog. There is also a small dog.

3. There is a movie house. There is also a theater.

Answers

1. 古い新聞がある / あります。古い雑誌もある / あります。
   Furui shinbun ga aru / arimasu. Furui zasshi mo aru / arimasu.

2. 大きい犬がいる / います。小さい犬もいる / います。
   Ōkii inu ga iru / imasu. Chiisai inu mo iru / imasu.

3. 映画館がある / あります。劇場もある / あります。
   Eigakan ga aru / arimasu. Gekijō mo aru / arimasu.

(a) There isn't any food.

(b) There is no interpreter.

(a) 食べ物が / は**ない** / **ありません**。
*Tabemono ga / wa **nai** / **arimasen**.*

(b) 通訳が / は**いない** / **いません**。
*Tsūyaku ga / wa **inai** / **imasen**.*

The negative form of the verb *aru* or *arimasu* is *nai* (not *aranai*) or *arimasen*, and the negative form of the verb *iru* or *imasu* is *inai* or *imasen*.

The particle *wa* may replace the particle *ga* in a negative sentence if the speaker wishes to suggest that although one person or thing (marked by *wa*) may be absent, other similar people or things are or will be present. For example, if *wa* is used instead of *ga* in (a) above, the speaker might be suggesting that although there is no food, there are drinks (or something else), whereas if *ga* is used, he or she would simply be stating that there is or will be no food, period. Likewise, (b) with *wa* instead of *ga* might suggest that other professionals, besides interpreters, are or will be present (although interpreters are not or will not be), whereas with *ga* the implication is that an interpreter is what is missing—an emphatic statement.

The particle *mo* can be used in a negative sentence to mean "either," in which case it replaces the subject-marker *ga* or the topic-marker *wa* (Example 3).

Examples

1. There isn't any interesting news.
おもしろいニュースがありません。
Omoshiroi nyūsu ga arimasen.

2. There aren't any tourists.

観光客はいません。

Kankōkyaku wa imasen.

3. There are no horses. There are no sheep, either.

馬がいない。羊もいない。

Uma ga inai. Hitsuji mo inai.

Practice

milk	牛乳	*gyūnyū*
adult	大人	*otona*
children	子供	*kodomo*
cat	猫	*neko*

Say the following in Japanese:

1. There isn't any milk.
2. There aren't any adults. There aren't any children, either.
3. There is no dog. There is no cat, either.

Answers

1. 牛乳 が / はない / ありません。
   Gyūnyū ga / wa nai / arimasen.

2. 大人 が / はいない / いません。子供もいない/ いません。
   Otona ga / wa inai / imasen. Kodomo mo inai / imasen.

3. 犬が / はいない / いません。猫もいない / いません。
   Inu ga / wa inai / imasen. Neko mo inai / imasen.

23

(a) There was an earthquake.

(b) There was a black bear.

(a) 地震があった / ありました。
   *Jishin ga **atta** / **arimashita**.*

(b) 黒い熊がいた / いました。
   *Kuroi kuma ga **ita** / **imashita**.*

To express the past tense, the verb *aru* or *arimasu* changes to *atta* or *arimashita*, and the verb *iru* or *imasu* changes to *ita* or *imashita*.

Examples

1. There was a traffic accident last night.
   ゆうべ交通事故がありました。
   Yūbe kōtsū jiko ga arimashita.

2. There were shoppers.
   買い物客がいました。
   Kaimonokyaku ga imashita.

3. There were elephants. There were also giraffes.
   象がいた。きりんもいた。
   Zō ga ita. Kirin mo ita.

Practice

flood	洪水	*kōzui*		monkey	猿	*saru*
last week	先週	*senshū*		celebrity	有名人	*yūmeijin*
horse	馬	*uma*				

Say the following in Japanese:

1. There was a flood last week.

2. There were horses. There were also monkeys.

3. There were celebrities.

---

1. 先週洪水があった / ありました。
   Senshū kōzui ga atta / arimashita.

2. 馬がいた / いました。猿もいた / いました。
   Uma ga ita / imashita. Saru mo ita / imashita.

3. 有名人がいた / いました。
   Yūmeijin ga ita / imashita.

24

(a) There was no shortcut.

(b) There were no passengers.

(a) 近道が / は**なかった** / **ありませんでした**。
   *Chikamichi ga / wa **nakatta** / **arimasen deshita**.*

(b) 乗客が / は**いなかった** / **いませんでした**。
   *Jōkyaku ga / wa **inakatta** / **imasen deshita**.*

In a negative sentence in the past tense, *atta* or *arimashita* changes to *nakatta* or *arimasen deshita*, and *ita* or *imashita* changes to *inakatta* or *imasen deshita*.

Examples

1. There weren't any cold drinks.
   冷たい飲み物が / はありませんでした。
   Tsumetai nomimono ga / wa arimasen deshita.

2. There were no young waitresses.

若いウエイトレスが / はいなかった。

Wakai ueitoresu ga / wa inakatta.

3. There were no buses. There were no taxis, either.

バスが / はなかった。タクシーもなかった。

Basu ga / wa nakatta. Takushī mo nakatta.

Practice

passerby	通行人	*tsūkōnin*
animal	動物	*dōbutsu*
gift shop	ギフトショップ	*gifuto shoppu*

Say the following in Japanese:

1. There were no passersby.

2. There were no dangerous animals.

3. There was no restaurant. There was no gift shop, either.

Answers

1. 通行人が / はいなかった / いませんでした。
   Tsūkōnin ga / wa inakatta / imasen deshita.

2. 危険な動物が/ はいなかった / いませんでした。
   Kikenna dōbutsu ga / wa inakatta / imasen deshita.

3. レストランが / はなかった / ありませんでした。ギフトショップもなかった / ありませんでした。
   Resutoran ga / wa nakatta / arimasen deshita. Gifuto shoppu mo nakatta / arimasen deshita.

(a) There are stamps and envelopes.

(b) There are cameramen and reporters (and others).

(a) 切手と封筒がある / あります。
   *Kitte **to** fūtō ga aru / arimasu.*

(b) カメラマンやレポーターがいる / います。
   *Kameraman **ya** repōtā ga iru / imasu.*

The particle *to* lists two or more items exhaustively, whereas the particle *ya* lists two or more items nonexhaustively, implying the existence of others.

Examples

1. There is a red sweater and a brown handbag.
   赤いセーターと茶色のハンドバッグがあります。
   Akai sētā to chairo no handobaggu ga arimasu.

2. There were cherry trees and pine trees and others.
   桜の木や松の木があった。
   Sakura no ki ya matsu no ki ga atta.

3. There are first and second-year students.
   1年生と2年生がいます。
   Ichi-nensei to ni-nensei ga imasu.

4. There were salesmen and buyers and others.
   セールスマンやバイヤーがいた。
   Sērusuman ya baiyā ga ita.

ring	指輪	*yubiwa*
necklace	ネックレス	*nekkuresu*
cake	ケーキ	*kēki*
old people	老人	*rōjin*

Say the following in Japanese:

1. There are rings and necklaces and whatnot.
2. There were delicious pies and cakes.
3. There were old people and young people and others.

Answers

1. 指輪やネックレスがある / あります。
   Yubiwa ya nekkuresu ga aru / arimasu.

2. おいしいパイとケーキがあった / ありました。
   Oishii pai to kēki ga atta / arimashita.

3. 老人や若い人がいた / いました。
   Rōjin ya wakai hito ga ita / imashita.

26

(a) There are lots of apples.

(b) There are five actors.

(a) りんごが**たくさん**ある / あります。
   *Ringo ga **takusan** aru / arimasu.*

(b) 俳優が**5人**いる / います。
   *Haiyū ga **go-nin** iru / imasu.*

To express quantity, adverbs such as *takusan* ("many"), *sukoshi* ("a few," "a little"), or *ōzei* ("many" in reference to people) are placed after the subject-marker, as in (a).

Quantity can also be described by specifying a number and adding a counter, as in (b). Japanese uses various kinds of counters, depending on the type of objects to be counted. For example, the counter *-hon* is used for long, cylindrical objects such as pencils or bottles; *-satsu* for books; *-hiki* for small animals; and *-mai* for thin, flat objects such as papers or blankets. Numbers with counters, like adverbs, come after the subject-marker.

NOTE: For a table of counters, see Appendix 2.

Examples

1. There are two beer bottles.
   ビールの瓶が2本あります。
   Bīru no bin ga ni-hon arimasu.

2. There were many sightseers.
   見物人が大勢いました。
   Kenbutsunin ga ōzei imashita.

3. There are four children and three dogs.
   子供が4人と犬が3匹いる。
   Kodomo ga yonin to inu ga san-biki iru.

4. There were six blankets.
   毛布が6枚ありました。
   Mōfu ga roku-mai arimashita.

water	水	*mizu*
inn	旅館	*ryokan*
five (inns)	5軒	*go-ken*
two (persons)	二人	*futari*

Say the following in Japanese:

1. There is a little water.
2. There were five inns.
3. There are two teachers and many children.

Answers

1. 水が少しある / あります。
   Mizu ga sukoshi aru / arimasu.

2. 旅館が5軒あった / ありました。
   Ryokan ga go-ken atta / arimashita.

3. 先生が二人と子供が大勢いる / います。
   Sensei ga futari to kodomo ga ōzei iru / imasu.

27

(a) There is a bookcase in this room.

(b) There are boys under the tree.

(a) この部屋**に**本箱がある / あります。
   *Kono heya **ni** honbako ga aru / arimasu.*

(b) 木**の下に**男の子がいる / います。
   *Ki **no shita ni** otoko no ko ga iru / imasu.*

The particle *ni* added to a noun or noun phrase indicates a location where someone or something exists. The following are some of the most commonly used locative phrases.

on/under the desk
机の上 / 下に
tsukue no ue/shita ni

near the station
駅の近く / そばに
eki no chikaku/soba ni

in front of/behind the store
店の前 / 後ろに
mise no mae/ushiro ni

beside the cabinet
キャビネットの横に
kyabinetto no yoko ni

inside/outside the room
部屋の中 / 外に
heya no naka/soto ni

beyond the river
川の向こうに
kawa no mukō ni

Ni can also be used with the demonstrative pronouns *koko* ("here"), *soko* ("there"), and *asoko* ("over there"), as in *koko ni arimasu* ("It is here").

NOTE: The particles *mo* ("also") and *wa* (the topic-marker) can be added to *ni*: *koko ni mo arimasu* ("It is here, too"; Example 4), *koko ni wa arimasu* ("It is here," implying "as far as this place is concerned"). When *wa* is added to *ni*, it makes the phrase describing location the topic of the sentence (Example 5).

Examples

1. There is a big pond over there.
   あそこに大きい池があります。
   Asoko ni ōkii ike ga arimasu.

2. There is a bus stop in front of the station.
   駅の前にバス停がある。
   Eki no mae ni basutei ga aru.

3. There are two guides near the entrance.

入り口のそばに案内人が二人います。

Iriguchi no soba ni annainin ga futari imasu.

4. There is a movie theater on this street. There is also one on the next street.

この通りに映画館がある。次の通りにもある。

Kono tōri ni eigakan ga aru. Tsugi no tōri ni mo aru.

5. On the third floor, there is a coffee shop.

3階には、コーヒーショップがあります。

Sangai ni wa, kōhī shoppu ga arimasu.

Practice

factory	工場	*kōjō*
copier	コピー機	*kopīki*
many (in reference to people)	大勢	*ōzei*
people	人	*hito*
various	色々な	*iroirona*

Say the following in Japanese:

1. There is a factory beyond the river.

2. There is a copier beside the cabinet.

3. There are many people over there.

4. In this pond, there are various fish.

Answers

1. 川の向こうに工場がある / あります。
   Kawa no mukō ni kōjō ga aru / arimasu.

2. キャビネットの横にコピー機がある / あります。
   Kyabinetto no yoko ni kopīki ga aru / arimasu.

3. あそこに人が大勢いる / います。
   Asoko ni hito ga ōzei iru / imasu.

4. この池 (の中) には、色々な魚がいる / います。
   Kono ike (no naka) ni wa, iroirona sakana ga iru / imasu.

28

(a) What is on the desk?

(b) Who is in the reception room?

(a) 机の上に**何が**ありますか。

   *Tsukue no ue ni **nani ga** arimasu ka.*

(b) 応接室に**だれが**いますか。

   *Ōsetsushitsu ni **dare ga** imasu ka.*

The interrogative pronouns *nani* ("what") and *dare* ("who") always serve as subjects and must, therefore, be marked by the particle *ga* (never by *wa*).

Examples

1. What is in this drawer?

   この引き出しの中に何がありますか。

   Kono hikidashi no naka ni nani ga arimasu ka.

   There are notebooks, pencils, erasers, and other things.

   ノートや鉛筆や消しゴムがあります。

   Nōto ya enpitsu ya keshigomu ga arimasu.

2. Who is in the next room?

隣の部屋にだれがいますか。

Tonari no heya ni dare ga imasu ka.

The department head and the secretary are.

部長と秘書がいます。

Buchō to hisho ga imasu.

Practice

refrigerator	冷蔵庫	*reizōko*
beer	ビール	*bīru*
juice	ジュース	*jūsu*
bridge	橋	*hashi*
woman	女の人	*onna no hito*
supermarket	スーパー	*sūpā*
gas station	ガソリンスタンド	*gasorinsutando*

Say the following in Japanese:

1. What is in the refrigerator?
   Beer, juice, and other things.

2. Who is on the bridge?
   A woman and some children are.

3. What is near the supermarket?
   A gas station is.

Answers

1. 冷蔵庫の中に何がありますか。
   Reizōko no naka ni nani ga arimasu ka.

   ビールやジュースがあります。
   Bīru ya jūsu ga arimasu.

2. 橋の上にだれがいますか。
   Hashi no ue ni dare ga imasu ka.

   女の人と子供がいます。
   Onna no hito to kodomo ga imasu.

3. スーパーの近くに何がありますか。
   Sūpā no chikaku ni nani ga arimasu ka.

   ガソリンスタンドがあります。
   Gasorin sutando ga arimasu.

29

(a) How many books are there?

(b) How many foreign students are there?

(a) 本は**何冊**ありますか。
   *Hon wa **nan-satsu** arimasu ka.*

(b) 留学生は**何人**いますか。
   *Ryūgakusei wa **nan-nin** imasu ka.*

The interrogative pronoun *nan* (= *nani*), combined with a counter, is used to express a question about quantity: "How many …?" The interrogative pronoun *ikutsu* ("how many") is used to ask the quantity of certain items such as apples and teacups, for which there is no specific counter. Such items are counted with native-Japanese numerals, or with Roman numerals pronounced in Japanese: *hitotsu, futatsu, mittsu,* etc. (Example 3). (For more on how to count in Japanese, see Appendix 1.)

1. How many cars are there in the parking lot?
   駐車場に車が何台ありますか。
   Chūshajō ni kuruma ga nandai arimasu ka.

   There are ten.
   10台あります。
   Jūdai arimasu.

2. How many fish are there in the water tank?
   水槽の中に魚が何匹いますか。
   Suisō no naka ni sakana ga nan-biki imasu ka.

   There are two red ones and three blue ones.
   赤い魚が2匹と青い魚が3匹います。
   Akai sakana ga ni-hiki to aoi sakana ga san-biki imasu.

3. How many apples are there in the basket?
   かごの中にりんごがいくつありますか。
   Kago no naka ni ringo ga ikutsu arimasu ka.

   There are five.
   5つあります。
   Itsutsu arimasu.

how many pairs	何足	*nan-zoku*
shoes	靴	*kutsu*
box	箱	*hako*
class	クラス	*kurasu*
male	男の	*otoko no*
female	女の	*onna no*
teacup	茶碗	*chawan*
table	テーブル	*tēburu*

Say the following in Japanese:

1. How many pairs of shoes are there in this box?
   There are two pairs.

2. How many students are in your class?
   There are two male students and five female students.

3. How many teacups are on the table?
   There are three.

---

1. この箱の中に靴が何足ありますか。
   Kono hako no naka ni kutsu ga nan-zoku arimasu ka.

   2足あります。
   Ni-soku arimasu.

2. あなたのクラスに学生が何人いますか。
   Anata no kurasu ni gakusei ga nan-nin imasu ka.

   男の学生が2人と女の学生が5人います。
   Otoko no gakusei ga futari to onna no gakusei ga go-nin imasu.

3. テーブルの上に茶碗がいくつありますか。
   Tēburu no ue ni chawan ga ikutsu arimasu ka.

   3つあります。
   Mittsu arimasu.

30

(a) Is anything there?
    No, there is nothing.

(b) Is anybody there?
    No, there is nobody.

(a) **何か**ありますか。

    Nani ka arimasu ka.

    いいえ、**何も**ありせん。

    Iie, nani mo arimasen.

(b) **だれか**いますか。

    Dare ka imasu ka.

    いいえ、**だれも**いません。

    Iie, dare mo imasen.

The interrogative pronouns *nani* ("what") and *dare* ("who") combine with the particle *ka* to mean "anything" or "anyone," respectively. Likewise, they can combine with the particle *mo* to mean "nothing" or "no one" in negative sentences. *Nani ka* (or *nani mo*) and *dare ka* (or *dare mo*) are usually sentence subjects, although they are not attended by the particle *ga* (Examples 1, 2). Note that these words may modify the modified nouns that follow them (Example 3), in which case their English translations may vary.

Examples

1. Is there anything on the shelf?

    棚の上に何かありますか。

    Tana no ue ni nani ka arimasu ka.

Yes, there is a round box.

ええ、丸い箱があります。

Ē, marui hako ga arimasu.

2. Was there anybody in the auditorium?

講堂にだれかいましたか。

Kōdō ni dare ka imashita ka.

No, there wasn't anyone.

いいえ、だれもいませんでした。

Iie, dare mo imasen deshita.

3. Were there any rare plants on that island?

その島に何か珍しい植物がありましたか。

Sono shima ni nani ka mezurashii shokubutsu ga arimashita ka.

Yes, there were many tropical plants.

はい、熱帯植物がたくさんありました。

Hai, nettai-shokubutsu ga takusan arimashita.

Practice

garden	庭	*niwa*
gardener	植木屋さん	*uekiya-san*
cabinet	キャビネット	*kyabinetto*
TV program	テレビ番組	*terebi bangumi*

Say the following in Japanese:

1. Is there anyone in the garden?
   Yes, a gardener and a boy are.

2. Is there anything behind the cabinet?
   Yes, there are two desks.

3. Were there any interesting TV programs?
   No, there were none.

/Answers/

1. 庭にだれかいますか。
   Niwa ni dare ka imasu ka.

   はい、植木屋さんと男の子がいます。
   Hai, uekiya-san to otoko no ko ga imasu.

2. キャビネットの後ろに何かありますか。
   Kyabinetto no ushiro ni nani ka arimasu ka.

   はい、机が2つあります。
   Hai, tsukue ga futatsu arimasu.

3. 何かおもしろいテレビ番組がありましたか。
   Nani ka omoshiroi terebi bangumi ga arimashita ka.

   いいえ、何もありませんでした。
   Iie, nani mo arimasen deshita.

31

(a) The document is on the table.

(b) The section chief is in the president's room.

(a) 書類**は**机の上**にある** / **あります**。
   *Shorui **wa** tsukue no ue **ni aru** / **arimasu**.*

(b) 課長**は**社長の部屋**にいる** / **います**。
   *Kachō **wa** shachō no heya **ni iru** / **imasu**.*

A noun followed by the particle *wa* is the topic of the sentence, and a noun coming after the topic and followed by the particle *ni* indicates where the topic (someone or something) is.

1. My car is in front of the hotel.
   私の車はホテルの前にあります。
   Watashi no kuruma wa hoteru no mae ni arimasu.

2. Mr. Johnson is in Osaka now.
   ジョンソンさんは今大阪にいます。
   Jonson-san wa ima Ōsaka ni imasu.

3. Kitchenware was on the fifth floor of the department store.
   台所用品はデパートの5階にあった。
   Daidokoro-yōhin wa depāto no go-kai ni atta.

Practice

| a while ago | さっき | *sakki* |
| secondhand bookshop | 古本屋 | *furuhon'ya* |

Say the following in Japanese:

1. Mr. Yamanaka is in the conference room now.
2. Mike was in the school library a while ago.
3. This dictionary was at the secondhand bookshop in Kanda.

Answers

1. 山中さんは今会議室にいる / います。
   Yamanaka-san wa ima kaigishitsu ni iru / imasu.

2. マイク (さん) はさっき学校の図書館にいた / いました。
   Maiku(-san) wa sakki gakkō no toshokan ni ita / imashita.

3. この辞書は神田の古本屋にあった / ありました。
   Kono jisho wa Kanda no furuhon'ya ni atta / arimashita.

(a) Where is the elevator?

(b) Where is Mr. Kimura?

(a) エレベーターは**どこにありますか**。
*Erebētā **wa doko ni arimasu ka.***

(b) 木村さん**はどこにいますか**。
*Kimura-san **wa doko ni imasu ka**.*

The interrogative pronoun *doko* ("where"), followed by the particle *ni*, is placed after the topic marked by *wa* to express a question about the location of the topic.

NOTE: The verb *arimasu* or *imasu*, one of which usually follows *doko ni*, may be replaced by *desu*, and *ni* dropped, when the meaning of the question or answer is clear from context (Examples 1, 2).

Examples

1. Where is today's newspaper?

   今日の新聞はどこにありますか / どこですか。
   Kyō no shinbun wa doko ni arimasu ka / doko desu ka.

   It's on the table.

   テーブルの上にあります / の上です。
   Tēburu no ue ni arimasu / no ue desu.

2. Where is the department head?

   部長はどこですか。
   Buchō wa doko desu ka.

He's in the next room.

隣の部屋です。

Tonari no heya desu.

3. Where were you last summer?

あなたは去年の夏どこにいましたか。

Anata wa kyonen no natsu doko ni imashita ka.

I was in Canada.

カナダにいました。

Kanada ni imashita.

Practice

restroom	お手洗い	*o-tearai*
elevator	エレベーター	*erebētā*
park	公園	*kōen*
taxi stand	タクシー乗り場	*takushī noriba*
station	駅	*eki*

Say the following in Japanese:

1. Where is the restroom?
   It's near the elevator.

2. Where were the children?
   They were in the park.

3. Where is the taxi stand?
   It's in front of the station.

1. お手洗いはどこにありますか / どこですか。
   O-tearai wa doko ni arimasu ka / doko desu ka.

   エレベーターのそばにあります / そばです。
   Erebētā no soba ni arimasu / soba desu.

2. 子供達はどこにいましたか。
   Kodomo-tachi wa doko ni imashita ka.

   公園にいました。
   Kōen ni imashita.

3. タクシー乗り場はどこにありますか / どこですか。
   Takushī noriba wa doko ni arimasu ka / doko desu ka.

   駅の前にあります / 前です。
   Eki no mae ni arimasu / mae desu.

33

> (a) Mr. Honda has gray hair.
>
> (b) Linda has children.

(a) 本田さん**には**白髪**がある** / **あります**。

   *Honda-san **ni wa** shiraga **ga aru** / **arimasu**.*

(b) リンダ (さん) **には**子供**がある** / **いる** / **あります** / **います**。

   *Rinda(-san) **ni wa** kodomo **ga aru** / **iru** / **arimasu** / **imasu**.*

The verbs *aru* and *iru* are used to express possession as well as existence (→ Pattern 21). *Aru* and *iru* are used for animate possession, and *aru* for inanimate possession. In statements about possession, such as (a) and (b) above, the topic and subject appear in the same sentence. The possessor is the topic (marked by the particle combination *ni wa*), and what is possessed is the subject (marked by the particle *ga*).

1. Mr. Hill has faults.

   ヒルさんには欠点があります。

   Hiru-san ni wa ketten ga arimasu.

2. I have three sons.

   私には息子が3人います。

   Watashi ni wa musuko ga san-nin imasu.

3. Ms. Machida has no children.

   町田さんには子供がありません / いません。

   Machida-san ni wa kodomo ga arimasen / imasen.

Practice

magnificent	立派な	*rippana*
now	今	*ima*
regular customer	常連	*jōren*

Say the following in Japanese:

1. He has a magnificent house.

2. My older brother has no job now.

3. That restaurant has many regular customers.

Answers

1. 彼には立派な家がある / あります。
   Kare ni wa rippana uchi ga aru / arimasu.

2. 兄には今仕事がない / ありません。
   Ani ni wa ima shigoto ga nai / arimasen.

3. あのレストランには常連が大勢いる / います。
   Ano resutoran ni wa jōren ga ōzei iru / imasu.

3 Making Comparisons

34

Today is colder than yesterday.

今日**のほうが**昨日**より**寒い / 寒いです。

*Kyō **no hō ga** kinō **yori** samui / samui desu.*

Japanese adjectives do not have a comparative form (a separate, inflected form for expressing comparison, as in English "colder," "taller," etc.). Instead, when comparing two items in Japanese, the phrase *no hō ga* (… *yori*), followed by an adjective, is used. In this pattern, the item that is the subject of the sentence (the thing that is "more"), and which is being compared to another item, is followed by *no hō ga*, and the item with which comparison is being made (if specified) comes next, followed by the particle *yori*. Finally, an adjective completes the sentence.

The word *hō* is a noun that literally means "side" or "alternative."

Examples

1. This room is quieter than the one upstairs.

   この部屋のほうが2階の部屋より静かです。

   Kono heya no hō ga ni-kai no heya yori shizuka desu.

2. Tonight's banquet was more enjoyable than last week's.

   今晩の宴会のほうが先週の（宴会）より愉快だった。

   Konban no enkai no hō ga senshū no (enkai) yori yukai datta.

3. Tokyo has a larger population than Osaka.

東京のほうが大阪より人口が多い。

Tōkyō no hō ga Ōsaka yori jinkō ga ōi.

Practice

vase	花瓶	*kabin*	⋮	leg	足	*ashi*
tall	背が高い	*se ga takai*	⋮	short	短い	*mijikai*

Say the following in Japanese:

1. This vase is prettier than that one.

2. Mr. Ogawa is taller than Mr. Kubo.

3. My dog has shorter legs than this dog.

Answers

1. この花瓶のほうがその花瓶よりきれいだ / きれいです。
   Kono kabin no hō ga sono kabin yori kirei da / kirei desu.

2. 小川さんのほうが久保さんより背が高い / 背が高いです。
   Ogawa-san no hō ga Kubo-san yori se ga takai / se ga takai desu.

3. 私の犬のほうがこの犬より足が短い/ 短いです。
   Watashi no inu no hō ga kono inu yori ashi ga mijikai / mijikai desu.

35

Mt. Fuji is the most beautiful mountain in Japan.

富士山は日本で一番美しい山だ / です。

*Fuji-san wa Nihon **de ichiban** utsukushii yama da / desu.*

To express the superlative form of an adjective, the adverb *ichiban* ("most," literally, "number one") is placed just before the adjective. The limit within which the comparison is made—the things among which one thing is the "most" or the "best"—is indicated by the particle *de*. If the limit is a group of people, however, the phrase *no naka de* ("among," "of all …") is used instead (Example 3).

Examples

1. This temple is the oldest in Nara.

   この寺は奈良で一番古いです。
   Kono tera wa Nara de ichiban furui desu.

2. Frank was the best student in the class.

   フランクはクラスで一番優秀な学生だった。
   Furanku wa kurasu de ichiban yūshūna gakusei datta.

3. Of all the secretaries, Ms. Yasuda is the most competent.

   秘書の中で、安田さんが一番有能です。
   Hisho no naka de, Yasuda-san ga ichiban yūnō desu.

Practice

Lake Biwa	びわ湖	*Biwa-ko*
lake	湖	*mizuumi*
novel	小説	*shōsetsu*
work (of art)	作品	*sakuhin*

Say the following in Japanese:

1. Lake Biwa is the largest lake in Japan.
2. This novel is the most famous of his works.
3. Of all our teachers, Ms. Sasaki is the kindest.

1. びわ湖は日本で一番大きい湖だ / です。
   Biwa-ko wa Nihon de ichiban ōkii mizuumi da / desu.

2. この小説は彼の作品の中で一番有名だ / 有名です。
   Kono shōsetsu wa kare no sakuhin no naka de ichiban yūmei da / yūmei desu.

3. 私達の先生の中で、佐々木先生が一番親切だ / 親切です。
   Watashi-tachi no sensei no naka de, Sasaki-sensei ga ichiban shinsetsu da / shinsetsu desu.

36

Which is sweeter, this pie or that pie?

That pie is sweeter.

このパイと そのパイと、 **どちらが** 甘いですか。
*Kono pai **to** sono pai **to**, **dochira ga** amai desu ka.*

そのパイ**のほうが**甘いですよ。
*Sono pai **no hō ga** amai desu **yo**.*

To ask a comparative question, the two items being compared are listed first, each accompanied by the particle *to* ("and"). Next comes the interrogative pronoun *dochira* ("which of the two") followed by the subject-marker *ga* and, finally, an adjective, the copula *desu*, and the question-marker *ka*. To answer such a question, simply state the answer, following it up with the phrase *no hō ga* and the appropriate adjective.

The particle *yo* at the end of a sentence indicates the speaker's strong conviction. To express conjecture ("is probably," "I guess"), *deshō* may be used in place of *desu* at the end of the sentence (Example 1).

NOTE: *Dotchi* is the colloquial form of *dochira* (Example 3).

1. Which is stronger, this cord or that cord?
   このひもとそのひもと、どちらが強いですか。
   Kono himo to sono himo to, dochira ga tsuyoi desu ka.

   That cord is stronger, I guess.
   そのひものほうが強いでしょう。
   Sono himo no hō ga tsuyoi deshō.

2. Who was stricter, your father or your mother?
   お父さんとお母さんと、どちらが厳しかったですか。
   O-tō-san to o-kā-san to, dochira ga kibishikatta desu ka.

   My mother was stricter.
   母のほうが厳しかったです。
   Haha no hō ga kibishikatta desu.

3. Which is more convenient, the subway or the bus?
   地下鉄とバスと、どっちが便利ですか。
   Chikatetsu to basu to, dotchi ga benri desu ka.

   The subway is more convenient, by far.
   地下鉄のほうが便利ですよ。
   Chikatetsu no hō ga benri desu yo.

Practice

paper	紙	*kami*
thick	厚い	*atsui*
today	今日	*kyō*
yesterday	昨日	*kinō*
sociable	社交的	*shakōteki*

Say the following in Japanese:

1. Which is thicker, this paper or that paper?
   That paper is thicker.

2. Which was more difficult, today's exam or yesterday's (exam)?
   Today's exam was more difficult, for sure.

3. Who is more sociable, Akiko or Keiko?
   Keiko is more sociable, I guess.

/Answers/

1. この紙とその紙と、どちらが厚いですか。
   Kono kami to sono kami to, dochira ga atsui desu ka.

   その紙のほうが厚いです。
   Sono kami no hō ga atsui desu.

2. 今日の試験と昨日の (試験) と、どちらが難しかったですか。
   Kyō no shiken to kinō no (shiken) to, dochira ga muzukashikatta desu ka.

   今日の試験のほうが難しかったですよ。
   Kyō no shiken no hō ga muzukashikatta desu yo.

3. 明子 (さん) と恵子 (さん) と、どっちが社交的ですか。
   Akiko(-san) to Keiko(-san) to, dotchi ga shakōteki desu ka.

   恵子 (さん) のほうが社交的でしょう。
   Keiko(-san) no hō ga shakōteki deshō.

37

Of these three, which is the most durable?

This red one is probably the most durable.

この3つの中で、どれが一番丈夫ですか。
*Kono mittsu **no naka de**, **dore ga** ichiban jōbu desu ka.*

この赤いのが一番丈夫でしょう。
*Kono akai **no** ga ichiban jōbu deshō.*

To ask a question in the superlative, the limit of the question is stated first and is indicated by the phrase *no naka de* ("among"). The interrogative pronoun *dore* ("which among many")—or *dare* ("who") if the limit is a group of people—comes next, followed by the particle *ga*. The question is completed with the adverb *ichiban* ("the most"), an adjective, the copula *desu*, and the question-marker *ka*. To answer such a question, simply state the answer, following it up with the subject-marker *ga*, the adverb *ichiban*, and the copula *desu* or *deshō*.

NOTE: the particle *no* ("one") attached to an adjective replaces a noun when the noun is understood from context (Example 1).

Examples

1. Of these machines, which one is the newest?

   この機械の中で、どれが一番新しいですか。

   Kono kikai no naka de, dore ga ichiban atarashii desu ka.

   That big one is the newest.

   その大きいのが一番新しいです。

   Sono ōkii no ga ichiban atarashii desu.

2. Of all our new employees, who is the most promising?

   新入社員の中で、だれが一番有望ですか。

   Shinnyū-shain no naka de, dare ga ichiban yūbō desu ka.

   Ms. Yamakawa is probably the most promising.

   山川さんが一番有望でしょう。

   Yamakawa-san ga ichiban yūbō deshō.

3. Who is the most diligent—Tom, Bill, or Sarah?

トム（さん）とビル（さん）とサラ（さん）の中で、だれが
一番勤勉ですか。

*Tomu(-san) to Biru(-san) to Sara(-san) no naka de, dare ga
ichiban kinben desu ka.*

Sarah is the most industrious.

サラ（さん）が一番勤勉です。

Sara(-san) ga ichiban kinben desu.

Practice

utensil	器具	*kigu*
easy to use	使いやすい	*tsukaiyasui*
composition	作文	*sakubun*
popular	人気がある	*ninki ga aru*

Say the following in Japanese:

1. Of these utensils, which one is the easiest to use?
   This light one is the easiest to use.

2. Among these compositions, which one is the best?
   That short one is probably the best.

3. Who is the most diligent—Yukiko, Sachiko, or Midori?
   Midori is the most diligent.

Answers

1. この器具の中で、どれが一番使いやすいですか。
   Kono kigu no naka de, dore ga ichiban tsukaiyasui desu ka.

   この軽いのが一番使いやすいです。
   Kono karui no ga ichiban tsukaiyasui desu.

2. この作文の中で、どれが一番いいですか。
   Kono sakubun no naka de, dore ga ichiban ii desu ka.

   その短いのが一番いいでしょう。
   Sono mijikai no ga ichiban ii deshō.

3. 由紀子（さん）と、幸子（さん）と、みどり（さん）の中で、だれが一番勤勉ですか。
   Yukiko(-san) to, Sachiko(-san) to, Midori(-san) no naka de, dare ga ichiban kinben desu ka.

   みどり（さん）が一番勤勉です。
   Midori(-san) ga ichiban kinben desu.

38

This painter is about as famous as Picasso.

この画家はピカソ（**と同じ**）**くらい**有名だ／有名です。
*Kono gaka wa Pikaso (**to onaji**) **kurai** yūmei da / yūmei desu.*

To describe one item (unknown to the listener) by saying that it is about the same as another (better known to the listener), the item that is less familiar is given as the topic, followed by the topic-marker *wa*. Next is the other, similar and better known item, followed by the phrase *to onaji kurai* ("about as … as"), then the adjective that fits both items. The phrase *to onaji kurai* can be shortened to just *kurai* or, colloquially, *gurai* (Examples 2, 3).

Examples

1. New York is about as humid as Tokyo now.

   今ニューヨークは東京（と同じ）くらい蒸し暑いです。
   Ima Nyū-yōku wa Tōkyō (to onaji) kurai mushiatsui desu.

2. My little brother is about as tall as me.

   弟は僕（と同じ）ぐらい背が高い。
   Otōto wa boku (to onaji) gurai se ga takai.

74

3. This watch is about as accurate as that one.

この時計はその時計（と同じ）ぐらい正確だ。

Kono tokei wa sono tokei (to onaji) gurai seikaku da.

Practice

diamond	ダイヤモンド	*daiyamondo*
boring	つまらない	*tsumaranai*
mountain road	山道	*yamamichi*
safe	安全な	*anzenna*

Say the following in Japanese:

1. This ring is about as expensive as a diamond.

2. This novel is about as boring as that one.

3. That mountain road is about as safe as this road.

Answers

1. この指輪はダイヤモンド（と同じ）くらい高い / 高いです。
   Kono yubiwa wa daiyamondo (to onaji) kurai takai / takai desu.

2. この小説はその小説（と同じ）ぐらいつまらない / つまらないです。
   Kono shōsetsu wa sono shōsetsu (to onaji) gurai tsumaranai / tsumaranai desu.

3. その山道はこの道（と同じ）ぐらい安全だ / 安全です。
   Sono yamamichi wa kono michi (to onaji) gurai anzen da / anzen desu.

39

This briefcase is not as heavy as that one.

このかばんはそのかばん**ほど**重く**ない** / 重く**ありません**。

*Kono kaban wa sono kaban **hodo** omoku **nai** / omoku **ari-masen**.*

In sentences that negate a comparison, the particle *hodo* ("to the degree") follows the item with which the topic (marked by the topic-marker *wa*) is being compared, and the sentence ends with an adjective in the negative form.

1. This report is not as detailed as Ms. Wada's report.

   このレポートは和田さんのレポートほど詳しくありません。

   Kono repōto wa Wada-san no repōto hodo kuwashiku arimasen.

2. This problem is not as important as that one.

   この問題はその問題ほど大切ではありません。

   Kono mondai wa sono mondai hodo taisetsu de wa arimasen.

3. This dog is not as intelligent as my dog.

   この犬は私の犬ほど賢くない。

   Kono inu wa watashi no inu hodo kashikoku nai.

coat	コート	*kōto*
brown	茶色の	*chairo no*
computer	コンピューター	*konpyūtā*
former/old	前の	*mae no*
thin	細い	*hosoi*

Say the following in Japanese:

1. This coat is not as soft as that brown one.

2. This computer is not as expensive as my old one.

3. I am not as thin as my older sister.

---

1. このコートはその茶色の (コート) ほど柔らかくない / 柔らかくありません。
   Kono kōto wa sono chairo no (kōto) hodo yawarakaku nai / yawarakaku arimasen.

2. このコンピューターは前の (コンピューター) ほど高くない / 高くありません。
   Kono konpyūtā wa mae no (konpyūtā) hodo takaku nai / takaku arimasen.

3. 私は姉ほど細くない / 細くありません。
   Watashi wa ane hodo hosoku nai / hosoku arimasen.

Describing Actions in the Present, Future, and Past

40

He gets up at 6 o'clock every morning.

彼は毎朝6時**に起きる** / **起きます**。

*Kare wa maiasa roku-ji **ni okiru** / **okimasu**.*

Japanese verbs use the same form for both the present and future tenses. The tense of the verb is made clear by the use of time adverbs or by context.

Like the copula (→ Pattern 1), Japanese verbs have plain and polite forms. The plain form, also called the dictionary form, is the form listed in dictionaries and generally used in writing and in speech among family and friends. The polite form, also called the *masu* form, is used mainly among adults who are not close friends, and in business.

Japanese verbs may be divided into three groups: Regular I, Regular II, and Irregular. These can be recognized as follows:

1. Regular I verbs: The dictionary form of a Regular I verb has a consonant plus an *u*-vowel ending: *ik**u*** ("go"), *yom**u*** ("read").

2. Regular II verbs: The dictionary form of a Regular II verb has a vowel (either *e* or *i*) and a *ru* ending: *tabe**ru*** ("eat"), *mi**ru*** ("see").
   EXCEPTIONS: Some verbs ending with *-eru* or *-iru* are Regular I verbs: *kae**ru*** ("return home"), *hashi**ru*** ("run").

3. Irregular verbs: There are only two Irregular verbs: *kuru* ("come") and *suru* ("do"). *Suru* combines with nouns to form verbs: *shigoto* ("work") → *shigoto suru* ("do work"), *doraibu* ("drive") → *doraibu suru* ("go for a drive").

The particle *ni* following a time-noun indicates the time at which someone or something does something or something happens. *Ni* is optional with the four seasons, *haru* ("spring"), *natsu* ("summer"), *aki* ("fall"), and *fuyu* ("winter"). And certain time-nouns that refer to broader time frames, rather than to specific times, do not take *ni*: *kyō* ("today"), *konshū* ("this week"), *raigetsu* ("next month"), etc.

Examples

1. The concert starts at 8 P.M.

   コンサートは午後8時に始まる。

   Konsāto wa gogo hachiji ni hajimaru.

2. The section chief will leave on Monday.

   課長は月曜日に出掛けます。

   Kachō wa getsuyōbi ni dekakemasu.

3. Mr. Sagawa will come next week.

   佐川さんは来週来ます。

   Sagawa-san wa raishū kimasu.

4. We travel in spring. / We will take a trip in the spring.

   私達は春 (に) 旅行します。

   Watashi-tachi wa haru (ni) ryokō shimasu.

Practice

what time	何時	*nanji*
begin	始まる	*hajimaru*
bank	銀行	*ginkō*
open	開く	*aku*
department head	部長	*buchō*
go on a business trip	出張する	*shutchō suru*

tomorrow	明日	*ashita*
every night	毎晩	*maiban*
go to bed	寝る	*neru*

Say the following in Japanese:

1. What time does school begin?
2. The bank opens at 9 o'clock.
3. The department head will make a business trip tomorrow.
4. The child goes to bed at 8 o'clock every night.

/Answers/

1. 学校は何時に始まりますか。
   Gakkō wa nan-ji ni hajimarimasu ka.

2. 銀行は9時に開く/開きます。
   Ginkō wa ku-ji ni aku / akimasu.

3. 部長は明日出張する / 出張します。
   Buchō wa ashita shutchō suru / shutchō shimasu.

4. 子供は毎晩8時に寝る / 寝ます。
   Kodomo wa maiban hachi-ji ni neru / nemasu.

41

I eat breakfast in the dining room.

食堂で朝ご飯を食べる / 食べます。
*Shokudō **de** asagohan **o** taberu / tabemasu.*

The particle *de* following a noun indicates the location where an action or event takes place (Examples 1, 2). *De* can be used with certain time-nouns, too, to indicate the time when an action or event takes place (Example 3).

The particle *o* following a noun, as in the above example, marks the noun as the direct object of a transitive verb. If the direct object is also the topic of the sentence (Example 3), the topic-marker *wa* replaces *o*.

Examples

1. Jeff reads newspapers in the library.

   ジェフさんは図書館で新聞を読みます。

   Jefu-san wa toshokan de shinbun o yomimasu.

2. There will be a movie in the auditorium in the afternoon.

   午後講堂で映画がある。

   Gogo kōdō de eiga ga aru.

3. As for this matter, I'll check into it later.

   この件は、後で調べます。

   Kono ken wa, ato de shirabemasu.

Practice

homework	宿題	*shukudai*		living room	居間	*ima*
sometimes	時々	*tokidoki*		lunch	昼ご飯	*hirugohan*
concert	コンサート	*konsāto*		classroom	教室	*kyōshitsu*
(public) hall	ホール	*hōru*				

Say the following in Japanese:

1. Jim does his homework at his friend's house.
2. There are sometimes concerts in this hall.
3. We watch TV in the living room.
4. As for lunch, I eat it in the classroom.

1. ジム（さん）は友達の家で宿題をする / します。
   Jimu(-san) wa tomodachi no uchi de shukudai o suru / shimasu.

2. このホールで時々コンサートがある / あります。
   Kono hōru de tokidoki konsāto ga aru / arimasu.

3. 私達は居間でテレビを見る / 見ます。
   Watashi-tachi wa ima de terebi o miru / mimasu.

4. 昼ご飯は、教室で食べる / 食べます。
   Hirugohan wa, kyōshitsu de taberu / tabemasu.

42

Mr. Sakai doesn't drink coffee. (IMPLYING: But he drinks tea.)

酒井さんはコーヒー**は飲まない** / **飲みません**。

*Sakai-san wa kōhī **wa nomanai** / **nomimasen**.*

In negative sentences, the verb form changes to the negative form. The dictionary, or plain, form changes to the *nai* form (→ Appendix 4), and the polite, or *masu*, form changes to the *masen* form.

The particle *wa* attached to the direct object in a negative sentence replaces the object-marker *o*, singling out the direct object as one item in contrast to another, similar item. The item with which the direct object is set in contrast can be specified (Example 3), or not (Examples 1, 2).

Examples

1. Mr. Abe doesn't speak Korean. (IMPLYING: But he speaks Chinese, etc.)

   阿部さんは韓国語は話しません。

   Abe-san wa Kankokugo wa hanashimasen.

2. Professor Ozaki doesn't teach mathematics. (IMPLYING: But he teaches science, etc.)

小崎先生は数学は教えない。

Ozaki-sensei wa sūgaku wa oshienai.

3. Masako plays tennis. She doesn't play golf.

正子（さん）はテニスはします。ゴルフはしません。

Masako(-san) wa tenisu wa shimasu. Gorufu wa shimasen.

Practice

meat	肉	*niku*
buy	買う	*kau*
wear	着る	*kiru*
sweater	セーター	*sētā*

Say the following in Japanese:

1. I don't buy meat at that store. (IMPLYING: I buy fish, etc. there.)
2. She drinks wine. She doesn't drink beer.
3. My younger sister doesn't wear red sweaters. (IMPLYING: But she wears sweaters of other colors.)

Answers

1. あの店で肉は買わない / 買いません。
   Ano mise de niku wa kawanai / kaimasen.

2. 彼女はワインは飲む / 飲みます。ビールは飲まない / 飲みません。
   Kanojo wa wain wa nomu / nomimasu. Bīru wa nomanai / nomimasen.

3. 妹は赤いセーターは着ない / 着ません。
   Imōto wa akai sētā wa kinai / kimasen.

43

Charles comes to school by bicycle every day.

チャールズ（さん）は毎日自転車で学校へ / に来る /
来ます。

*Chāruzu(-san) wa mainichi jitensha **de** gakkō **e** / **ni** kuru / kimasu.*

The particle *e* or *ni* following a noun indicates the direction in which an action proceeds. It means "to," "toward," "in the direction of," etc.

The particle *de* following a noun—with this phrase then followed by a verb—indicates the means used to perform an action.

The contrastive *wa* may be added to the particles *e, ni* (Example 4), or *de*; *wa* is added to these particles, instead of replacing them as it does *o*.

Examples

1. Mr. Hill will return (home) to Texas by car next week.

   ヒルさんは来週車でテキサスへ帰る。

   Hiru-san wa raishū kuruma de Tekisasu e kaeru.

2. Where is Helen going?

   ヘレンさんはどこへ行きますか。

   Heren-san wa doko e ikimasu ka.

3. We are going to Hawaii by boat next summer.

   来年の夏、船でハワイに行きます。

   Rainen no natsu, fune de Hawai ni ikimasu.

4. This afternoon I'll go to the bank. Not to the post office.

午後、銀行へ行きます。郵便局へは行きません。

Gogo, ginkō e ikimasu. Yūbinkyoku e wa ikimasen.

Practice

sightseeing bus	観光バス	*kankōbasu*
train	電車	*densha*
airplane	飛行機	*hikōki*
morning	朝	*asa*

Say the following in Japanese:

1. Where are you going by the sightseeing bus?

2. He comes to the office by train every day. Not by car.

3. I'm going to Hakata on the 9 o'clock plane tomorrow morning.

Answers

1. 観光バスでどこへ行きますか。
   Kankōbasu de doko e ikimasu ka.

2. 彼は毎日電車で会社に来る / 来ます。車では来ない / 来ません。
   Kare wa mainichi densha de kaisha ni kuru / kimasu. Kuruma de wa konai / kimasen.

3. 明日の朝、9時の飛行機で博多へ行く/ 行きます。
   Ashita no asa, ku-ji no hikōki de Hakata e iku / ikimasu.

44

I leave home at 8 o'clock in the morning.

朝8時に家を出る / 出ます。

*Asa hachi-ji ni uchi **o** deru / demasu.*

The particle *o* following a noun indicates a point of departure for an action.

1. Bill will graduate from college next year.

   ビルは来年大学を卒業する。

   Biru wa rainen daigaku o sotsugyō suru.

2. Mr. Kinoshita gets off the train at Shinjuku.

   木下さんは新宿で電車を降ります。

   Kinoshita-san wa Shinjuku de densha o orimasu.

3. What time will you check out of the hotel?

   何時にホテルをチェックアウトしますか。

   Nanji ni hoteru o chekkuauto shimasu ka.

Practice

| quit | 辞める | *yameru* |
| March | 3月 | *san-gatsu* |

Say the following in Japanese:

1. Ms. Hayashi will quit the company in March.
2. What time does the bus leave the hotel?

Answers

1. 林さんは3月に会社を辞める / 辞めます。
   Hayashi-san wa san-gatsu ni kaisha o yameru / yamemasu.

2. バスは何時にホテルを出ますか。
   Basu wa nan-ji ni hoteru o demasu ka.

45

John will enter a Japanese company.

ジョン(さん)は日本の会社に入る / 入ります。

*Jon(-san) wa Nihon no kaisha **ni** hairu / hairimasu.*

The particle *ni* following a noun indicates a point of entry for an action, or for the arrival of someone or something.

Examples

1. I get on the bus in front of the station.

   駅前でバスに乗ります。

   Ekimae de basu ni norimasu.

2. Sam will join (literally, "enter") the judo club soon.

   サムはもうすぐ柔道クラブに入る。

   Samu wa mō sugu jūdo kurabu ni hairu.

3. Mr. White will arrive at the airport this evening.

   ホワイトさんは今晩空港に着く。

   Howaito-san wa konban kūkō ni tsuku.

4. On which platform does the express (train) arrive?

   急行はどのホームに着きますか。

   Kyūkō wa dono hōmu ni tsukimasu ka.

   It's platform No. 6.

   6番ホームです。

   Roku-ban hōmu desu.

| next spring | 来春 | *raishun* | : | bug | 虫 | *mushi* |
| kindergarten | 幼稚園 | *yōchien* | : | gate | ゲート | *gēto* |

Say the following in Japanese:

1. My son will enter kindergarten next spring.

2. Sometimes bugs come into my room.

3. At which gate does the airplane arrive?
   Gate No. 8.

Answers

1. 息子は来春幼稚園に入る / 入ります。
   Musuko wa raishun yōchien ni hairu / hairimasu.

2. 時々虫が部屋に入る / 入ります。
   Tokidoki mushi ga heya ni hairu / hairimasu.

3. 飛行機はどのゲートに着きますか。
   Hikōki wa dono gēto ni tsukimasu ka.

   8番ゲートです。
   Hachi-ban gēto desu.

46

I am just about to go out.

今出掛ける**ところだ** / です。
*Ima dekakeru **tokoro da** / **desu**.*

To express that an action is about to take place, the dictionary, or plain, form of a verb is used, followed by the phrase *tokoro da* (or *tokoro desu*). The noun *tokoro* ("place") in this expression means "state" or "moment."

1. My mother is just about to eat breakfast.

   母は朝ご飯を食べるところです。

   Haha wa asagohan o taberu tokoro desu.

2. The ship is just about to enter the port.

   船は港に入るところだ。

   Fune wa minato ni hairu tokoro da.

3. The passengers are just about to get off the bus.

   乗客はバスを降りるところです。

   Jōkyaku wa basu o oriru tokoro desu.

Practice

| CD | CD | *shīdī* | auditorium | 講堂 | *kōdō* |
| listen | 聞く | *kiku* | | | |

Say the following in Japanese:

1. I am just about to listen to a CD.

2. The train is about to leave the station.

3. The students are just about to enter the auditorium.

Answers

1. 今CDを聞くところだ / です。
   Ima shīdī o kiku tokoro da / desu.

2. 電車は駅を出るところだ / です。
   Densha wa eki o deru tokoro da / desu.

3. 学生は講堂に入るところだ / です。
   Gakusei wa kōdō ni hairu tokoro da / desu.

47

I traveled with my friend last month.

先月友達と旅行した / 旅行しました。
*Sengetsu tomodachi **to** ryokō **shita** / ryokō **shimashita**.*

To express that an action or event has taken place, or took place, the dictionary form of a verb changes to the *ta* (or *da*) form (→ Appendix 4), and the *masu* form changes to *mashita*, to form the past tense.

The particle *to* following a noun means "with": it indicates a person (or an animal) with whom an action is performed. The word *issho ni* ("together") is often used with *to*, immediately following it (Example 1).

Examples

1. I went to the amusement park with the children.
   子供と一緒に遊園地へ行きました。
   Kodomo to issho ni yūenchi e ikimashita.

2. Hiroshi played with a dog in the park.
   宏は公園で犬と遊んだ。
   Hiroshi wa kōen de inu to asonda.

3. Last night I had a meal with Frank at a restaurant.
   ゆうべフランクとレストランで食事をした。
   Yūbe Furanku to resutoran de shokuji o shita.

4. Midori married an American last year.
   みどりさんは去年アメリカ人と結婚しました。
   Midori-san wa kyonen Amerikajin to kekkon shimashita.

tennis	テニス	*tenisu*	talk	話す	*hanasu*
Saturday	土曜日	*doyōbi*	lobby	ロビー	*robī*
fight	けんかする	*kenka suru*			

Say the following in Japanese:

1. I played tennis with my older brother on Saturday.

2. Sometimes I fought with my younger brother.

3. I talked with my friend in the lobby of the hotel.

Answers

1. 土曜日に兄とテニスをした / しました。
   Doyōbi ni ani to tenisu o shita / shimashita.

2. 時々弟とけんかした / けんかしました。
   Tokidoki otōto to kenka shita / kenka shimashita.

3. ホテルのロビーで友達と話した / 話しました。
   Hoteru no robī de tomodachi to hanashita / hanashimashita.

48

(a) The party started at 7 o'clock.

(b) I walked to the zoo.

(a) パーティーは7時**から**始まった / 始まりました。
   *Pātī wa shichi-ji **kara** hajimatta / hajimarimashita.*

(b) 動物園**まで**歩いた / 歩きました。
   *Dōbutsuen **made** aruita / arukimashita.*

The particle *kara* ("from") or *made* ("to, until"), each coming after a noun, indicates a starting point or an ending point, respectively, in time or space.

1. I studied in the library from 2 o'clock to 4 o'clock.

図書館で2時から4時まで勉強しました。

Toshokan de ni-ji kara yo-ji made benkyō shimashita.

2. This ship came from Alaska.

この船はアラスカから来た。

Kono fune wa Arasuka kara kita.

3. I took the subway to Meguro.

目黒まで地下鉄に乗りました。

Meguro made chikatetsu ni norimashita.

4. I went with Frank as far as the airport.

フランクさんと一緒に空港まで行きました。

Furanku-san to issho ni kūkō made ikimashita.

Practice

work	働く	*hataraku*
Monday	月曜日	*getsuyōbi*
Friday	金曜日	*kin'yōbi*
taxi	タクシー	*takushī*
read	読む	*yomu*
beginning	初め	*hajime*
end	終わり	*owari*

Say the following in Japanese:

1. She worked at a supermarket from Monday through Friday.

2. I took a taxi from the airport to the hotel.

3. As for this book, I read it from beginning to end.

1. 彼女は月曜日から金曜日までスーパーで働いた / 働きました。
   Kanojo wa getsuyōbi kara kin'yōbi made sūpā de hataraita / hatarakimashita.

2. 空港からホテルまでタクシーに乗った / 乗りました。
   Kūkō kara hoteru made takushī ni notta / norimashita.

3. この本は、初めから終わりまで読んだ / 読みました。
   Kono hon wa, hajime kara owari made yonda / yomimashita.

49

My father has just gotten up.

父は今起きた**ところだ** / **です**。
*Chichi wa ima okita **tokoro da** / **desu**.*

To express that an action has just been completed, the *ta* (or *da*) form of a verb is used, followed by the phrase *tokoro da* (or *tokoro desu*).

Examples

1. I have just finished my homework.
   宿題を終えたところです。
   Shukudai o oeta tokoro desu.

2. The train has just come out of a tunnel.
   列車はトンネルを出たところだ。
   Ressha wa tonneru o deta tokoro da.

3. Mr. Nelson has just returned (home) to America.
   ネルソンさんはアメリカへ帰ったところです。
   Neruson-san wa Amerika e kaetta tokoro desu.

package	小包	*kozutsumi*
arrive	着く	*tsuku*
start/begin	始める	*hajimeru*
project	プロジェクト	*purojekuto*
sell	売る	*uru*

Say the following in Japanese:

1. This package has just arrived.

2. We have just started a new project.

3. Mr. Kimura has just sold his house.

Answers

1. この小包は今着いたところだ / です。
   Kono kozutsumi wa ima tsuita tokoro da / desu.

2. 新しいプロジェクトを始めたところだ / です。
   Atarashii purojekuto o hajimeta tokoro da / desu.

3. 木村さんは家を売ったところだ / です。
   Kimura-san wa uchi o utta tokoro da / desu.

50

That child sleeps with the lights on.

その子は電気をつけた**まま**寝る / 寝ます。
*Sono ko wa denki o tsuketa **mama** neru / nemasu.*

To express that someone or something (the subject) remains in a certain state after performing an action, the noun *mama* is used. *Mama* is preceded by a verb in the *ta* (or *da*) form (→ Appendix 4) and is followed by another verb (in any tense) to indicate that the subject performs another action while in this unaltered state.

1. He ate the cake standing up.

   彼は立ったままケーキを食べた。

   Kare wa tatta mama kēki o tabeta.

2. My roommate often goes out leaving the TV on.

   ルームメートはよくテレビをつけたまま出掛けます。

   Rūmumēto wa yoku terebi o tsuketa mama dekakemasu.

3. The boy answered with both hands in his pockets.

   少年は両手をポケットに入れたまま答えた。

   Shōnen wa ryōte o poketto ni ireta mama kotaeta.

Practice

| tea | お茶 | *o-cha* | open | 開ける | *akeru* |
| window | 窓 | *mado* | put on (a hat) | かぶる | *kaburu* |

Say the following in Japanese:

1. She drank tea with her coat on.
2. Sometimes I sleep with the window open.
3. The student entered the auditorium with a hat on.

Answers

1. 彼女はコートを着たままお茶を飲んだ / 飲みました。
   Kanojo wa kōto o kita mama o-cha o nonda / nomimashita.

2. 時々私は窓を開けたまま寝る / 寝ます。
   Tokidoki watashi wa mado o aketa mama neru / nemasu.

3. 学生は帽子をかぶったまま講堂に入った / 入りました。
   Gakusei wa bōshi o kabutta mama kōdō ni haitta / hairimashita.

51

I study while listening to music.

音楽を聞き**ながら**勉強する / 勉強します。

*Ongaku o kiki**nagara** benkyō suru / benkyō shimasu.*

The particle *nagara* expresses simultaneous actions: one subject performs one main action while also performing another, secondary action. The secondary action is given first, and the form of the verb used—the form that comes before nagara—is the stem (the *masu* form without *masu*).

Examples

1. Mr. Suzuki reads reports while smoking.

鈴木さんはたばこを吸いながらレポートを読みます。

Suzuki-san wa tabako o suinagara repōto o yomimasu.

2. I watched TV with my friend while drinking beer.

ビールを飲みながら友達とテレビを見た。

Bīru o nominagara tomodachi to terebi o mita.

3. The teacher explained while showing slides.

先生はスライドを見せながら説明しました。

Sensei wa suraido o misenagara setsumei shimashita.

Practice

word	言葉	*kotoba*	use	使う	*tsukau*
memorize	覚える	*oboeru*	telephone	電話	*denwa*
walk	歩く	*aruku*	hamburger	ハンバーガー	*hanbāgā*
write	書く	*kaku*			

Say the following in Japanese:

1. Dan memorizes words while walking.

2. Anne wrote a composition in Japanese while using a dictionary.

3. I talked with Sam on the phone while eating a hamburger.

/Answers/

1. ダン(さん)は歩きながら言葉を覚える / 覚えます。
   Dan(-san) wa arukinagara kotoba o oboeru / oboemasu.

2. アン(さん)は辞書を使いながら日本語で作文を書いた / 書きました。
   An(-san) wa jisho o tsukainagara Nihongo de sakubun o kaita / kakimashita.

3. ハンバーガーを食べながらサム(さん)と電話で話した / 話しました。
   Hanbāgā o tabenagara Samu(-san) to denwa de hanashita / hanashimashita.

52

The cherry blossoms will begin to bloom in March.

桜の花は3月に咲き**始める** / 咲き**始めます**。
*Sakura no hana wa san-gatsu ni saki**hajimeru** / saki**hajime-masu**.*

A compound verb meaning "begin to do" can be formed using the verb *hajimeru* ("begin"). *Hajimeru* is attached, as an auxiliary, to a verb in its stem form, to indicate that someone or something begins to do something.

/Examples/

1. It began to rain. / Rain began to fall.

雨が降り始めました。

Ame ga furihajimemashita.

2. The train finally began to move.

電車はやっと動き始めた。

Densha wa yatto ugokihajimeta.

3. Jim has just started to date Michiko.

ジムは道子と付き合い始めたところだ。

Jimu wa Michiko to tsukiaihajimeta tokoro da.

Practice

snow	雪	*yuki*
collect	集める	*atsumeru*
practice	練習する	*renshū suru*
piano	ピアノ	*piano*

Say the following in Japanese:

1. It began to snow. / Snow began to fall.

2. I have just started to collect stamps.

3. I will begin to practice the piano, starting tomorrow.

Answers

1. 雪が降り始めた / 降り始めました。
   Yuki ga furihajimeta / furihajimemashita.

2. 切手を集め始めたところだ / です。
   Kitte o atsumehajimeta tokoro da / desu.

3. 明日からピアノを練習し始める / 練習し始めます。
   Ashita kara piano o renshū shihajimeru / renshū shihajimemasu.

53

He will finish writing his thesis soon.

彼はもうすぐ論文を書き**終わる** / 書き**終わります**。
Kare wa mō sugu ronbun o kakiowaru / kakiowarimasu.

A compound verb meaning "finish doing" can be formed using the verb *owaru* ("finish"). *Owaru* is attached, as an auxiliary, to a verb in its stem form to indicate that someone or something finishes doing something.

Examples

1. My husband finished eating his breakfast.
   主人は朝ご飯を食べ終わりました。
   Shujin wa asagohan o tabeowarimashita.

2. The police finished investigating the case.
   警察はその事件を調べ終わった。
   Keisatsu wa sono jiken o shirabeowatta.

3. I have just finished reading this history book.
   この歴史の本を読み終わったところです。
   Kono rekishi no hon o yomiowatta tokoro desu.

Practice

wash	洗う	*arau*
mow	刈る	*karu*
lawn	芝生	*shibafu*

Say the following in Japanese:

1. He finished washing his car.

2. My father has just finished mowing the lawn.

3. The section chief has just finished speaking.

---

1. 彼は車を洗い終わった / 洗い終わりました。
   Kare wa kuruma o araiowatta / araiowarimashita.

2. 父は芝生を刈り終わったところだ / です。
   Chichi wa shibafu o kariowatta tokoro da / desu.

3. 課長は話し終わったところだ / です。
   Kachō wa hanashiowatta tokoro da / desu.

54

I didn't eat breakfast this morning.

今朝、朝ご飯を食べ**なかった** / 食べ**ませんでした**。
*Kesa, asagohan o tabe**nakatta** / tabe**masen deshita**.*

To express the negative past tense, the *nai* of the *nai* form changes to *nakatta*, and the *masen* of the *masen* form changes to *masen deshita*.

Examples

1. Mr. Kida didn't come to the office today.

   木田さんは今日会社へ来ませんでした。
   Kida-san wa kyō kaisha e kimasen deshita.

2. I didn't shop at the department store yesterday.

昨日デパートで買い物しなかった。

Kinō depāto de kaimono shinakatta.

3. Bill didn't dance with Beth at last night's party.

ビルはゆうべのパーティーでベスと踊らなかった。

Biru wa yūbe no pātī de Besu to odoranakatta.

Practice

weekend	週末	*shūmatsu*
swim	泳ぐ	*oyogu*
movie	映画	*eiga*
last month	先月	*sengetsu*

Say the following in Japanese:

1. He didn't swim on the weekend.

2. Last month I didn't see a movie.

3. They didn't eat at the hotel's restaurant.

Answers

1. 彼は週末 (に) 泳がなかった / 泳ぎませんでした。
   Kare wa shūmatsu (ni) oyoganakatta. / oyogimasen deshita.

2. 先月は映画を見なかった / 見ませんでした。
   Sengetsu wa eiga o minakatta / mimasen deshita.

3. 彼らはホテルのレストランで食べなかった / 食べませんでした。
   Kare-ra wa hoteru no resutoran de tabenakatta / tabemasen deshita.

55

I went to the park yesterday, but not today.

昨日は公園へ行った / 行きました**が**、今日**は**行かな
かった / 行きませんでした。

*Kinō wa kōen e itta / ikimashita **ga**, kyō **wa** ikanakatta / ikimasen deshita.*

The particle *ga* is used as a conjunction that combines two sentences. It
means "but" (and sometimes "and" when loosely combining two sentences)
and is often used to introduce a contrast. The repeated use of the particle
wa after a noun in a sentence with a conjunctive *ga* is contrastive. This
contrastive *wa* can be added to nouns or noun phrases that already have
a particle attached (Examples 1, 2, 3).

| Examples |

1. I swam in the pool, but not in the ocean.

   プールでは泳いだが、海では泳がなかった。

   Pūru de wa oyoida ga, umi de wa oyoganakatta.

2. My older sister went to Paris, but not to Rome.

   姉はパリへは行きましたが、 ローマへは行きません
   でした。

   *Ane wa Pari e wa ikimashita ga, Rōma e wa ikimasen
   deshita.*

3. Mr. Suda traveled by train, but not by plane.

須田さんは列車では旅行したが、飛行機では旅行しなかった。

Suda-san wa ressha de wa ryokō shita ga, hikōki de wa ryokō shinakatta.

review (lessons)	復習する	*fukushū suru*
last night	ゆうべ	*yūbe*
tonight	今晩	*konban*
bar	バー	*bā*
golf	ゴルフ	*gorufu*

Say the following in Japanese:

1. I reviewed (my lesson) last night, but not tonight.

2. He drank at home, but not at a bar.

3. Mr. Miki played golf with the section chief, but not with the president.

Answers

1. ゆうべは復習した / しましたが、今晩はしなかった / しませんでした。
   Yūbe wa fukushū shita / shimashita ga, konban wa shinakatta / shimasen deshita.

2. 彼は家では飲んだ / 飲みましたが、バーでは飲まなかった / 飲みませんでした。
   Kare wa uchi de wa nonda / nomimashita ga, bā de wa nomanakatta / nomimasen deshita.

3. 三木さんは課長とはゴルフをした / しましたが、社長とはしなかった / しませんでした。
   Miki-san wa kachō to wa gorufu o shita / shimashita ga, shachō to wa shinakatta / shimasen deshita.

5

Actions: in Progress, Completed, Successive, Simultaneous, and Miscellaneous

56

I am eating breakfast right now.

今、朝ご飯を食べている / 食べています。
Ima, asagohan o tabete iru / tabete imasu.

The *te* form of a verb (→Appendix 4), followed by the verb *iru* or *imasu* ("exist"), expresses the present progressive tense. Here *iru* or *imasu* is used as an auxiliary.

Examples

1. Kazuo is playing in the yard with his dog.
   和夫は庭で犬と遊んでいる。
   Kazuo wa niwa de inu to asonde iru.

2. I am listening to music and drinking tea.
   私はお茶を飲みながら音楽を聞いています。
   Watashi wa o-cha o nominagara ongaku o kiite imasu.

3. Ms. Tamura was making a phone call a while ago.
   田村さんはさっき電話をかけていました。
   Tamura-san wa sakki denwa o kakete imashita.

Practice

cookies	クッキー	*kukkī*	rewrite	書き直す	*kakinaosu*
bake	焼く	*yaku*			

Say the following in Japanese:

1. My older sister is baking cookies in the kitchen now.

2. Sam is reading a newspaper and using a dictionary.

3. Mr. Sasaki was rewriting the report a while ago.

---

1. 姉は今台所でクッキーを焼いている / 焼いていますます。
   Ane wa ima daidokoro de kukkī o yaite iru / yaite imasu.

2. サム (さん) は辞書を使いながら新聞を読んでいる / 読んでいます。
   Samu(-san) wa jisho o tsukainagara shinbun o yonde iru / yonde imasu.

3. 佐々木さんはさっきレポートを書き直していた / 書き直していました。
   Sasaki-san wa sakki repōto o kakinaoshite ita / kakinaoshite imashita.

57

Birds are flying in the sky.

鳥が空を飛んでいる / 飛んでいます。
*Tori ga sora **o** tonde iru / tonde imasu.*

The particle *o* following a noun and coming before a motion verb (a verb that expresses movement) indicates the space or distance through, upon, or along which the action expressed by the verb takes place.

Examples

1. Small fish are swimming along the bottom of the river.
   小さい魚が川の底を泳いでいる。
   Chiisai sakana ga kawa no soko o oyoide iru.

2. Many people were walking along the street in front of the station.

大勢の人が駅前の道を歩いていた。

Ōzei no hito ga ekimae no michi o aruite ita.

3. The bus is crossing the bridge.

バスが橋を渡っている。

Basu ga hashi o watatte iru.

Practice

seagull	かもめ	*kamome*
ocean/sea	海	*umi*
beach/seashore	海岸	*kaigan*
run	走る	*hashiru*
left side	左側	*hidarigawa*

Say the following in Japanese:

1. Seagulls were flying over the ocean.

2. A young man is walking along the beach.

3. Cars are running on the left side of the street.

Answers

1. かもめが海の上を飛んでいた / 飛んでいました。
   Kamome ga umi no ue o tonde ita / tonde imashita.

2. 若い男の人が海岸を歩いている / 歩いています。
   Wakai otoko no hito ga kaigan o aruite iru / aruite imasu.

3. 車が道の左側を走っている / 走っています。
   Kuruma ga michi no hidarigawa o hashitte iru / hashitte imasu.

58

The kids are doing nothing but watching TV.

子供達はテレビを見て**ばかりいる** / 見て**ばかりいます**。
*Kodomo-tachi wa terebi o mite **bakari iru** / mite **bakari imasu**.*

The particle *bakari* ("only"), coming between the *te* form of a verb and the auxiliary verb *iru* or *imasu*, expresses a repeated or an ongoing action. This pattern is used to express disapproval.

Examples

1. Mr. Izumi was doing nothing but drinking beer at the party.
   泉さんはパーティーでビールを飲んでばかりいた。
   Izumi-san wa pātī de bīru o nonde bakari ita.

2. My roommate is doing nothing but reading manga.
   ルームメートは漫画を読んでばかりいる。
   Rūmumēto wa manga o yonde bakari iru.

3. The cat is doing nothing but sleeping on the sofa all day long.
   猫は一日中ソファの上で寝てばかりいます。
   Neko wa ichinichijū sofa no ue de nete bakari imasu.

Practice

poem	詩	*shi*
take	とる	*toru*
picture/photo	写真	*shashin*
camera	カメラ	*kamera*

Say the following in Japanese:

1. She was doing nothing but watching movies.

2. My older brother was doing nothing but writing poems.

3. My son is doing nothing but taking pictures with his new camera.

Answers

1. 彼女は映画を見てばかりいた / 見てばかりいました。
   Kanojo wa eiga o mite bakari ita / mite bakari imashita.

2. 兄は詩を書いてばかりいた / 書いてばかりいました。
   Ani wa shi o kaite bakari ita / kaite bakari imashita.

3. 息子は新しいカメラで写真を撮ってばかりいる / 撮ってばかりいます。
   Musuko wa atarashii kamera de shashin o totte bakari iru / totte bakari imasu.

59

My parents live in Boston.

両親はボストンに住んでいる / 住んでいます。
*Ryōshin wa Bosuton **ni** sun**de iru** / sun**de imasu**.*

With certain verbs, the *te iru* form (→ Pattern 56) can express an action that takes place over a period of time—a regular or habitual action like "living" in a place or "working" for a company. The particle *ni* used with such verbs to express such meanings indicates the place where the static action (i.e., "living," "working," etc.) occurs (Example 1).

Examples

1. Ms. Olson works for a Japanese company.

   オルソンさんは日本の会社に勤めている。
   Oruson-san wa Nihon no kaisha ni tsutomete iru.

2. My daughter Akiko goes to drama school.

娘の秋子は演劇学校に行っています。

Musume no Akiko wa engeki gakkō ni itte imasu.

3. Mr. Young was teaching English at high school.

ヤングさんは高校で英語を教えていた。

Yangu-san wa kōkō de Eigo o oshiete ita.

Practice

commute	通う	*kayou*
university	大学	*daigaku*
subway	地下鉄	*chikatetsu*
the Foreign Ministry	外務省	*gaimushō*

Say the following in Japanese:

1. I commute to the university by subway.

2. My friend Kazuko was working for the Foreign Ministry.

3. Where does Mr. Rice live?

Answers

1. 私は地下鉄で大学に通っている / 通っています。
   Watashi wa chikatetsu de daigaku ni kayotte iru / kayotte imasu.

2. 友達の和子さんは外務省に勤めていた / 勤めていました。
   Tomodachi no Kazuko-san wa gaimushō ni tsutomete ita / tsutomete imashita.

3. ライスさんはどこに住んでいますか。
   Raisu-san wa doko ni sunde imasu ka.

60

The door of the conference room is open.

会議室のドアが開い**ている** / 開い**ています**。
*Kaigishitsu no doa ga ai**te iru** / ai**te imasu**.*

The *te iru* form (→ Pattern 56) can also express matter-of-factly a state of being that is the result of a previous action.

Examples

1. The bus is stopped over there. (PREVIOUS ACTION: "stop," "come to a stop")

   あそこにバスが止まっている。

   Asoko ni basu ga tomatte iru.

2. Mr. Kubo is wearing a brown suit. (PREVIOUS ACTION: "put on")

   久保さんは茶色の背広を着ています。

   Kubo-san wa chairo no sebiro o kite imasu.

3. Mr. Yamada has come, but Mr. Saeki hasn't come yet.

   山田さんは来ていますが、佐伯さんはまだ来ていま
   せん。

   Yamada-san wa kite imasu ga, Saeki-san wa mada kite imasen.

Practice

wear (shoes)	はく	*haku*
white	白い	*shiroi*
be closed	閉まる	*shimaru*
get married	結婚する	*kekkon suru*

Say the following in Japanese:

1. The child is wearing white shoes.

2. The windows of the classroom are closed.

3. My older brother is married, but my younger brother isn't yet.

---

1. 子供は白い靴をはいている / はいています。
   Kodomo wa shiroi kutsu o haite iru / haite imasu.

2. 教室の窓が閉まっている / 閉まっています。
   Kyōshitsu no mado ga shimatte iru / shimatte imasu.

3. 兄は結婚している / していますが、弟はまだ結婚していない / していません。
   Ani wa kekkon shite iru / shite imasu ga, otōto wa mada kekkon shite inai / shite imasen.

61

The lights in the hallway have been turned on.

廊下の電気がつけ**てある** / つけ**てあります**。
*Rōka no denki ga tsuke**te aru** / tsuke**te arimasu**.*

The *te* form of a verb, followed by the verb *aru* or *arimasu* ("exist"), expresses a state of being that is the result of a previous, deliberate action. Only transitive verbs can be used in this pattern, and the subject of the sentence must be inanimate.

Examples

1. Posters have been put on the wall.

   壁にポスターが張ってある。
   Kabe ni posutā ga hatte aru.

2. This room has been cleaned.

この部屋は掃除してあります。

Kono heya wa sōji shite arimasu.

3. These cups have been washed.

このコップは洗ってあります。

Kono koppu wa aratte arimasu.

Practice

entrance	入り口	*iriguchi*
close	閉める	*shimeru*
blackboard	黒板	*kokuban*

Say the following in Japanese:

1. As for the door of the entrance, it has been closed.

2. Kanji are written on the blackboard.

3. As for this report, it has been read.

Answers

1. 入り口のドアは閉めてある / 閉めてあります。
   Iriguchi no doa wa shimete aru / shimete arimasu.

2. 黒板に漢字が書いてある / 書いてあります。
   Kokuban ni kanji ga kaite aru / kaite arimasu.

3. このレポートは読んである / 読んであります。
   Kono repōto wa yonde aru / yonde arimasu.

62

I bought drinks for tomorrow's picnic.

明日のピクニック**のために**飲み物を買っ**ておいた** /
買っ**ておきました**。

*Ashita no pikunikku **no tame ni** nomimono o kat**te oita** /
kat**te okimashita**.*

The *te* form of a verb, followed by the verb *oku* or *okimasu* ("put"), expresses an action done deliberately for a future convenience. Here *oku* or *okimasu* is used as an auxiliary and is conventionally written in hiragana, not kanji.

The phrase *no tame ni*—consisting of the particle *no*, the noun *tame* ("benefit"), and the particle *ni*—indicates the beneficiary of an action (Example 3) and means "for" or "for the benefit of."

Examples

1. I'll check the price of the article beforehand.

   前もって品物の値段を調べておきます。

   Mae motte shinamono no nedan o shirabete okimasu.

2. I reserved a table (for us) at the restaurant.

   レストランのテーブルを予約しておきましたよ。

   Resutoran no tēburu o yoyaku shite okimashita yo.

3. He collected Japanese stamps for his friend in America.

   彼はアメリカの友達のために日本の切手を集めておいた。

   Kare wa Amerika no tomodachi no tame ni Nihon no kitte o atsumete oita.

clean	掃除する	*sōji suru*
guest	お客さま	*o-kyaku-sama*
plot/storyline	筋	*suji*
play	劇	*geki*
order	注文する	*chūmon suru*
five (books)	5冊	*go-satsu*

Say the following in Japanese:

1. I cleaned the room for tonight's guests.
2. I read the plot of that play beforehand.
3. I ordered five copies of this book yesterday.

Answers

1. 今晩のお客さまのために部屋を掃除しておいた / 掃除しておきました。
   Konban no o-kyaku-sama no tame ni heya o sōji shite oita / sōji shite oki-mashita.

2. 前もってその劇の筋を読んでおいた / 読んでおきました。
   Mae motte sono geki no suji o yonde oita / yonde okimashita.

3. 昨日この本を5冊注文しておいた / 注文しておきました。
   Kinō kono hon o go-satsu chūmon shite oita / chūmon shite okimashita.

63

We have already completed the project.

私達はもうプロジェクトを仕上げ**てしまった** / 仕上げ
てしまいました。

*Watashi-tachi wa mō purojekuto o shiage**te shimatta** /
shiage**te shimaimashita**.*

The *te* form of a verb, followed by the verb *shimau* ("finish," "put away"), expresses with emphasis the completion of an action and, in some cases, may imply a sense of regret for an action one has taken or an event that has occurred (Example 3). *Shimau* here is used as an auxiliary.

Examples

1. He finished writing that novel in one year.
   彼は1年でその小説を書いてしまった。
   Kare wa ichi-nen de sono shōsetsu o kaite shimatta.

2. Takashi ate up all the cookies.
   孝はクッキーをみんな食べてしまいました。
   Takashi wa kukkī o minna tabete shimaimashita.

3. I have completely forgotten (to do) my homework.
   すっかり宿題を忘れてしまった。
   Sukkari shukudai o wasurete shimatta.

Practice

be late	遅れる	*okureru*
class	授業	*jugyō*
go abroad	外国へ行く	*gaikoku e iku*
tidy up	片付ける	*katazukeru*

Say the following in Japanese:

1. Jim was late for class.
2. My older sister has gone abroad.
3. I've already finished tidying up the room.

1. ジム（さん）は授業に遅れてしまった / 遅れてしまいました。
   Jimu(-san) wa jugyō ni okurete shimatta / okurete shimaimashita.

2. 姉は外国へ行ってしまった / 行ってしまいました。
   Ane wa gaikoku e itte shimatta / itte shimaimashita.

3. もう部屋を片付けてしまった / 片付けてしまいました。
   Mō heya o katazukete shimatta / katazukete shimaimashita.

64

I ate sashimi for the first time (to see what it was like).

初めて刺身を食べてみた / 食べてみました。
Hajimete sashimi o tabete mita / tabete mimashita.

The *te* form of a verb, followed by the verb *miru* ("see"), expresses the subject's attempt at doing something to see what it is like. Here *miru* is used as an auxiliary and by convention is written in hiragana, not kanji.

Examples

1. Jim took the Bullet Train from Tokyo to Osaka (to see what it is like).

   ジムは東京から大阪まで新幹線に乗ってみた。
   Jimu wa Tōkyō kara Ōsaka made shinkansen ni notte mita.

2. Judy tried on a Japanese kimono for the first time.

   ジュディさんは初めて日本の着物を着てみました。
   Judī-san wa hajimete Nihon no kimono o kite mimashita.

3. As for this matter, I will consult with my teacher (to see what he/she thinks about it).

この事は先生と相談してみます。

Kono koto wa sensei to sōdan shite mimasu.

Practice

new product	新製品	*shinseihin*
bread	パン	*pan*
bakery	パン屋	*panya*

Say the following in Japanese:

1. Mr. Brown lived in a Japanese house (to see what it was like).

2. I'll use this new product (to see what it is like).

3. I bought some bread at the new bakery, for the first time (to see what it was like).

Answers

1. ブラウンさんは日本の家に住んでみた / 住んでみました。
   Buraun-san wa Nihon no ie ni sunde mita / sunde mimashita.

2. この新製品を使ってみる / 使ってみます。
   Kono shinseihin o tsukatte miru / tsukatte mimasu.

3. 新しいパン屋で初めてパンを買ってみた / 買ってみました。
   Atarashii pan'ya de hajimete pan o katte mita / katte mimashita.

65

The dog is running away.

犬が走って**いく** / 走って**いきます**。

Inu ga hashitte iku / hashitte ikimasu.

The *te* form of a verb, followed by the verb *iku* or *ikimasu* ("go"), expresses an action that moves away from the location of the speaker, or moves into the future. Here *iku* or *ikimasu* is used as an auxiliary and by convention is written in hiragana, not kanji.

Examples

1. He left the room suddenly. (VIEWPOINT: The speaker is or was in the room when the person left, thus the direction of his/her leaving is or was away from the speaker.)

   彼は急に部屋を出ていった。

   Kare wa kyū ni heya o dete itta.

2. Every year, Janet returns to her (home) country for Christmas. (VIEWPOINT: The speaker no doubt remains in the country from which Janet leaves, and that country is probably his/her home country.)

   毎年ジャネットさんはクリスマスに国へ帰っていきます。

   Mainen, Janetto-san wa kurisumasu ni kuni e kaette ikimasu.

3. This city's population will gradually increase.

   この町の人口はだんだん増えていく。

   Kono machi no jinkō wa dandan fuete iku.

Practice

grow (of tree)	育つ	*sodatsu*
pass (by)	通る	*tōru*
bird	鳥	*tori*
that direction	あちら	*achira*

Say the following in Japanese:

1. This tree will grow gradually.
2. A bus passed by the front of this building.
3. The bird flew away in that direction.

---

1. この木はだんだん育っていく / 育っていきます。
   Kono ki wa dandan sodatte iku / sodatte ikimasu.

2. バスがこのビルの前を通っていった / 通っていきました。
   Basu ga kono biru no mae o tōtte itta / tōtte ikimashita.

3. 鳥があちらへ飛んでいった / 飛んでいきました。
   Tori ga achira e tonde itta / tonde ikimashita.

66

The sky has cleared up.

空が晴れてきた / 晴れてきました。
Sora ga harete kita / harete kimashita.

The *te* form of a verb, followed by the verb *kuru* or *kimasu* ("come"), expresses an action that moves toward the location of the speaker, or proceeds up to a current point in time. Here *kuru* or *kimasu* is used as an auxiliary and by convention is written in hiragana, not kanji.

Examples

1. A little bird sometimes comes into the room through the window.

   小鳥が時々窓から部屋に入ってくる.

   Kotori ga tokidoki mado kara heya ni haitte kuru.

2. The section chief has started to gain weight recently.

課長は最近太ってきました。

Kachō wa saikin futotte kimashita.

3. Sales have declined since last month.

先月から売り上げが減ってきた。

Sengetsu kara uriage ga hette kita.

Practice

get thin/lose weight	やせる	*yaseru*
suddenly	急に	*kyūni*
wind	風	*kaze*
blow	吹く	*fuku*
do one's best	がんばる	*ganbaru*

Say the following in Japanese:

1. She started to lose weight suddenly.

2. A cold wind started to blow.

3. We have done our best up to now.

Answers

1. 彼女は急にやせてきた / やせてきました。
   Kanojo wa kyū ni yasete kita / yasete kimashita.

2. 冷たい風が吹いてきた / 吹いてきました。
   Tsumetai kaze ga fuite kita / fuite kimashita.

3. 私達は今までがんばってきた / がんばってきました。
   Watashi-tachi wa ima made ganbatte kita / ganbatte kimashita.

67

He drinks coffee and leaves home before 8 o'clock.

彼はコーヒーを飲ん**で**8時前に家を出る / 出ます。

*Kare wa kōhī o non**de** hachi-ji mae ni uchi o deru / demasu.*

The *te* form of a verb is used to link two or more actions in the order of their occurrence. The tense of a sentence with the *te* form used in this way is determined by the final verb.

NOTE: In formal speech and writing, the stem form replaces the *te* form.

Examples

1. Ken got off the bus at Shinjuku and entered a bookstore.

   ケンは新宿でバスを降りて本屋に入った。

   Ken wa Shinjuku de basu o orite hon'ya ni haitta.

2. She gets up early in the morning, jogs, and eats breakfast.

   彼女は朝早く起きて、ジョギングをして、朝ご飯を食べる。

   Kanojo wa asa hayaku okite, jogingu o shite, asagohan o taberu.

3. I went to Ginza with my friend and had a meal at a high-class restaurant.

   友達と銀座へ行って高級レストランで食事をした。

   Tomodachi to Ginza e itte kōkyū resutoran de shokuji o shita.

aquarium	水族館	*suizokukan*
turn off	消す	*kesu*
electricity/lights	電気	*denki*

Say the following in Japanese:

1. I went to the aquarium and saw various fish.

2. I closed the windows, turned off the lights, and went to bed.

3. Mr. Honda sold his old car and bought a new one.

Answers

1. 水族館へ行って色々な魚を見た / 見ました。
   Suizokukan e itte iroirona sakana o mita / mimashita.

2. 窓を閉めて、電気を消して寝た / 寝ました。
   Mado o shimete, denki o keshite neta / nemashita.

3. 本田さんは古い車を売って新しいのを買った / 買いました。
   Honda-san wa furui kuruma o utte atarashii no o katta / kaimashita.

68

After eating dinner, I went for a walk.

晩ご飯を食べ**てから**散歩した / 散歩しました。
*Bangohan o tabe**te kara** sanpo shita / sanpo shimashita.*

The *te* form of a verb, followed by the particle *kara* ("after"), expresses a temporal relation between one action and another: after doing one thing (or after one thing happens), one does another thing (or another thing happens). The tense of a sentence with *te kara* is determined by the final verb.

1. Yukiko plays tennis after school finishes.

由紀子(さん)は学校が終わってからテニスをします。

Yukiko(-san) wa gakkō ga owatte kara tenisu o shimasu.

2. He got his license after he bought the car.

彼は車を買ってから免許をとった。

Kare wa kuruma o katte kara menkyo o totta.

3. After graduating from high school, Ben joined the Air Force.

ベンは高校を卒業してから空軍に入った。

Ben wa kōkō o sotsugyō shite kara kūgun ni haitta.

learn	習う	*narau*
take off (article of clothing)	脱ぐ	*nugu*
do prep work (for a class)	予習する	*yoshū suru*

Say the following in Japanese:

1. Mr. Ross went to Japan after he had learned Japanese.
2. He took his hat off after entering the room.
3. Bill practiced kanji after he did his prep work.

---

1. ロスさんは日本語を習ってから日本へ行った / 行きました。
   Rosu-san wa Nihongo o naratte kara Nihon e itta / ikimashita.

2. 彼は部屋に入ってから帽子を脱いだ / 脱ぎました。
   Kare wa heya ni haitte kara bōshi o nuida / nugimashita.

3. ビル(さん)は予習してから漢字を練習した / 練習しました。
   Biru(-san) wa yoshū shite kara kanji o renshū shita / renshū shimashita.

69

He always takes a shower before going to bed.

彼はいつも寝る**前に**シャワーを浴びる / 浴びます。

*Kare wa itsumo neru **mae ni** shawā o abiru / abimasu.*

The dictionary form of a verb, followed by the phrase *mae ni* ("before"), indicates a temporal relation between one action and another: before doing one thing (or before one thing happens), one does another thing (or another thing happens.) The tense of a sentence with *mae ni* is determined by the final verb.

| Examples |

1. The students close the classroom windows before going home.

   学生は家へ帰る前に教室の窓を閉めます。

   Gakusei wa uchi e kaeru mae ni kyōshitsu no mado o shimemasu.

2. I stopped by a bakery before I went to the bank.

   銀行へ行く前にパン屋に寄った。

   Ginkō e iku mae ni pan'ya ni yotta.

3. Kazuo sharpens his pencils before he studies.

   和夫さんは勉強する前に鉛筆を削ります。

   Kazuo-san wa benkyō suru mae ni enpitsu o kezurimasu.

Practice

| exercise | 運動する | *undō suru* | die | 死ぬ | *shinu* |
| hand | 手 | *te* | | | |

Say the following in Japanese:

1. I exercise before I swim.

2. Hiroko always washes her hands before she eats.

3. He died (regretfully) before he had finished writing the book.

---

1. 泳ぐ前に運動する / 運動します。
   Oyogu mae ni undō suru / undō shimasu.

2. 弘子 (さん) はいつも食べる前に手を洗う / 洗います。
   Hiroko(-san) wa itsumo taberu mae ni te o arau / araimasu.

3. 彼は本を書き終わる前に死んでしまった / 死んでしまいました。
   Kare wa hon o kakiowaru mae ni shinde shimatta / shinde shimaimashita.

70

She wears glasses when she reads the newspaper.

彼女は新聞を読む**時**(**に**)めがねをかける / かけます。
*Kanojo wa shinbun o yomu **toki** (**ni**) megane o kakeru / kakemasu.*

The dictionary form of a verb, followed by the noun *toki* ("time"), and, optionally, the particle *ni*, indicates the time at which an action (expressed by another verb, at the end of the sentence) takes place. *Toki* in this pattern can mean "when" (example above) or "before" (Example 1).

The *te iru* and *ta* forms (including *te ita*) can also be used with *toki*, but when they are, the meaning of the *toki* phrase sometimes changes. When the *te iru* form is used, the meaning is closer to "while" (Example 2), and when the *ta* form is used, the meaning can be "when" (Example 3) or "after" (Example 4).

NOTE: If the verb in the main clause is in the past tense, the verb in the subordinate clause (the *toki* clause) may be in either the present or the past tense.

1. Before I go to bed, I brush my teeth.

    寝る時 (に) 歯を磨きます。

    Neru toki (ni) ha o migakimasu.

2. The boy found a wallet while walking in the park.

    少年は公園を歩いている時 / 歩いていた時 (に) 財布を見つけた。

    Shōnen wa kōen o aruite iru toki / aruite ita toki (ni) saifu o mitsuketa.

3. When we went to Hawaii, we went by boat.

    私達はハワイへ行った時 (に) 船で行きました。

    Watashi-tachi wa Hawai e itta toki (ni) fune de ikimashita.

4. When/After I get up in the morning, I wash my face.

    朝起きた時 (に) 顔を洗います。

    Asa okita toki (ni) kao o araimasu.

Practice

guidebook	ガイドブック	*gaidobukku*
people	人	*hito*
knock	ノックする	*nokku suru*
change money	両替する	*ryōgae suru*
error	間違い	*machigai*

Say the following in Japanese:

1. When I travel, I buy a guidebook.
2. When he enters the rooms of others, he doesn't knock.
3. When/After I've arrived at the airport, I'll change money.
4. When/While I was reading the report, I found an error.

/Answers/

1. 旅行する時 (に) ガイドブックを買う / 買います。
   Ryokō suru toki (ni) gaidobukku o kau / kaimasu.

2. 彼は人の部屋に入る時 (に) ノックしない / ノックしません。
   Kare wa hito no heya ni hairu toki (ni) nokku shinai / nokku shimasen.

3. 空港に着いた時 (に) 両替する / 両替します。
   Kūkō ni tsuita toki (ni) ryōgae suru / ryōgae shimasu.

4. レポートを読んでいる / 読んでいた時 (に) 間違いを見つけた / 見つけました。
   Repōto o yonde iru / yonde ita toki (ni) machigai o mitsuketa / mitsukemashita.

71

When Ms. Noda came, I was writing a letter.

野田さん**が**来た時 (に) 私**は**手紙を書いていた / 書いていました。

*Noda-san **ga** kita toki (ni) watashi **wa** tegami o kaite ita / kaite imashita.*

If there are two subjects in a sentence involving a verb followed by *toki* (→ Pattern 70), the one in the subordinate clause (the *toki* clause) is marked by the particle *ga*, and the one in the main clause by *wa*.

1. When I go to Paris, Kazuko will go to London.

   私がパリへ行く時 (に) 和子さんはロンドンへ行きます。

   Watashi ga Pari e iku toki (ni) Kazuko-san wa Rondon e ikimasu.

2. When I was taking a bath, the telephone rang.

   私が風呂に入っている / 入っていた時 (に) 電話が鳴った。

   Watashi ga furo ni haitte iru / haitte ita toki (ni) denwa ga natta.

3. When Frank left of the building, a car accident occurred.

   フランクがビルを出た時 (に) 車の事故が起こった。

   Furanku ga biru o deta toki (ni) kuruma no jiko ga okotta.

Practice

gardener	植木屋	*uekiya*
branch	枝	*eda*
next-door neighbor	隣の人	*tonari no hito*
cut	切る	*kiru*
smoke	たばこを吸う	*tabako o suu*
always	いつも	*itsumo*

Say the following in Japanese:

1. When I telephoned, Ms. Kida wasn't at home.
2. When/While/As the gardener was cutting the branches of the tree, the next-door neighbor came/showed up.
3. When he smokes, I always open the window.

1. 私が電話した時 (に) 木田さんは家にいなかった / いませんでした。
   Watashi ga denwa shita toki (ni) Kida-san wa uchi ni inakatta / imasen deshita.

2. 植木屋さんが木の枝を切っている / 切っていた時(に) 隣の人が来た / 来ました。
   Uekiya-san ga ki no eda o kitte iru / kitte ita toki (ni) tonari no hito ga kita / kimashita.

3. 彼がたばこを吸う時 (に) 私はいつも窓を開ける / 開けます。
   Kare ga tabako o suu toki (ni) watashi wa itsumo mado o akeru / akemasu.

72

While I was talking with my friend, my child was playing outside.

私が友達と話し**ている間**子供は外で遊んでいた / 遊んでいました。

*Watashi ga tomodachi to hanashi**te iru aida** kodomo wa soto de asonde ita / asonde imashita.*

The *te iru* form of a verb, followed by the noun *aida* ("space"), indicates the time during which an action (expressed by another verb, at the end of the sentence) takes place. In this pattern the actions in the main clause and the subordinate clause (the *aida* clause) cover the same span of time. If *aida* is followed by the particle *ni*, it implies that the action in the main clause occurs within the time span of the action in the *aida* clause (Examples 2, 3).

Examples

1. Kenji was teaching judo (all the) while he was in America.
   健二(さん)はアメリカにいる間、柔道を教えていた。
   Kenji(-san) wa Amerika ni iru aida, jūdō o oshiete ita.

2. Misako reads books while her children are sleeping.

美佐子（さん）は子供が寝ている間に本を読みます。

Misako(-san) wa kodomo ga nete iru aida ni hon o yomi-masu.

3. Ms. Brown learned Japanese flower arrangement while she lived in Kyoto.

ブラウンさんは京都に住んでいる間に日本の生け花を習った。

Buraun-san wa Kyōto ni sunde iru aida ni Nihon no ikebana o naratta.

Practice

cook	料理する	*ryōri suru*
shop	買い物する	*kaimono suru*
disappear	いなくなる	*inakunaru*

Say the following in Japanese:

1. While I was cooking, my younger sister was cleaning the room.

2. While my son was traveling, his dog died.

3. While I was shopping, my child disappeared.

Answers

1. 私が料理している間、妹は部屋を掃除していた / 掃除していました。
   Watashi ga ryōri shite iru aida, imōto wa heya o sōji shite ita / sōji shite imashita.

2. 息子が旅行している間に犬が死んだ / 死にました。
   Musuko ga ryokō shite iru aida ni inu ga shinda / shinimashita.

3. 私が買い物している間に子供がいなくなった / いなくなりました。
   Watashi ga kaimono shite iru aida ni kodomo ga inaku natta / inaku narimashita.

73

I was reading a magazine in the lobby until he came.

彼が来る**まで**ロビーで雑誌を読んでいた / 読んでいました。

*Kare ga kuru **made** robī de zasshi o yonde ita / yonde imashita.*

The dictionary form of a verb, followed by the particle *made* ("until"), indicates a temporal limit for an action. The tense of a sentence with *made* used in this way is determined by the final verb.

Examples

1. Mr. White had lived in an apartment until he bought a house.

   ホワイトさんは家を買うまでアパートに住んでいた。

   Howaito-san wa uchi o kau made apāto ni sunde ita.

2. I'll wait here until the rain stops.

   雨が止むまでここで待ちます。

   Ame ga yamu made koko de machimasu.

3. I won't buy anything until I completely pay off my debts.

   借金を払ってしまうまで何も買いません。

   Shakkin o haratte shimau made nani mo kaimasen.

Practice

get/become fixed	直る	*naoru*
terminal station	終点	*shūten*
final exam(s)	期末試験	*kimatsu shiken*
be over	終わる	*owaru*

Say the following in Japanese:

1. I commuted to school by subway until my car got fixed.

2. He was sleeping until the train arrived at the terminal station.

3. I won't play tennis until final exams are over.

---

1. 車が直るまで地下鉄で学校に通った / 通いました。
   Kuruma ga naoru made chikatestu de gakkō ni kayotta / kayoimashita.

2. 彼は電車が終点に着くまで寝ていた / 寝ていました。
   Kare wa densha ga shūten ni tsuku made nete ita / nete imashita.

3. (私は) 期末試験が終わるまでテニスをしない / しません。
   (Watashi wa) kimatsu shiken ga owaru made tenisu o shinai / shimasen.

74

It will take two months before the project is completed.

プロジェクトが完成する**までに**2か月かかる / かかり
ます。

*Purojekuto ga kansei suru **made ni** ni-kagetsu kakaru / kakari-masu.*

The dictionary form of a verb, followed by the particle combination *made ni* ("before/by/until the time when"), indicates another temporal limit for an action. The tense of a sentence with *made ni* is determined by the final verb.

Examples

1. I'll go to Osaka to see my friend before school starts.

   学校が始まるまでに友達に会いに大阪へ行きます。

   Gakkō ga hajimaru made ni tomodachi ni ai ni Ōsaka e ikimasu.

2. By the time the plane arrived in Chicago, I had read a novel.

飛行機がシカゴに着くまでに小説を読んでしまった。

Hikōki ga Shikago ni tsuku made ni shōsetsu o yonde shimatta.

3. I'll check these papers (in advance) before the section chief returns from his trip.

課長が旅行から戻るまでにこの書類を調べておきます。

Kachō ga ryokō kara modoru made ni kono shorui o shirabete okimasu.

summer vacation	夏休み	*natsuyasumi*
once more	もう一度	*mō ichido*
go fishing	釣りに行く	*tsuri ni iku*

Say the following in Japanese:

1. I'll go fishing once more before the summer vacation ends.

2. He had bought a house by the time he got married.

3. I had cleaned the room (in advance) before my guests came.

Answers

1. 夏休みが終わるまでにもう一度釣りに行く/ 行きます。
   Natsuyasumi ga owaru made ni mō ichido tsuri ni iku / ikimasu.

2. 彼は結婚するまでに家を買った / 買いました。
   Kare wa kekkon suru made ni uchi o katta / kaimashita.

3. お客さんが来るまでに部屋を掃除しておいた / 掃除しておきました。
   O-kyaku-san ga kuru made ni heya o sōji shite oita / sōji shite okimashita.

75

> We ride motorboats on the lake and catch fish in it.
> (IMPLYING: And we do other lake activities, too.)

私達は湖でモーターボートに乗っ**たり**、魚を釣っ**たり**
する / します。

*Watachi-tachi wa mizuumi de mōtābōto ni not**tari**, sakana o
tsut**tari suru / shimasu**.*

The *tari* form of a verb (formed by adding *ri* to the *ta* form) is used repeatedly within a sentence, with the final occurrence accompanied by the verb *suru* ("do"), to express a number of alternative or indefinite actions in no particular sequence. A sentence with this pattern means, in essence, "do such things as …".

[Examples]

1. Last night at the bar, they did things like drink, eat, and sing.

   彼らはゆうべバーで飲んだり、食べたり、歌ったりした。

   Kare-ra wa yūbe bā de nondari, tabetari, utattari shita.

2. On the weekends, Mr. Wada does things like wash his car and mow the lawn.

   和田さんは週末に車を洗ったり、芝生を刈ったりします。

   Wada-san wa shūmatsu ni kuruma o arattari, shibafu o kattari shimasu.

3. In Tokyo, Lisa watched Japanese movies and went to art museums (and did other things there, too).

   リサは東京で日本映画を見たり、美術館へ行ったりした。

   Risa wa Tōkyō de Nihon eiga o mitari, bijutsukan e ittari shita.

Practice

sushi	すし	*sushi*
make	作る	*tsukuru*
gather	拾う	*hirou*
shell	貝	*kai*

Say the following in Japanese:

1. Tomorrow I'll do things like make sushi and bake cookies.

2. Tom did things like practice kanji and memorize words.

3. We did things like swim in the ocean and gather shells at the beach.

Answers

1. 明日すしを作ったり、クッキーを焼いたりする / します。
   Ashita sushi o tsukuttari, kukkī o yaitari suru / shimasu.

2. トム(さん)は漢字を練習したり、言葉を覚えたりした / しました。
   Tomu(-san) wa kanji o renshū shitari, kotoba o oboetari shita / shimashita.

3. 私達は海で泳いだり、海岸で貝を拾ったりした / しました。
   Watashi-tachi wa umi de oyoidari, kaigan de kai o hirottari shita / shimashita.

76

He not only teaches English but also writes novels.

彼は英語を教える**ばかりでなく**小説**も**書く / 書きます。
*Kare wa Eigo o oshieru **bakari de naku** shōsetsu **mo** kaku / kakimasu.*

The dictionary form of a verb, followed by the phrase *bakari de naku ... (mo)* ("not only ... but also ..."), is used to make an additional statement about the subject of the sentence, and to deny that what is stated in the first part of the sentence (up until *bakari*) is the entire truth.

NOTE: The *ta* form should be used in place of the dictionary form before *bakari* if one is speaking about past actions or events (Example 3).

Examples

1. She not only plays the piano but also composes.

   彼女はピアノを弾くばかりでなく作曲もします。

   Kanojo wa piano o hiku bakari de naku sakkyoku mo shimasu.

2. He not only eats a lot but also drinks a lot.

   あの人はよく食べるばかりでなくよく飲む。

   Ano hito wa yoku taberu bakari de naku yoku nomu.

3. Today, not only did I do some shopping, I also saw a movie.

   今日は買い物をしたばかりでなく映画も見ました。

   Kyō wa kaimono o shita bakari de naku eiga mo mimashita.

Practice

hard	よく	*yoku*
fix	直す	*naosu*
vacuum cleaner	掃除機	*sōjiki*
paint	塗る	*nuru*
kitchen	台所	*daidokoro*
wall	壁	*kabe*

Say the following in Japanese:

1. Sam not only studies hard but also plays a lot.

2. I not only review (for class) every day, but also do prep work.

3. Not only did he fix the vacuum cleaner, he also painted the kitchen walls.

---

1. サム（さん）はよく勉強するばかりでなくよく遊ぶ／遊びます。
   Samu(-san) wa yoku benkyō suru bakari de naku yoku asobu / asobimasu.

2. 毎日復習するばかりでなく予習もする／します。
   Mainichi fukushū suru bakari de naku yoshū mo suru / shimasu.

3. 彼は掃除機を直したばかりでなく台所の壁も塗った／塗りました。
   Kare wa sōjiki o naoshita bakari de naku daidokoro no kabe mo nutta / nurimashita.

77

I went to the library to return some books.

図書館へ本を返し**に行った / 行きました**。

*Toshokan e hon o kaeshi **ni itta** / **ikimashita**.*

The combination of the particle *ni* after the stem of the *masu* form of a verb, and a motion verb such as *iku* ("go"), *kuru* ("come"), *kaeru* ("return"), *hairu* ("enter"), or *deru* ("leave"), expresses the idea of "go to do something," "come to do something," etc. This idea can also be expressed with *ni* coming after a noun (instead of after the stem of the *masu* form of a verb) that refers to an activity, such as *kaimono* ("shopping") or *kankō* ("sightseeing"; Example 3).

Examples

1. Mr. Jackson entered a coffee shop to drink coffee.

   ジャクソンさんはコーヒーを飲みに喫茶店に入った。

   Jakuson-san wa kōhī o nomi ni kissaten ni haitta.

   OR

   ジャクソンさんは喫茶店にコーヒーを飲みに入った。

   Jakuson-san wa kissaten ni kōhī o nomi ni haitta.

2. Sandra came to Japan to study Japanese.

   サンドラさんは日本語を勉強しに日本へ来ました。

   Sandora-san wa Nihongo o benkyō shi ni Nihon e kimashita.

   OR

サンドラさんは日本へ日本語を勉強しに来ました。
Sandora-san wa Nihon e Nihongo o benkyō shi ni kimashita.

3. We'll go sightseeing by bus on Sunday.

私達は日曜日にバスで観光に行きます。

Watashi-tachi wa nichiyōbi ni basu de kankō ni ikimasu.

Practice

ticket	切符	*kippu*
ask questions	質問する	*shitsumon suru*
exhibition	展覧会	*tenrankai*

Say the following in Japanese:

1. I went to the station to buy a train ticket.

2. A student came to ask questions.

3. I'll go to the exhibition with my friend tomorrow.

Answers

1. 電車の切符を買いに駅へ行った / 行きました。
   Densha no kippu o kai ni eki e itta / ikimashita.

   OR

   駅へ電車の切符を買いに行った / 行きました。
   Eki e densha no kippu o kai ni itta / ikimashita.

2. 学生が質問しに来た / 来ました。
   Gakusei ga shitsumon shi ni kita / kimashita.

3. 明日友達と展覧会に行く / 行きます。
   Ashita tomodachi to tenrankai ni iku / ikimasu.

   OR

   明日展覧会に友達と行く / 行きます。
   Ashita tenrankai ni tomodachi to iku / ikimasu.

78

Mr. Morita is using the subway to get to the company.

森田さんは会社に行く**のに**地下鉄を使っている / 使っています。

*Morita-san wa kaisha ni iku **noni** chikatetsu o tsukatte iru / tsukatte imasu.*

The particle *noni* following the dictionary form of a verb indicates the purpose or intention for which an action is taken or a condition exists. It means "to" or "in order to" and implies a process.

Examples

1. I need a dictionary to write compositions in Japanese.
   日本語で作文を書くのに辞書が要ります。
   Nihongo de sakubun o kaku noni jisho ga irimasu.

2. It takes me one hour to get to the airport from here.
   ここから空港へ行くのに1時間かかる。
   Koko kara kūkō e iku noni ichi-jikan kakaru.

3. This is a good place to live.
   ここは住むのにいい所です。
   Koko wa sumu noni ii tokoro desu.

chopsticks	はし	*hashi*
correct	直す	*naosu*
thirty minutes	３０分	*san-jup-pun*
department store	デパート	*depāto*
place	所	*tokoro*
shop	買い物する	*kaimono suru*

Say the following in Japanese:

1. Japanese people use chopsticks to eat.

2. It took me thirty minutes to correct the errors in the report.

3. A department store is a convenient place to shop.

Answers

1. 日本人は食べるのにはしを使う / 使います。
   Nihonjin wa taberu noni hashi o tsukau / tsukaimasu.

2. レポートの間違いを直すのに３０分かかった / かかりました。
   Repōto no machigai o naosu noni san-jup-pun kakatta / kakarimashita.

3. デパートは買い物するのに便利な所だ / です。
   Depāto wa kaimono suru noni benrina tokoro da / desu.

79

He is working part-time in order to travel.

彼は旅行する**ために**アルバイトしている / アルバイト
しています。

*Kare wa ryōkō suru **tame ni** arubaito shite iru / arubaito shite imasu.*

The phrase *tame ni* (→ Pattern 62) following the dictionary form of a verb indicates the purpose of an action. It is interchangeable with *noni* when a process is implied ("get married" in Example 1, "translate" in Example 2).

Examples

1. I am saving money in order to get married.

結婚するために / 結婚するのにお金をためています。

Kekkon suru tame ni / kekkon suru noni o-kane o tamete imasu.

2. Scott bought a dictionary in order to translate Japanese newspapers.

スコット（さん）は日本の新聞を訳すために / のに辞書を買った。

Sukotto(-san) wa Nihon no shinbun o yakusu tame ni / noni jisho o katta.

3. June studied hard in order to pass the exam.

ジュンは試験に合格するためによく勉強した。

Jun wa shiken ni gōkako suru tame ni yoku benkyō shita.

Practice

live/stay alive	生きる	*ikiru*
support	養う	*yashinau*
family	家族	*kazoku*

Say the following in Japanese:

1. We eat in order to live.

2. He is working hard to support his family.

3. Masao worked part-time in order to buy a new computer.

1. 生きるために食べる / 食べます。
   Ikiru tame ni taberu / tabemasu.

2. 彼は家族を養うために / 養うのによく働いています / 働いている。
   Kare wa kazoku o yashinau tame ni / yashinau noni yoku hataraite imasu / hataraite iru.

3. 正夫(さん)は新しいコンピューターを買うために / 買うのにアルバイトした / アルバイトしました。
   Masao(-san) wa atarashii konpyūtā o kau tame ni / kau noni arubaito shita / arubaito shimashita.

80

The train stopped due to the snow.

雪で列車が止まった / 止まりました。

*Yuki **de** ressha ga tomatta / tomarimashita.*

A noun followed by the particle *de* ("due to") indicates a cause or reason for an action.

/Examples/

1. Bill was absent from school due to illness.

   ビルは病気で学校を休んだ。

   Biru wa byōki de gakkō o yasunda.

2. Many trees fell due to the strong wind.

   強い風で木がたくさん倒れました。

   Tsuyoi kaze de ki ga takusan taoremashita.

3. Mr. Mishima caused a car accident due to carelessness.

三島さんは不注意で車の事故を起こした。

Mishima-san wa fuchūi de kuruma no jiko o okoshita.

Practice

heat	暑さ	*atsusa*
collapse	倒れる	*taoreru*
be hospitalized	入院する	*nyūin suru*

Say the following in Japanese:

1. She collapsed due to the heat.
2. Many people died due to the earthquake.
3. Mr. Kihara was hospitalized due to illness.

Answers

1. 彼女は暑さで倒れた / 倒れました。
   Kanojo wa atsusa de taoreta / taoremashita.

2. 地震で大勢の人が死んだ / 死にました。
   Jishin de ōzei no hito ga shinda / shinimashita.

3. 木原さんは病気で入院した / 入院しました。
   Kihara-san wa byōki de nyūin shita / nyūin shimashita.

81

I'll take medicine so that my fever goes down.

熱が下がる**ように**薬を飲む / 飲みます。

*Netsu ga sagaru **yō ni** kusuri o nomu / nomimasu.*

The phrase *yō ni* ("so that") coming after the dictionary or negative (*nai*) form of a verb indicates the purpose of or motive for an action.

Examples

1. I went to the station by taxi so that I would be there in time for the train.

電車に間に合うように駅へタクシーで行きました。

Densha ni maniau yō ni eki e takushī de ikimashita.

2. We are doing our best to achieve the goal.

目的を達成するようにがんばっています。

Mokuteki o tassei suru yō ni ganbatte imasu.

3. Mike gets up early every morning so as not to be late for school.

マイクは学校に遅れないように毎朝早く起きる。

Maiku wa gakkō ni okurenai yō ni maiasa hayaku okiru.

4. I made a note so that I wouldn't forget.

忘れないようにメモをとった。

Wasurenai yō ni memo o totta.

Practice

catch a cold	風邪を引く	*kaze o hiku*
slowly	ゆっくり	*yukkuri*
understand	分かる	*wakaru*

Say the following in Japanese:

1. I wore a coat so that I wouldn't catch a cold.

2. Jim did his best so that he would pass the exam.

3. Dan spoke slowly in English so that Akira would understand.

---

1. 風邪を引かないようにコートを着た / 着ました。
   Kaze o hikanai yō ni kōto o kita / kimashita.

2. ジム (さん) は試験に合格するようにがんばった / がんばりました。
   Jimu(-san) wa shiken ni gōkaku suru yō ni ganbatta / ganbarimashita.

3. ダン (さん) は明が分かるようにゆっくり英語で話した / 話しました。
   Dan(-san) wa Akira ga wakaru yō ni yukkuri Eigo de hanashita / hanashimashita.

82

(a) He's going fishing, so I'll go, too.

(b) I'm sleepy because I ate too much.

(a) 彼が釣りに行く**から**、私も行く / 行きます。
   *Kare ga tsuri ni iku **kara**, watashi mo iku / ikimasu.*

(b) 食べすぎた**から** / **ので**眠くなった / 眠くなりました。
   *Tabesugita **kara** / **node** nemuku natta / nemuku narimashita.*

Verbal predicates in the present, past, or negative forms, followed by the conjunctive particle *kara* or *node* ("because"), express a reason or cause. *Kara* is used primarily to express subjective reasons and excuses, while *node* is used for stating objective reasons and causes. Unlike *kara*, *node* does not project the speaker's personal opinion, and therefore cannot be followed by a statement of belief, or by a command or an invitation.

The plain style of speech is normally used before *kara* or *node*, but the *masu* form may be used in very polite speech (Example 3).

Examples

1. Haruko won't attend the reception, so I won't, either.

春子 (さん) がレセプションに出席しないから、私も
(出席) しない。

Haruko(-san) ga resepushon ni shusseki shinai kara, watashi mo (shussekī) shinai.

2. Nora's grades went up because she studied hard.

ノラ (さん) はよく勉強したから/ので、成績が上がっ
た。

Nora(-san) wa yoku benkyō shita kara / node, seiseki ga agatta.

3. There was an accident along the way, so I was late for the meeting.

途中で事故がありましたので会議に遅れました。

Tochū de jiko ga arimashita node kaigi ni okuremashita.

Practice

purse/handbag	ハンドバッグ	*handobaggu*
have time	時間がある	*jikan ga aru*
visit	訪ねる	*tazuneru*
be absent from school	学校を休む	*gakkō o yasumu*

Say the following in Japanese:

1. My older sister is going to buy a purse, so I'll buy one, too.

2. Because I had time in Kyoto, I visited Professor Okano.

3. Jim caught a cold; that's why he was absent from school.

1. 姉がハンドバッグを買うから私も買う / 買います。
   Ane ga handobaggu o kau kara watashi mo kau / kaimasu.

2. 京都で時間があったから / あったので、岡野先生を訪ねた / 訪ねました。
   Kyōto de jikan ga atta kara / atta node, Okano-sensei o tazuneta / tazunemashita.

3. ジム（さん）は風邪を引いたから / 引いたので学校を休んだ / 休みました。
   Jimu(-san) wa kaze o hiita kara / hiita node gakkō o yasunda / yasumi-mashita.

83

> (a) The water is cold, so I won't swim (in it).
>
> (b) The flowers were pretty, so I took a picture of them.

(a) 水が冷たい**から** / **ので**泳がない / 泳ぎません。
   *Mizu ga tsumetai **kara** / **node** oyoganai / oyogimasen.*

(b) 花がきれいだった**から** / **ので**写真を撮った / 撮りました。
   *Hana ga kirei datta **kara** / **node** shashin o totta / torimashita.*

Here we have the same pattern as in 82 above, only with adjectival predicates instead of verbal ones. The same usage rules apply. However, it is important to note that if the predicate before *node* is a *na*-adjective in the present tense, *na*, rather than *da*, is used (Example 2). Also, if the predicate of the main clause is in the past tense, the tense of the *kara* or *node* clause may be either present or past (Example 3).

Examples

1. I am busy that day, so I will not go.
   その日は忙しいから行きません。
   Sono hi wa isogashii kara ikimasen.

2. Because this park is quiet, I often come here to read books.

この公園は静かだから / 静かなのでよく本を読みに
来る。

*Kono kōen wa shizuka da kara / shizukana node yoku hon
o yomi ni kuru.*

3. As for this doll, I bought it because it was inexpensive.

この人形は安い / 安かったから / ので買いました。

Kono ningyō wa yasui / yasukatta kara / node kaimashita.

Practice

weather	天気	*tenki*
bad	悪い	*warui*
painter	画家	*gaka*
painting/picture	絵	*e*
expensive	高い	*takai*
hot	暑い	*atsui*

Say the following in Japanese:

1. The weather is bad, so I won't play tennis.

2. That painter is famous, so his paintings are expensive.

3. It was hot, so I slept with the windows open.

Answers

1. 天気が悪いからテニスをしない / しません。
   Tenki ga warui kara tenisu o shinai / shimasen.

2. あの画家は有名だから / 有名なので彼の絵は高い / 高いです。
   Ano gaka wa yūmei da kara / yūmeina node kare no e wa takai / takai desu.

3. 暑い / 暑かったから / ので窓を開けたまま寝た / 寝ました。
   Atsui / atsukatta kara / node mado o aketa mama neta / nemashita.

84

Why won't you go to the party?

I have an exam tomorrow.

どうして / なぜパーティーに行かない**のです**か。
*Dōshite / naze pāti ni ikanai **no desu** ka.*

明日試験があるのです。
Ashita shiken ga aru no desu.

Dōshite and *naze* are interrogative adverbs used to inquire about a reason or cause. *Naze* is more formal than *dōshite*. The phrase *no da* or *no desu* (literally, "It is that …"), placed at the end of a sentence, is used as a convention for offering a reason or explanation—or, in the case of *no desu* followed by the question-marker *ka*, for asking for a reason or cause. In conversation, *no da* or *no desu* often becomes *n da* or *n desu*. In ordinary, plain-stlye speech, male speakers usually use *n da* (Example 3) and female speakers usually use *no* (Example 4), in both declarative statements and questions.

Examples

1. Why were you late for class?
   なぜ授業に遅れたのですか。
   Naze jugyō ni okureta no desu ka.

   My alarm clock didn't go off.
   目覚まし時計が鳴らなかったのです。
   Mezamashi dokei ga naranakatta no desu.

2. What are you reading?
   何を読んでいるんですか。
   Nani o yonde iru n desu ka.

I'm reading a detective novel. It's very interesting.

探偵小説を読んでいるんです。とてもおもしろいん
ですよ。

Tantei shōsetsu o yonde iru n desu. Totemo omoshiroi n desu yo.

3. Why didn't you come last night?

どうしてゆうべ来なかったんだ？

Dōshite yūbe konakatta n da?

My son suddenly got ill.

息子が急に病気になったんだ。

Musuko ga kyū ni byōki ni natta n da.

4. Yasuko, why don't you eat?

安子さん、どうして食べないの？

Yasuko-san, dōshite tabenai no?

(The food) doesn't taste good.

おいしくないの。

Oishiku nai no.

Practice

girl	女の子	*onna no ko*
cry	泣く	*naku*
lonely	寂しい	*sabishii*
drink too much	飲みすぎる	*nomisugiru*
wait	待つ	*matsu*
my boyfriend	彼	*kare*

Say the following in Japanese:

1. Why is that girl crying?
   She's lonely.

2. (man speaking) Why did you become ill?
   (man replying) I drank too much.

3. (woman speaking) Kazuko, who are you waiting for?
   (woman replying) I'm waiting for my boyfriend.

---

1. なぜ / どうしてあの女の子は泣いているのですか。
   Naze / dōshite ano onna no ko wa naite iru no desu ka.

   寂しいのです。
   Sabishii no desu.

2. どうして病気になったんだ?
   Dōshite byōki ni natta n da?

   飲みすぎたんだ。
   Nomisugita n da.

3. 和子さん、だれを待っているの?
   Kazuko-san, dare o matte iru no?

   彼を待っているの。
   Kare o matte iru no.

7 Commands, Requests, Suggestions, Approval, Disapproval, Prohibition, and Obligation

85

Practice some more.

もっと練習し**なさい**。

*Motto renshū shi**nasai**.*

The stem of the *masu* form of a verb, followed by *nasai*, expresses a command. This pattern is used mainly by teachers and parents when speaking to their students or children. *Nasai* is the imperative form of the honorific verb *nasaru* ("do") and is used here as an auxiliary verb.

Examples

1. Wear this, since it is cold.

   寒いからこれを着なさい。

   Samui kara kore o kinasai.

2. Brush your teeth before you go to bed.

   寝る前に歯を磨きなさい。

   Neru mae ni ha o migakinasai.

3. Review this lesson once more.

   もう一度この課を復習しなさい。

   Mō ichido kono ka o fukushū shinasai.

as much as possible	できるだけ	*dekiru dake*
be careful	気をつける	*ki o tsukeru*
bell	ベル	*beru*
ring	鳴る	*naru*

Say the following in Japanese:

1. Speak in Japanese as much as possible.

2. Be careful; the wind is strong.

3. Study in the classroom until the bell rings.

Answers

1. できるだけ日本語で話しなさい。
   Dekiru dake Nihongo de hanashi nasai.

2. 風が強いから気をつけなさい。
   Kaze ga tsuyoi kara ki o tsuke nasai.

3. ベルが鳴るまで教室で勉強しなさい。
   Beru ga naru made kyōshitsu de benkyō shinasai.

86

Please wait here.

どうぞこちらでお待ちください。
*Dōzo kochira de **o**-machi **kudasai**.*

The stem of the *masu* form of a verb, with the honorific prefix *o-*, is followed by *kudasai* to express a polite request, usually one directed at a social superior or customer. *Kudasai* is the polite imperative form of the honorific verb *kudasaru* ("give") and is used here as an auxiliary verb. Usually the adverb *dōzo* ("please") is used with *kudasai*, at the beginning of the sentence.

To express a polite request using a noun-plus-*suru* verb, *kudasai* follows the noun, and the stem of *suru* is dropped altogether (Example 3).

Generally speaking, the prefix *o-* attaches to native-Japanese verbs (Examples 1, 2), and *go-* to verbs of Chinese origin (Example 3).

Examples

1. Please come in.

   どうぞお入りください。

   Dōzo o-hairi kudasai.

2. Have a nice weekend.

   どうぞいい週末をお過ごしください。

   Dōzo ii shūmatsu o o-sugoshi kudasai.

3. Please explain once more.

   どうぞもう一度ご説明ください。

   Dōzo mō ichido go-setsumei kudasai.

Practice

sit down	座る	*suwaru*
check	調べる	*shiraberu*
data	データ	*dēta*

Say the following in Japanese:

1. Please sit down.
2. Please check this data.
3. Please ask questions.

1. どうぞお座りください。
   Dōzo o-suwari kudasai.

2. （どうぞ）このデータをお調べください。
   (Dōzo) kono dēta o o-shirabe kudasai.

3. どうぞご質問ください。
   Dōzo go-shitsumon kudasai.

87

Please close the door.

ドアを閉めて**ください**。
Doa o shimete kudasai.

The *te* form of a verb, followed by *kudasai*, expresses a polite request or command, usually one directed at a social equal or subordinate.

Examples

1. Please tell me the meaning of this kanji.

   この漢字の意味を教えてください。

   Kono kanji no imi o oshiete kudasai.

2. I'm busy, so please help me.

   忙しいから手伝ってください。

   Isogashii kara tetsudatte kudasai.

3. Please mail this package by 3 o'clock.

   3時までにこの小包を出してください。

   San-ji made ni kono kozutsumi o dashite kudasai.

hurry	急ぐ	*isogu*
carry	運ぶ	*hakobu*
chair	いす	*isu*
conference room	会議室	*kaigishitsu*
finish	済ませる	*sumaseru*
work	仕事	*shigoto*

Say the following in Japanese:

1. There's no time, so please hurry.

2. Please carry this chair to the conference room.

3. Please finish this work by tomorrow.

Answers

1. 時間がないから急いでください。
   Jikan ga nai kara isoide kudasai.

2. このいすを会議室に運んでください。
   Kono isu o kaigishitsu ni hakonde kudasai.

3. 明日までにこの仕事を済ませてください。
   Ashita made ni kono shigoto o sumasete kudasai.

88

Please don't park your car on this street.

この通りに車を止め**ないでください**。
*Kono tōri ni kuruma o tome**nai de kudasai**.*

The negative form of a verb, followed by the particle *de* and *kudasai*, expresses a negative request or command ("Please don't ...") directed at a social equal or subordinate.

1. Please don't use your cell phones on the train.

   電車の中で携帯電話を使わないでください。

   Densha no naka de keitai denwa o tsukawanai de kudasai.

2. It's cold, so please don't open the window.

   寒いから窓を開けないでください。

   Samui kara mado o akenai de kudasai.

3. Please don't throw away these papers yet.

   この書類はまだ捨てないでください。

   Kono shorui wa mada sutenai de kudasai.

Practice

forget	忘れる	*wasureru*
promise	約束	*yakusoku*
loudly	大声で	*ōgoe de*

Say the following in Japanese:

1. Please don't forget your promise.
2. Please don't smoke in this room.
3. Please don't talk loudly.

Answers

1. 約束を忘れないでください。
   Yakusoku o wasurenai de kudasai.

2. この部屋でたばこを吸わないでください。
   Kono heya de tabako o suwanai de kudasai.

3. 大声で話さないでください。
   Ōgoe de hanasanai de kudasai.

89

Would you please lend me your dictionary?

辞書を貸してくださいませんか。
Jisho o kashite kudasaimasen ka.

The *te* form of a verb, followed by the phrase *kudasaimasen ka*, expresses a very polite request made to a social superior. The negative question form *kudasaimasen ka* ("Won't you give me …?") is more polite than *kudasai*.

Examples

1. Would you please show me that sample?
   その見本を見せてくださいませんか。
   Sono mihon o misete kudasaimasen ka.

2. Would you please write a letter of recommendation?
   推薦状を書いてくださいませんか。
   Suisenjō o kaite kudasaimasen ka.

3. Would you please change the place for the picnic?
   ピクニックの場所を変えてくださいませんか。
   Pikunikku no basho o kaete kudasaimasen ka.

Practice

attend	出席する	*shusseki suru*
graduation ceremony	卒業式	*sotsugyōshiki*
cancel	取り消す	*torikesu*
order	注文	*chūmon*
contact	連絡する	*renraku suru*

Say the following in Japanese:

1. Would you please attend the graduation ceremony?
2. Would you please cancel the order?
3. Would you please contact me by 3 o'clock tomorrow?

---

1. 卒業式に出席してくださいませんか。
   Sotsugyōshiki ni shusseki shite kudasaimasen ka.

2. 注文を取り消してくださいませんか。
   Chūmon o torikeshite kudasaimasen ka.

3. 明日3時までに連絡してくださいませんか。
   Ashita san-ji made ni renraku shite kudasaimasen ka.

90

Would you please not leave magazines here?

ここに雑誌を置か**ないでくださいませんか**。
*Koko ni zasshi o oka**nai de kudasaimasen ka**.*

The negative form of a verb, followed by the particle *de* and *kudasaimasen ka*, expresses a polite negative request ("Would you please not …?) directed at a social superior.

Examples

1. Would you please not take pictures in this building?

   この建物の中で写真を撮らないでくださいませんか。

   Kono tatemono no naka de shashin o toranai de kudasaimasen ka.

2. Would you please not erase the kanji on the blackboard?

黒板の漢字を消さないでくださいませんか。

Kokuban no kanji o kesanai de kudasaimasen ka.

3. As for this matter, would you please not announce it yet?

この事は、まだ発表しないでくださいませんか。

Kono koto wa, mada happyō shinai de kudasaimasen ka.

Practice

move	動かす	ugokasu
desk	机	tsukue
matter/issue	事	koto
decide on	決める	kimeru
banquet	宴会	enkai

Say the following in Japanese:

1. Would you please not move this desk?
2. As for this issue, would you please not decide on it now?
3. Would you please not be late for tonight's banquet?

Answers

1. この机を動かさないでくださいませんか。
   Kono tsukue o ugokasanai de kudasaimasen ka.

2. この事は、今決めないでくださいませんか。
   Kono koto wa, ima kimenai de kudasaimasen ka.

3. 今晩の宴会に遅れないでくださいませんか。
   Konban no enkai ni okurenai de kudasaimasen ka.

91

Please tell Ms. Takeda to come/not to come.

竹田さん**に**来る / 来**ないように**言ってください。
*Takeda-san **ni** kuru / ko**nai yō ni** itte kudasai.*

The dictionary or negative (*nai*) form of a verb, followed by *yō ni*, is placed before a command or request to make it indirect. The particle *ni* coming after "Takeda-san" in the above example marks the indirect object of the sentence—the person to or for whom the action is performed.

Examples

1. Please ask Mr. Miller to translate this article into English.

   ミラーさんにこの記事を英語に訳すように頼んでください。

   Mirā-san ni kono kiji o Eigo ni yakusu yō ni tanonde kudasai.

2. Please tell the children not to stay up late.

   子供達に遅くまで起きていないように言ってください。
   Kodomo-tachi ni osoku made okite inai yō ni itte kudasai.

3. Would you please advise Mr. Kojima to participate in the marathon?

   小島さんにマラソンに参加するように勧めてくださいませんか。

   Kojima-san ni marason ni sanka suru yō ni susumete kudasaimasen ka.

submit	提出する	*teishutsu suru*
student (in middle school or high school)	生徒	*seito*
hallway	廊下	*rōka*

Say the following in Japanese:

1. Please tell the students to submit their reports.

2. Please tell the students not to run in the hallway.

3. Would you please ask Ms. Hayashi not to use this computer?

Answers

1. 学生にレポートを提出するように言ってください。
   Gakusei ni repōto o teishutsu suru yō ni itte kudasai.

2. 生徒達に廊下を走らないように言ってください。
   Seito-tachi ni rōka o hashiranai yō ni itte kudasai.

3. 林さんにこのコンピューターを使わないように頼んでくださいませんか。
   Hayashi-san ni kono konpyūtā o tsukawanai yō ni tanonde kudasaimasen ka.

92

Let's go to see the parade.

パレードを見に**行こう** / **行きましょう**。
*Parēdo o mi ni **ikō** / **ikimashō**.*

The volitional form of a verb expresses an invitation or a suggestion. The plain volitional form is obtained as follows:

Regular I verbs: The final syllable of the dictionary form changes from one ending in *u* to one ending in *o* and is elongated.

au ("meet")	→ *aō* ("let's meet")
iku ("go")	→ *ikō* ("let's go")
oygu ("swim")	→ *oyogō* ("let's swim")
hanasu ("speak")	→ *hanasō* ("let's speak")
matsu ("wait")	→ *matō* ("let's wait")
asobu ("play")	→ *asobō* ("let's play")
yomu ("read")	→ *yomō* ("let's read")
kaeru ("return")	→ *kaerō* ("let's return")

Regular II verbs: The final *ru* of the dictionary form changes to *yō*.

miru ("see")	→ *miyō* ("let's see")
taberu ("eat")	→ *tabeyō* ("let's eat")

Irregular verbs:

kuru ("come")	→ **koyō** ("let's come")
suru ("do")	→ **shiyō** ("let's do")

The polite volitional form of a verb is the same as the *masu* form, only with *mashō* replacing *masu*: *ikimashō* ("let's go"), *mimashō* ("let's see"), etc.

The plain volitional form is used mainly by men, whereas the polite volitional form is used by both men and women.

Examples

1. Let's rest here for a while.

ここでしばらく休みましょう。

Koko de shibaraku yasumimashō.

2. Let's celebrate Mr. Murata's promotion at the bar.

バーで村田さんの昇進を祝おう。

Bā de Murata-san no shōshin o iwaō.

3. Let's study hard so that we won't fail the exam.

試験に落第しないようによく勉強しましょう。

Shiken ni rakudai shinai yō ni yoku benkyō shimashō.

| dine out | 外食する | *gaishoku suru* |
| sweets | お菓子 | *o-kashi* |

Say the following in Japanese:

1. Let's dine out tonight.

2. Let's wait here until the meeting is over.

3. Let's buy sweets (in advance), since guests are coming.

Answers

1. 今晩外食しよう / 外食しましょう。
   Konban gaishoku shiyō / gaishoku shimashō.

2. 会議が終わるまでここで待とう / 待ちましょう。
   Kaigi ga owaru made koko de matō / machimashō.

3. お客さまが来るから、お菓子を買っておこう / 買っておきましょう。
   O-kyaku-sama ga kuru kara, o-kashi o katte okō / katte okimashō.

93

Let's not buy a new car.

新しい車は買わ**ないでおこう** / 買わ**ないでおきましょう**。

*Atarashii kuruma wa kawa**nai de okō** / kawa**nai de okimashō**.*

The negative form of a verb, followed by the particle *de* and *okō* or *okimashō*, which is the volitional form of the verb *oku* ("put"), is used to express a suggestion that involves inaction by both the speaker and the listener.

1. It's warm, so let's not turn on the heater.

   暖かいからヒーターをつけないでおきましょう。

   Atatakai kara hītā o tsukenai de okimashō.

2. Let's not take the subway, because it's crowded now.

   今、混んでいるから地下鉄に乗らないでおこう。

   Ima, konde iru kara chikatetsu ni noranai de okō.

3. As for this issue, let's not decide on it until Mr. Yano returns.

   この事は、矢野さんが帰るまで決めないでおきましょう。

   Kono koto wa, Yano-san ga kaeru made kimenai de oki-mashō.

Practice

take (someone somewhere)	連れて行く	*tsurete iku*
take (something somewhere)	持って行く	*motte iku*
leave	出掛ける	*dekakeru*
stop (of rain)	止む	*yamu*

Say the following in Japanese:

1. Let's not take the children to the party.
2. It's not cold, so let's not take coats with us.
3. Let's not leave until the rain stops.

Answers

1. 子供達はパーティーに連れて行かないでおこう / 連れて行かないでおきましょう。
   Kodomo-tachi wa pātī ni tsurete ikanai de okō / tsurete ikanai de okimashō.

2. 寒くないからコートは持って行かないでおこう / 持って行かないでおきましょう。
   Samuku nai kara kōto wa motte ikanai de okō / motte ikanai de okimashō.

3. 雨が止むまで出掛けないでおこう / 出掛けないでおきましょう。
Ame ga yamu made dekakenai de okō / dekakenai de okimashō.

94

Shall we have sandwiches (or something)?

サンドイッチでも食べようか / 食べましょうか。
*Sandoitchi **demo tabeyō ka** / **tabemashō ka**.*

The plain or polite volitional form of a verb, followed by the particle *ka*, is used to express a suggestion in the form of a question: "Shall I …?" or "Shall we …?" Similar to this construction but more polite is the negative polite question *masen ka* (Example 3).

The particle *demo* in a sentence involving a suggestion indicates a thing offered up as a suggestion, but only as one of a number of possibilities. It replaces the direct-object marker *o*.

Examples

1. Shall we have coffee or something?

   コーヒーでも飲もうか。
   Kōhī demo nomō ka.

2. Shall we go by taxi, since it's raining?

   雨が降っているからタクシーで行きましょうか。
   Ame ga futte iru kara takushī de ikimashō ka.

3. Wouldn't you (like to) invite our teacher to the party?

   私達の先生をパーティーに招待しませんか。
   Watashi-tachi no sensei o pātī ni shōtai shimasen ka.

| souvenir | お土産 | *o-miyage* |
| noisy | やかましい | *yakamashii* |

Say the following in Japanese:

1. Shall we buy souvenirs (or something) at that gift shop?
2. Shall I turn off the TV, since it's noisy?
3. Wouldn't you like to go to the picnic with us?

Answers

1. あのギフトショップでお土産でも買おうか / 買いましょうか。
   Ano gifuto shoppu de o-miyage demo kaō ka / kaimashō ka.

2. やかましいからテレビを消そうか / 消しましょうか。
   Yakamashii kara terebi o kesō ka / keshimashō ka.

3. 私達と一緒にピクニックに行きませんか。
   Watashi-tachi to issho ni pikunikku ni ikimasen ka.

95

How about asking your teacher?

先生に聞い**たらどう**？
*Sensei ni kii**tara dō**?*

The *tara* form of a verb (formed by adding *ra* to the *ta* form), followed by the interrogative adverb *dō* ("how"), is used in casual conversation to express a suggestion: "How about …?" *Dō* may be omitted.

1. How about taking medicine before going to bed?

   寝る前に薬を飲んだらどう？

   Neru mae ni kusuri o nondara dō?

2. How about waiting a little longer?

   もう少し待ったら？

   Mō sukoshi mattara?

3. How about paying in cash?

   現金で払ったら？

   Genkin de harattara?

Practice

swim	泳ぐ	*oyogu*	sing	歌う	utau
pool	プール	*pūru*	song	歌	*uta*
college	大学	*daigaku*			

Say the following in Japanese:

1. How about swimming in the pool?
2. How about teaching English at a college?
3. How about singing Japanese songs at the party?

Answers

1. プールで泳いだら（どう）？
   Pūru de oyoidara (dō)?

2. 大学で英語を教えたら（どう）？
   Daigaku de Eigo o oshietara (dō)?

3. パーティーで日本の歌を歌ったら（どう）？
   Pātī de Nihon no uta o uttatara (dō)?

96

You had better eat more vegetables.

もっと野菜を食べた**ほうがいい / いいです**。
*Motto yasai o tabeta **hō ga ii** / **ii desu**.*

The *ta* form of a verb, followed by the phrase *hō ga ii*, is used to give advice. It corresponds to the English "had better do."

NOTE: The sentence-final particles *ne* and *yo* are frequently used when giving advice, either to soften a suggestion (as with *ne* in Example 1) or to give force to it (as with *yo* in Example 2).

Examples

1. Bill had better study kanji harder, don't you think?
   ビルはもっと漢字を勉強したほうがいいね。
   Biru wa motto kanji o benkyō shita hō ga ii ne.

2. You had better hurry so that you won't be late for your flight.
   フライトに遅れないように急いだほうがいいですよ。
   Furaito ni okurenai yō ni isoida hō ga ii desu yo.

3. You had better apply for a passport now (in advance).
   今パスポートを申請しておいたほうがいい。
   Ima pasupōto o shinsei shite oita hō ga ii.

Practice

| interesting | おもしろい | *omoshiroi* | loan | ローン | *rōn* |
| pay (off) | 払う | *harau* | regularly | きちんと | *kichin to* |

Say the following in Japanese:

1. That play is interesting, so you had better go to see it.

2. You had better pay off the loan regularly.

3. We had better buy the concert tickets in advance.

Answers

1. あの劇はおもしろいから、見に行ったほうがいい / いいです。
   Ano geki wa omoshiroi kara, mi ni itta hō ga ii / ii desu.

2. ローンをきちんと払ったほうがいい / いいですよ。
   Rōn o kichin to haratta hō ga ii / ii desu yo.

3. コンサートの切符を買っておいたほうがいい / いいですね。
   Konsāto no kippu o katte oita hō ga ii / ii desu ne.

97

You had better not drink too much coffee.

コーヒーを飲みすぎ**ないほうがいい / いいです**。
*Kōhī o nomisugi**nai hō ga ii / ii desu**.*

The *nai* form of a verb, followed by the phrase *hō ga ii*, is used to give advice about what one ought not do. It corresponds to the English "had better not do" or "ought not do."

Examples

1. You had better not climb that mountain, as it is dangerous.
   危険だからあの山には登らないほうがいい。
   Kiken da kara ano yama ni wa noboranai hō ga ii.

2. You had better not associate with that kind of man.

あんな男とは付き合わないほうがいいよ。

Anna otoko to wa tsukiawanai hō ga ii yo.

3. We had better not oppose the section chief's opinion.

課長の意見に反対しないほうがいいですね。

Kachō no iken ni hantai shinai hō ga ii desu ne.

Practice

believe	信じる	*shinjiru*
words	言葉	*kotoba*
rent	借りる	*kariru*
that kind of	あんな	*anna*

Say the following in Japanese:

1. You had better not go home yet.

2. You had better not believe his words.

3. We had better not rent that kind of apartment.

Answers

1. まだ帰らないほうがいい / いいですね。
   Mada kaeranai hō ga ii / ii desu ne.

2. 彼の言葉を信じないほうがいい / いいですよ。
   Kare no kotoba o shinjinai hō ga ii / ii desu yo.

3. あんなアパートは借りないほうがいい / いいですね。
   Anna apāto wa karinai hō ga ii / ii desu ne.

(a) It is all right if you write in pencil.

(b) It is all right if the price is high.

(a) 鉛筆で書い**てもいい / いいです**。
*Enpitsu de kaite **mo ii** / **ii desu**.*

(b) 値段は高く**てもいい / いいです**。
*Nedan wa takaku**te mo ii** / **ii desu**.*

The *te* form of a verb or an adjective—or the negative *te* form (*nakute* for verbs, *ku nakute* for *i*-adjectives, and *de nakute* for *na*-adjectives)—followed directly by *mo ii*, is used to grant or ask permission to do something, or to express approval of a condition (Example 3). If one is asking permission to do something (or asking to be allowed not to do something, as the case may be), the question-marker *ka* is used at the end of the sentence (Examples 2, 4).

NOTE: *Kamaimasen* ("I don't mind") and *yorshii desu* (a politer form of *ii desu*, meaning "good," "all right") may be used in place of *mo ii*.

| Examples |

1. It is all right if you take a day off tomorrow.
   明日休んでもいいですよ。
   Ashita yasunde mo ii desu yo.

2. Do you mind if I borrow this magazine?
   この雑誌を借りてもかまいませんか。
   Kono zasshi o karite mo kamaimasen ka?

3. It is all right if the furniture is not new.

家具は新しくなくてもいいです。

Kagu wa atarashiku nakute mo ii desu.

4. Is is all right if I don't take the exam?

試験を受けなくてもよろしいですか。

Shiken o ukenakute mo yoroshii desu ka.

Practice

come in/enter	入る	*hairu*
meeting	会議	*kaigi*
large/spacious	広い	*hiroi*

Say the following in Japanese:

1. May I come in?
2. It is all right if you don't attend the meeting.
3. Is it all right if I use this chair?
4. It is all right if the room is not large.

Answers

1. 入ってもいいですか / かまいませんか。
   Haitte mo ii desu ka / kamaimasen ka.

2. 会議に出席しなくてもいい/ いいです。
   Kaigi ni shusseki shinakute mo ii / ii desu.

3. このいすを使ってもかまいませんか。
   Kono isu o tsukatte mo kamaimasen ka.

4. 部屋は広くなくてもいい / いいです。
   Heya wa hiroku nakute mo ii / ii desu.

99

> You must not watch TV in this room.

この部屋でテレビを見**てはいけない / いけません**。
*Kono heya de terebi o mi**te wa ikenai / ikemasen**.*

The *te* form of a verb, followed by *wa ikenai* or *wa ikemasen*, is used to tell someone that he or she should not, or is not allowed to, do something.

NOTE: The verb *komaru* ("be troubled") or the *na*-adjective *dame da* ("no good," "useless") may be used in place of *ikenai* (Examples 2, 3).

Examples

1. The water is dirty, so you must not swim in the river.
   水が汚いから川で泳いではいけません。
   Mizu ga kitanai kara kawa de oyoide wa ikemasen.

2. You must not go to bed leaving the TV on.
   テレビをつけたまま寝てはだめですよ。
   Terebi o tsuketa mama nete wa dame desu yo.

3. You must not throw away these papers yet.
   まだこの書類を捨てては困ります。
   Mada kono shorui o sutete wa komarimasu.

Practice

quit one's job	仕事を辞める	*shigoto o yameru*
misunderstand	誤解する	*gokai suru*
right side	右側	*migigawa*
street	道	*michi*

Say the following in Japanese:

1. You must not quit your job now.

2. You must not misunderstand my words.

3. You must not drive on the right side of the street.

/Answers/

1. 今仕事を辞めてはいけない /いけません。
   Ima shigoto o yamete wa ikenai / ikemasen.

2. 私の言葉を誤解してはいけない / いけません。
   Watashi no kotoba o gokai shite wa ikenai / ikemasen.

3. 道の右側を運転してはいけない / いけません。
   Michi no migigawa o unten shite wa ikenai / ikemasen.

100

(a) I have to get up early every morning.

(b) The office must be spacious.

(c) Schools must be safe.

(a) 毎朝早く起き**なければならない / なりません**。
   *Maiasa hayaku oki**nakereba naranai** / **narimasen**.*

(b) オフィスは広く**なければならない / なりません**。
   *Ofisu wa hiroku **nakereba naranai** / **narimasen**.*

(c) 学校は安全で**なければならない / なりません**。
   *Gakkō wa anzen de **nakereba naranai** / **narimasen**.*

The stem of the *nai* form of a verb (the form without *nai*), followed by the phrase *nakereba naranai* ("must," "have to"), expresses the speaker's belief that an action is necessary, often because of an obligation or a duty. Similarly with adjectives, the *ku* form of an *i*-adjective or the *te* form of a *na*-adjective, followed by this same phrase, expresses the speaker's belief that a state or condition is necessary, though not necessarily because of an obligation or a duty (Example 3).

Examples

1. I must stop by a supermarket on the way home.
   帰りにスーパーに寄らなければなりません。
   Kaeri ni sūpā ni yoranakereba narimasen.

2. Fruit must be fresh.
   果物は新しくなければならない。
   Kudamono wa atarashiku nakereba naranai.

3. The hotel must be quiet.
   ホテルは静かでなければならない。
   Hoteru wa shizuka de nakereba naranai.

Practice

store clerk	店員	*ten'in*
postpone	延期する	*enki suru*
trip	旅行	*ryokō*
sumo wrestler	相撲取り	*sumōtori*

Say the following in Japanese:

1. Store clerks must be kind.
2. I have to postpone my trip.
3. Sumo wrestlers must be big.

1. 店員は親切でなければならない / なりません。
   Ten'in wa shinsetsu de nakereba naranai / narimasen.

2. 私は旅行を延期しなければならない / なりません。
   Watashi wa ryokō o enki shinakereba naranai / narimasen

3. 相撲取りは大きくなければならない / なりません。
   Sumōtori wa ōkiku nakereba naranai / narimasen.

101

> (a) I don't have to do homework tonight.
>
> (b) The report doesn't have to be detailed.
>
> (c) The ceremony doesn't have to be gorgeous.

(a) 今晩宿題を**しなくてもいい** / **いいです**。
*Konban shukudai o shi**nakute mo ii** / **ii desu**.*

(b) レポートは詳しく**なくてもいい** / **いいです**。
*Repōto wa kuwashiku **nakute mo ii** / **ii desu**.*

(c) 式は豪華で**なくてもいい** / **いいです**。
*Shiki wa gōka de **nakute mo ii** / **ii desu**.*

The negative *te* form of a verb (*nakute*), followed by *mo ii*, expresses the speaker's belief that an action is not necessary. And the negative *te* form of an *i*-adjective (*ku nakute*) or a *na*-adjective (*de nakute*), followed by this same phrase, expresses the speaker's belief that a state is not necessary.

1. We are not busy, so we don't have to work overtime.

忙しくないから残業しなくてもいいです。

Isogashiku nai kara zangyō shinakute mo ii desu.

2. You don't have to finish this work by tomorrow.

この仕事は明日までに済ませなくてもいいですよ。

Kono shigoto wa ashita made ni sumasenakute mo ii desu yo.

3. The apartment doesn't have to be near the station.

アパートは駅に近くなくてもいい。

Apāto wa eki ni chikaku nakute mo ii.

4. The hotel doesn't have to be high-class.

ホテルは高級でなくてもいいです。

Hoteru wa kōkyū de nakute mo ii desu.

Practice

turn on	つける	*tsukeru*
composition	作文	*sakubun*
long	長い	*nagai*
answer	答え	*kotae*
perfect	完全な	*kanzenna*

Say the following in Japanese:

1. It's not cold, so we don't have to turn on the heater.

2. The composition doesn't have to be long.

3. The answers don't have to be perfect.

1. 寒くないからヒーターをつけなくてもいい / いいです。
   Samuku nai kara hītā o tsukenakute mo ii / ii desu.

2. 作文は長くなくてもいい / いいです。
   Sakubun wa nagaku nakute mo ii / ii desu.

3. 答えは完全でなくてもいい / いいです。
   Kotae wa kanzen de nakute mo ii / ii desu.

8

Expressing Ability, Preference, Desire, Intention, Resolution, and Experience

102

Mr. Hill can speak Chinese.

ヒルさんは中国語を話す**ことができる** / **できます**。
*Hiru-san wa Chūgokugo o hanasu **koto ga dekiru** / **deki-masu**.*

The dictionary form of a verb, followed by the phrase *koto ga dekiru* ("can," "be able to"), expresses ability or potential. Grammatically, the noun *koto* ("thing") in this pattern functions to turn the verb coming before it into a gerund, so that the sentence above, with the topic, means, literally, "As for Mr. Hill, speaking Chinese is possible."

A shorter potential form also exists in Japanese. The shorter forms for the three verb types are obtained as follows:

Regular I verbs: The final syllable of the dictionary form changes from one ending in *u* to one ending in *eru*.

au ("meet")	→ *aeru* ("can meet")
iku ("go")	→ *ikeru* ("can go")
oyogu ("swim")	→ *oyogeru* ("can swim")
hanasu ("speak")	→ *hanaseru* ("can speak")
matsu ("wait")	→ *materu* ("can wait")
asobu ("play")	→ *asoberu* ("can play")
yomu ("read")	→ *yomeru* ("can read")
kaeru ("return")	→ *kaereru* ("can return")

Regular II verbs: The final *ru* of the dictionary form changes to *rareru.*

| *mi**ru*** ("see") | → *mi**rareru*** ("can see") |
| *tabe**ru*** ("eat") | → *tabe**rareru*** ("can eat") |

Irregular verbs:

| **kuru** ("come") | → **korareru** ("can come") |
| **suru** ("do") | → **dekiru** ("can do") |

The direct object of a potential verb is marked by *o* with the *koto ga dekiru* pattern, but by *ga* with the shorter potential form.

Examples

1. She can play Chopin.

彼女はショパンを弾くことができる / ショパンが弾ける。

Kanojo wa Shopan o hiku koto ga dekiru / Shopan ga hikeru.

2. You can get to the museum in ten minutes by car.

博物館まで車で10分で行くことができます / 行けます。

Hakubutsukan made kuruma de jup-pun de ikukoto ga dekimasu / ikemasu.

3. Mr. Brown can make speeches in Japanese.

ブラウンさんは日本語で演説することができる / 演説ができる。

Buraun-san wa Nihongo de enzetsu suru koto ga dekiru / enzetsu ga dekiru.

4. Can you come by 8 o'clock?

8時までに来ることができますか / 来られますか。

Hachi-ji made ni kuru koto ga dekimasu ka / koraremasu ka.

alone	一人で	*hitori de*
fast	速く	*hayaku*

Say the following in Japanese:

1. Anne is able to go shopping alone.
2. Dan can sing Japanese songs.
3. Can this dog swim fast?

Answers

1. アン (さん) は一人で買い物に行くことができる / できます。
   An(-san) wa hitori de kaimono ni iku koto ga dekiru / dekimasu.

   OR

   アン (さん) は一人で買い物に行ける / 行けます。
   An(-san) wa hitori de kaimono ni ikeru / ikemasu.

2. ダン (さん) は日本の歌を歌うことができる / できます。
   Dan(-san) wa Nihon no uta o utau koto ga dekiru / dekimasu.

   OR

   ダン (さん) は日本の歌が歌える / 歌えます。
   Dan(-san) wa Nihon no uta ga utaeru / utaemasu.

3. この犬は速く泳ぐことができますか / 泳げますか。
   Kono inu wa hayaku oyogu koto ga dekimasu ka / oyoge masu ka.

103

I have reached the point where I can read kanji.

漢字が読める**ようになった** / **なりました**。
*Kanji ga yomeru **yō ni natta** / **narimashita**.*

The potential form of a verb, followed by the phrase *yō ni naru* ("reach the point where …"), expresses achievement of an ability or a potential: someone becomes capable of something after a process or length of time.

The dictionary or *nai* form of a verb may be used in place of the potential form in this same pattern to express the same notion (Example 2), or to express a change in a situation (Example 3), state, or condition.

Examples

1. He has finally reached the point where he can write a letter in Japanese.

   彼はやっと日本語で手紙が書けるようになった。

   Kare wa yatto Nihongo de tegami ga kakeru yō ni natta.

2. Our neighbor's baby has learned to walk by herself.

   隣の赤ちゃんは一人で歩くようになりました。

   Tonari no akachan wa hitori de aruku yō ni narimashita.

3. Linda doesn't date Jim anymore.

   リンダはジムとデートしないようになった。

   Rinda wa Jimu to dēto shinai yō ni natta.

Practice

| feeling | 気持ち | *kimochi* |

Say the following in Japanese:

1. I have come to understand her feelings.
2. Mr. Tada has reached the point where he no longer smokes.
3. I have finally reached the point where I can use the computer.

1. 彼女の気持ちが分かるようになった / なりました。
   Kanojo no kimochi ga wakaru yō ni natta / narimashita.

2. 多田さんはたばこを吸わないようになった / なりました。
   Tada-san wa tabako o suwanai yō ni natta / narimashita.

3. やっとコンピューターが使えるようになった / なりました。
   Yatto konpyūtā ga tsukaeru yō ni natta / narimashita.

104

> (a) I can see a lake in the distance. (IMPLYING: A lake can be seen in the distance.)
>
> (b) I can hear music. (IMPLYING: Music can be heard.)

(a) 遠くに湖が**見える** / **見えます**。
*Tōku ni mizuumi ga **mieru** / **miemasu**.*

(b) 音楽が**聞こえる** / **聞こえます**。
*Ongaku ga **kikoeru** / **kikoemasu**.*

The verbs *mieru* ("can be seen") and *kikoeru* ("can be heard") indicate that something is passively or spontaneously visible or audible. These verbs are different from *mirareru* ("can see") and *kikeru* ("can hear")—the potential forms of the verbs *miru* and *kiku*—in that the latter indicate that one can see or hear something by virtue of the quality of one's eyesight or hearing, not by the nature of what happens to be in one's field of vision or within earshot.

Examples

1. One can see stars in the (night) sky. (IMPLYING: Stars are visible.)
   夜空に星が見える。
   Yozora ni hoshi ga mieru.

2. It's cloudy today, so we can't see Mt. Fuji.

今日は曇っているので富士山が見えません。

Kyō wa kumotte iru node Fuji-san ga miemasen.

3. The cries of birds could be heard in the woods.

森の中で鳥の鳴き声が聞こえた。

Mori no naka de tori no nakigoe ga kikoeta.

4. This place is so quiet I can't hear anything.

ここはとても静かで何も聞こえない。

Koko wa totemo shizuka de nani mo kikoenai.

Practice

siren	サイレン	*sairen*
old	古い	*furui*
temple	お寺	*o-tera*
window	窓	*mado*
sound	音	*oto*
wind	風	*kaze*
all night (long)	一晩中	*hitobanjū*

Say the following in Japanese:

1. I can hear sirens.
2. An old temple could be seen from the window.
3. I can't see anything from here.
4. The sound of wind could be heard all night long.

1. サイレンが聞こえる / 聞こえます。
   Sairen ga kikoeru / kikoemasu.

2. 窓から古いお寺が見えた / 見えました。
   Mado kara furui o-tera ga mieta / miemashita.

3. ここからは何も見えない / 見えません。
   Koko kara wa nani mo mienai / miemasen.

4. 一晩中風の音が聞こえた / 聞こえました。
   Hitobanjū kaze no oto ga kikoeta / kikoemashita.

105

(a) Mr. Harris is good at golf.

(b) Jim is good at memorizing words.

(a) ハリスさんはゴルフ**が上手だ** / **上手です**。
   *Harisu-san wa gorufu **ga jōzu da** / **jōzu desu**.*

(b) ジム(さん)は言葉を覚える**のが早い** / **早いです**。
   *Jimu(-san) wa kotoba o oboeru **no ga hayai** / **hayai desu**.*

The adjectives *jōzuna* ("skillful") and *hayai* ("quick"), as well as their antonyms *hetana* ("lousy") and *osoi* ("slow"), are often used as predicates to describe a person's ability to do something. The particle *no* following the dictionary form of a verb, as in (b) above, turns the verb into a gerund.

Examples

1. This child is good at making paper airplanes.
   この子は紙で飛行機を作るのが上手だ。
   Kono ko wa kami de hikōki o tsukuru no ga jōzu da.

2. My older sister was bad at cooking.

姉は料理が下手でした。

Ane wa ryōri ga heta deshita.

3. He is always quick to hand in his exams.

彼はいつも答案を出すのが早い。

Kare wa itsumo tōan o dasu no ga hayai.

Practice

French	フランス語	*furansugo*
make/give a speech	スピーチをする	*supīchi o suru*
return	返す	*kaesu*

Say the following in Japanese:

1. Ms. Kawase is good at French.

2. Mr. Mori was bad at making speeches.

3. Professor Sada is slow at returning exams.

4. The section chief is good (= quick) at finding errors.

Answers

1. 川瀬さんはフランス語が上手だ / 上手です。
   Kawase-san wa Furansugo ga jōzu da / jōzu desu.

2. 森さんはスピーチ (をするの) が下手だ / 下手です。
   Mori-san wa supīchi (o suru no) ga heta da / heta desu.

3. 佐田先生は答案を返すのが遅い / 遅いです。
   Sada-sensei wa tōan o kaesu no ga osoi / osoi desu.

4. 課長は間違いを見つけるのが早い / 早いです。
   Kachō wa machigai o mitsukeru no ga hayai / hayai desu.

(a) Ken likes jazz.

(b) Bill doesn't like to listen to music.

(a) ケン（さん）はジャズが**好きだ / 好きです**。
   *Ken(-san) wa jazu **ga suki da / suki desu**.*

(b) ビル（さん）は音楽を聞くのが**嫌いだ / 嫌いです**。
   *Biru(-san) wa ongaku o kiku no **ga kirai da / kirai desu**.*

The *na*-adjectives *sukina* ("favorite," "preferred") and *kiraina* ("disliked") are often used as predicates to express one's preference for or dislike of someone or something. To express love or hate, the prefix *dai-* is added to these words: *dai-suki da* ("love"), *dai-kirai da* ("hate").

NOTE: The particle *ga* changes to *wa* when two items are contrasted (Example 4).

Examples

1. Mr. Cook likes Japanese food.

   クックさんは日本の食べ物が好きです。
   Kukku-san wa Nihon no tabemono ga suki desu.

2. Takashi loves to play with his dog.

   孝は犬と遊ぶのが大好きだ。
   Takashi wa inu to asobu no ga daisuki da.

3. My younger brother hates to mow the lawn.

   弟は芝生を刈るのが大嫌いです。
   Otōto wa shibafu o karu no ga daikirai desu.

4. My grandmother likes fish, but she doesn't like meat.

祖母は魚は好きですが、肉は嫌いです。

Sobo wa sakana wa suki desu ga, niku wa kirai desu.

Practice

chocolate	チョコレート	*chokorēto*
decorate	飾る	*kazaru*
sports	スポーツ	*supōtsu*

Say the following in Japanese:

1. Children love chocolate.
2. She likes to decorate rooms.
3. He likes sports but dislikes music.

Answers

1. 子供はチョコレートが大好きだ / 大好きです。
   Kodomo wa chokorēto ga daisuki da / daisuki desu.

2. 彼女は部屋を飾るのが好きだ / 好きです。
   Kanojo wa heya o kazaru no ga suki da / suki desu.

3. 彼はスポーツは好きだ / ですが音楽は嫌いだ / 嫌いです。
   Kare wa supōtsu wa suki da / desu ga ongaku wa kirai da / kirai desu.

> (a) I want a stereo.
>
> (b) My son wants a bicycle.

(a) 私はステレオ**が欲しい** / 欲しいです。
　　*Watashi wa sutereo **ga hoshii** / hoshii desu.*

(b) 息子は自転車**を欲しがっている** / 欲しがっています。
　　*Musuko wa jitensha **o hoshigatte iru** / hoshigatte imasu.*

The *i*-adjective *hoshii* ("desirable") is used as a predicate to express a first person's desire for something, with the object of desire marked by the particle *ga*. This adjective is also used in interrogative sentences to inquire about a second person's desire (Example 2). In speaking about a third person's desire, however, a different word must be used: *hoshigatte iru*, which is the present-progressive form of the verb *hoshigaru*, meaning, literally, "show signs of wanting." The particle *o* is used with *hoshigatte iru* to mark the object of desire (Example 3).

| Examples |

1. I want a big house.

   （私は）大きい家が欲しい。
   (Watashi wa) ōkii uchi ga hoshii.

2. What do you want now?

   今、何が欲しいですか。
   Ima, nani ga hoshii desu ka.

3. Sandra wanted a pearl necklace.

サンドラは真珠のネックレスを欲しがっていた。

Sandora wa shinju no nekkuresu o hoshigatte ita.

earring	イヤリング	*iyaringu*
scooter	スクーター	*sukūtā*
red	赤い	*akai*
sweater	セーター	*sētā*

Say the following in Japanese:

1. I want pearl earrings.

2. Dan wants a scooter.

3. Midori wanted a red sweater.

---

1. (私は) 真珠のイヤリングが欲しい / 欲しいです。
   (Watashi wa) shinju no iyaringu ga hoshii / hoshii desu.

2. ダン (さん) はスクーターを欲しがっている / 欲しがっています。
   Dan(-san) wa sukūtā o hoshigatte iru / hoshigatte imasu.

3. 緑 (さん) は赤いセーターを欲しがっていた / 欲しがっていました。
   Midori(-san) wa akai sētā o hoshigatte ita / hoshigatte imashita.

108

I want him to write the report.

私は彼にレポートを書いてほしい / 書いてほしいです。

*Watashi wa kare **ni** repōto **o** kai**te hoshii** / kai**te hoshii desu.***

The *te* form of a verb followed by the *i*-adjective *hoshii* ("desirable") expresses one's desire to have someone do something. This pattern is used with the first person in declarative sentences, and with the second person in interrogative sentences (Example 2).

NOTE: The person who is indirect object of the sentence (indicated by the particle *ni*) should not be of a higher social status than the speaker or the person whose desire is being spoken about.

Examples

1. I want you to read this letter.

   あなたにこの手紙を読んでほしいです。
   Anata ni kono tegami o yonde hoshii desu.

2. Who do you want to teach you tennis?

   あなたはだれにテニスを教えてほしいですか。
   Anata wa dare ni tenisu o oshiete hoshii desu ka.

3. I want my parents to go with me.

   私は両親に私と一緒に行ってほしい。
   Watashi wa ryōshin ni watashi to issho ni itte hoshii.

Practice

pass around	回す	*mawasu*
everybody	みんな	*minna*
read	読む	*yomu*
book	本	*hon*

Say the following in Japanese:

1. I want you to pass this around to everybody.
2. Who do you want to read this book?
3. I want Akiko to go shopping with me.

1. これをみんなに回してほしい / ほしいです。
   Kore o minna ni mawashite hoshii / hoshii desu.

2. あなたはだれにこの本を読んでほしいですか。
   Anata wa dare ni kono hon o yonde hoshii desu ka.

3. 私は秋子（さん）に（私と）一緒に買い物に行ってほしい / ほしいです。
   Watashi wa Akiko(-san) ni (watashi to) issho ni kaimono ni itte hoshii / hoshii desu.

109

(a) I want to eat a steak now.

(b) My wife wants to go to the opera.

(a) 私は今ステーキを / が食べ**たい** / 食べ**たいです**。
   *Watashi wa ima sutēki o / ga tabe**tai** / tabe**tai desu**.*

(b) 家内はオペラに行き**たがっている** / 行き**たがって います**。
   *Kanai wa opera ni iki**tagatte iru** / iki**tagatte imasu**.*

The stem of the *masu* form of a verb, followed by the auxiliary adjective *tai*, expresses a first person's desire to do something, or a second person's in interrogative sentences. If the root verb to which *tai* attaches is transitive, the direct object of the sentence can be marked by either *ga* or *o*.

A third person's desire to do something is expressed by the use of the auxiliary verb *tagatte iru* following the *masu* stem of a verb, as in (b).

Examples

1. I want to see that movie once more.

   私はもう一度あの映画を / が見たいです。
   Watashi wa mō ichido ano eiga o / ga mitai desu.

2. What do you want to do during summer vacation?

あなたは夏休みに何を / がしたいですか。

Anata wa natsuyasumi ni nani o / ga shitai desu ka.

3. Mr. Kida wanted to climb Mt. Everest.

木田さんはエベレスト山に登りたがっていた。

Kida-san wa Eberesuto-zan ni noboritagatte ita.

Practice

keep (pets)	飼う	*kau*
white	白い	*shiroi*
cat	猫	*neko*
camping	キャンプ	*kyanpu*

Say the following in Japanese:

1. I want (to keep) a white cat.

2. What do you want to see in Kyoto?

3. My son wants go camping with his friends.

Answers

1. 私は白い猫を / が飼いたい / 飼いたいです。
   Watashi wa shiroi neko o / ga kaitai / kaitai desu.

2. あなたは京都で何を / が見たいですか。
   Anata wa Kyōto de nani o / ga mitai desu ka.

3. 息子は友達と一緒にキャンプに行きたがっている / 行きたがっています。
   Musuko wa tomodachi to issho ni kyanpu ni ikitagatte iru / ikitagatte imasu.

110

He intends to become a doctor.

彼は医者になる**つもり**だ / です。
*Kare wa isha ni naru **tsumori** da / desu.*

The dictionary form of a verb, followed by *tsumori*, expresses a person's intention to do something. *Tsumori* ("intention") is a pseudo noun (a noun that cannot be used alone, without a modifier) and is usually accompanied by the copula *da* or *desu*.

To express an intention not to do something, the verb before *tsumori* can be made negative (Example 2), or *tsumori* itself can be made negative: *tsumori wa nai* ("have no intention"; Example 3).

Examples

1. We intend to spend Christmas in Hawaii.

   私達はクリスマスをハワイで過ごすつもりです。

   Watashi-tachi wa kurisumasu o Hawai de sugosu tsumori desu.

2. I don't intend to travel this summer.

   今年の夏は旅行しないつもりだ。

   Kotoshi no natsu wa ryokō shinai tsumori da.

3. She has no intention of getting married now.

   彼女は今結婚するつもりはない。

   Kanojo wa ima kekkon suru tsumori wa nai.

next month	来月	*raigetsu*
move	移る	*utsuru*
retire	引退する	*intai suru*
participate	参加する	*sanka suru*
marathon	マラソン	*marason*

Say the following in Japanese:

1. I intend to move to a new apartment next month.

2. My father has no intention of retiring yet.

3. I don't intend to participate in the marathon.

Answers

1. 来月新しいアパートに移るつもりだ / です。
   Raigetsu atarashii apāto ni utsuru tsumori da / desu.

2. 父はまだ引退するつもりはない / ありません。
   Chichi wa mada intai suru tsumori wa nai / arimasen.

3. マラソンに参加しないつもりだ / です。
   Marason ni sanka shinai tsumori da / desu.

111

I think I'll teach English to Japanese students.

日本の学生に英語を**教えようと思う / 思います**。
*Nihon no gakusei ni Eigo o **oshieyō to omou** / **omoimasu**.*

The volitional form of a verb, followed by *to omou* ("I think ...") or *to omotte iru* ("I am thinking ..."), expresses a course of action the speaker is intending to take, or is considering taking. The particle *to*, which is used to mark quotations, is used here to mark the content of the action *omou*.

1. I think I'll sell my car.

车を売ろうと思う。

Kuruma o urō to omou.

2. I'm thinking of inviting Judy to the concert.

ジュディ(さん) をコンサートに誘おうと思っています。

Judī(-san) o konsāto ni sasoō to omotte imasu.

3. Since I am free this afternoon, I'm thinking of going out.

午後ひまだから、出掛けようと思っている。

Gogo hima da kara, dekakeyō to omotte iru.

Practice

graduate school	大学院	*daigakuin*
airline company	航空会社	*kōkū-gaisha*
letter	手紙	*tegami*

Say the following in Japanese:

1. I think I'll go to graduate school.
2. I'm thinking of working for an airline company.
3. I think I'll write a letter to my mother.

Answers

1. 大学院に行こうと思う / 思います。
   Daigakuin ni ikō to omou / omoimasu.

2. 航空会社に勤めようと思っている / 思っています。
   Kōkū-gaisha ni tsutomeyō to omotte iru / omotte imasu.

3. 母に手紙を書こうと思う / 思います。
   Haha ni tegami o kakō to omou / omoimasu.

112

I decided to work in Japan.

私は日本で働くことにした / しました。

*Watashi wa Nihon de hataraku **koto ni shita** / **shimashita**.*

The dictionary form of a verb, followed by *koto ni suru* ("decide to …"), expresses a decision to do something. The present-progressive form of this phrase, *koto ni shite iru*, is used to expresses a decision to do something regularly, i.e., to make a habit or rule of something (Example 2).

To express a decision to not do something, the negative (*nai*) form of a verb is used in place of the dictionary form (Example 3).

Examples

1. I decided to quit my job.

   私は仕事を辞めることにした。

   Watashi wa shigoto o yameru koto ni shita.

2. I make it a rule to jog every morning.

   毎朝ジョギングをすることにしています。

   Maiasa jogingu o suru koto ni shite imasu.

3. I decided not to attend the class reunion.

   クラス会に出席しないことにしました。

   Kurasukai ni shusseki shinai koto ni shimashita.

Practice

cherry-blossom viewing	（お）花見	*(o-)hanami*
weekend	週末	*shūmatsu*
stay the night	泊まる	*tomaru*

Say the following in Japanese:

1. We decided to go cherry-blossom viewing by bus.

2. I make it a rule to play golf on weekends.

3. I decided not to stay the night in Osaka.

/Answers/

1. 私達はバスで（お）花見に行くことにした / しました。
   Watashi-tachi wa basu de (o-)hanami ni iku koto ni shita / shimashita.

2. 私は週末にゴルフをすることにしている / しています。
   Watashi wa shūmatsu ni gorufu o suru koto ni shite iru / shite imasu.

3. 大阪で泊まらないことにした / しました。
   Ōsaka de tomaranai koto ni shita / shimashita.

113

It will be arranged that Mr. Oda will take charge of the project.

小田さんがプロジェクトを担当する**ことになる** /
なります。

*Oda-san ga purojekuto o tantō suru **koto ni naru** / **narimasu**.*

The dictionary form of a verb, followed by *koto ni naru* ("It will be decided that ..."), expresses some decision or arrangement made by others, rather than by the speaker. The present-progressive form of this phrase, *koto ni natte iru*, is used to express the idea that a decision or arrangement has already been made, and the result is in effect (Example 3).

To express a decision made by others to not do something, the negative (*nai*) form of a verb is used in place of the dictionary form (Example 4).

Examples

1. It has been decided that Mr. Yagi will go on a business trip tomorrow.

八木さんが明日出張することになった。

Yagi-san ga ashita shutchō suru koto ni natta.

2. The store will close at 7 P.M. starting next month. (IMPLYING: That's the way things will be arranged).

この店は来月から午後7時に閉まることになります。

Kono mise wa raigetsu kara gogo shichi-ji ni shimaru koto ni narimasu.

3. I am supposed to see the (company) president at 2 o'clock.

2時に社長に会うことになっています。

Ni-ji ni shachō ni au koto ni natte imasu.

4. It has been decided that he won't participate in the Olympics.

彼はオリンピックに参加しないことになった。

Kare wa Orinpikku ni sanka shinai koto ni natta.

Practice

hire	雇う	*yatou*
be transferred	転勤する	*tenkin suru*
Wednesday	水曜日	*suiyōbi*

Say the following in Japanese:

1. They will hire two clerks. (IMPLYING: That's the way things will be arranged.)

2. It has been decided that my husband will be transferred to Kobe.

3. I'm supposed to return the books by Wednesday.

4. It has been decided that Professor Mori won't teach that class.

/Answers/

1. 店員を二人雇うことになる / なります。
   Ten'in o futari yatou koto ni naru / narimasu.

2. 主人は神戸に転勤することになった / なりました。
   Shujin wa Kōbe ni tenkin suru koto ni natta / narimashita.

3. 水曜日までに本を返すことになっている / います。
   Suiyōbi made ni hon o kaesu koto ni natte iru / imasu.

4. 森先生はそのクラスを教えないことになった / なりました。
   Mori-sensei wa sono kurasu o oshienai koto ni natta / narimashita.

114

There are times when I do homework in the train.

電車の中で宿題をする**ことがある** / **あります**。
*Densha no naka de shukudai o suru **koto ga aru** / **arimasu**.*

The dictionary form of a verb, followed by *koto ga aru* ("there are times when …"), expresses that an action or a situation occurs occasionally.

To express that a usual or an expected action or situation occasionally does not occur, this same pattern is used, only with the negative (*nai*) form of a verb in place of the dictionary form (Example 3).

1. There are times when I watch baseball games on TV.

   テレビで野球の試合を見ることがある。

   Terebi de yakyū no shiai o miru koto ga aru.

2. There are times when Dan beats Hiroshi in judo.

   柔道でダンさんが宏さんを負かすことがあります。

   Jūdō de Dan-san ga Hiroshi-san o makasu koto ga arimasu.

3. There are times when Helen does not prepare (for class).

   ヘレンは予習しないことがある。

   Heren wa yoshū shinai koto ga aru.

pizza	ピザ	*piza*
oversleep	寝過ごす	*nesugosu*

Say the following in Japanese:

1. There are times when I order a pizza.

2. There are times when Sam oversleeps.

3. There are times when I don't eat breakfast.

---

1. ピザを注文することがある / あります。

   Piza o chūmon suru koto ga aru / arimasu.

2. サム (さん) は寝過ごすことがある / あります。

   Samu(-san) wa nesugosu koto ga aru / arimasu.

3. 朝ご飯を食べないことがある / あります。

   Asagohan o tabenai koto ga aru / arimasu.

115

I have been to China.

私は中国へ**行ったことがある / あります**。
*Watashi wa Chūgoku e **itta koto ga aru / arimasu**.*

The *ta* form of a verb, followed by *koto ga aru*, expresses experience: someone has had the experience of doing something or being somewhere.

To express a lack of experience doing something or being somewhere, *koto ga/wa nai* is used in place of *koto ga aru* (Example 3).

Examples

1. I have taught songs to children.

   私は子供に歌を教えたことがある。
   Watashi wa kodomo ni uta o oshieta koto ga aru.

2. She has ridden a horse before.

   彼女は馬に乗ったことがあります。
   Kanojo wa uma ni notta koto ga arimasu.

3. Mr. Olson hasn't seen Kabuki before.

   オルソンさんは歌舞伎を見たことが / はない。
   Oruson-san wa kabuki o mita koto ga / wa nai.

Practice

many times	何度も	*nando mo*
drive	運転する	*unten suru*
ski	スキー	*skī*

Say the following in Japanese:

1. He has seen that movie many times.

2. She hasn't driven a car before.

3. My older brother has been to Hokkaido to ski.

---

1. 彼は何度もその映画を見たことがある / あります。
   Kare wa nando mo sono eiga o mita koto ga aru / arimasu.

2. 彼女は車を運転したことが / はない / ありません。
   Kanojo wa kuruma o unten shita koto ga / wa nai / arimasen.

3. 兄は北海道へスキーに行ったことがある / あります。
   Ani wa Hokkaidō e sukī ni itta koto ga aru / arimasu.

9 Describing the Actions of Giving and Receiving

116

I will give a present to Sachiko.

私は幸子（さん）にプレゼントを**あげる** / **あげます**。
*Watashi wa Sachiko(-san) ni purezento o **ageru** / **agemasu**.*

There are several verbs for "give" in Japanese, and each reflects a relationship between the person giving and the one receiving. The three basic verbs used to describe the action of one person giving something to another (where the recipient is not the speaker) are *ageru*, *sashiageru*, and *yaru*. *Ageru* is used when the social status of the giver is about equal to that of the recipient (Example 1), while the humble polite *sashiageru* is used when the status of the recipient is higher than that of the giver (Example 2). *Yaru*, on the other hand, is used when the status of the recipient is lower than that of the giver. *Yaru* is used among close friends, for example, or when the recipient is a child, animal, or plant (Example 3).

In a sentence that expresses the action of giving with any of the verbs described above, the indirect object—the recipient, marked by the particle *ni*—cannot be in the first person.

Examples

1. I gave Janet a vase.

私はジャネットに花瓶をあげた。
Watashi wa Janetto ni kabin o ageta.

2. I'll give the section chief a souvenir from Kyoto.

私は課長に京都のお土産を差し上げます。

Watashi wa kachō ni Kyōto no o-miyage o sashiagemasu.

3. My grandfather gave water to the plants this morning.

祖父は今朝植木に水をやりました。

Sofu wa kesa ueki ni mizu o yarimashita.

Practice

boyfriend	彼	*kare*
tie	ネクタイ	*nekutai*
peanut	ピーナッツ	*pīnattsu*
monkey	猿	*saru*

Say the following in Japanese:

1. Masako gave her boyfriend a tie.
2. I'll give my teacher a book.
3. The child gave some peanuts to the monkeys.

Answers

1. 正子さんは彼にネクタイをあげた / あげました。
   Masako-san wa kare ni nekutai o ageta / agemashita.

2. 私は先生に本を差し上げる / 差し上げます。
   Watashi wa sensei ni hon o sashiageru / sashiagemasu.

3. 子供は猿にピーナッツをやった / やりました。
   Kodomo wa saru ni pīnattsu o yatta / yarimashita.

117

I sometimes lend Rita my dictionary.

私は時々リタさんに辞書を貸して**あげる** / 貸してあ**げます**。

*Watashi wa tokidoki Rita-san ni jisho o kashite **ageru** / kashite **agemasu**.*

The *te* form of a verb, followed by *ageru*, *sashiageru*, or *yaru*, expresses someone's doing a favorable action for someone else. *Ageru* is used when the social status of the recipient of the action is about equal to that of the doer (Example 1), *sashiageru* when the his or her status is higher than that of the doer (Example 2), and *yaru* when the his or her status is lower than that of the doer (Examples 3). *Ageru*, *sashiageru*, and *yaru* are all used as auxiliaries here.

In this pattern neither the direct object marked by the particle *o*, nor the indirect object marked by *ni*, can be the first person.

Examples

1. I sent my friend some Japanese stamps.

   私は友達に日本の切手を送ってあげた。

   Watashi wa tomodachi ni Nihon no kitte o okutte ageta.

2. I drove my teacher home.

   私は先生を車で家まで送って差し上げました。

   Watashi wa sensei o kuruma de uchi made okutte sashiage-mashita.

3. My husband bought our son a toy airplane.

主人は息子におもちゃの飛行機を買ってやった。

Shujin wa musuko ni omocha no hikōki o katte yatta.

(photo)copy	コピーする	*kopī suru*
article	記事	*kiji*
fireworks display	花火大会	*hanabi taikai*

Say the following in Japanese:

1. I copied the article for John.

2. I took pictures for Professor Tanaka.

3. My husband took the children to a fireworks display.

Answers

1. 私はジョン（さん）に記事をコピーしてあげた / コピーしてあげました。
   Watashi wa Jon(-san) ni kiji o kopī shite ageta / kopī shite agemashita.

2. 私は田中先生に写真を撮って差し上げた / 差し上げました。
   Watashi wa Tanaka-sensei ni shashin o totte sashiageta / sashiage-mashita.

3. 主人は子供を花火大会に連れて行ってやった / 連れて行ってやりました。
   Shujin wa kodomo o hanabi taikai ni tsureteitte yatta / tsureteitte yari-mashita.

118

I received a postcard from my friend.

私は友達に / から葉書を**もらった** / **もらいました**。

*Watashi wa tomodachi ni / kara hagaki o **moratta** / **moraimashita**.*

The verbs *morau* and *itadaku* (both meaning "receive") express a person's receiving something from someone. *Morau* is used when the recipient's social status is about equal to or higher than that of the giver (Example 1), while the humble polite *itadaku* is used when the social status of the recipient is lower than that of the giver (Example 2).

In this pattern the indirect object (the giver) is marked by the particle *ni* or *kara*. However, if the giver is an impersonal institution, *kara* must be used (Example 3). The giver, in any case, cannot be in the first person when the verb *morau* is used.

Examples

1. Mr. White got a Kabuki ticket from Mr. Abe.

   ホワイトさんは阿部さんに / から歌舞伎の切符をもらった。

   Howaito-san wa Abe-san ni / kara kabuki no kippu o moratta.

2. I received some pears from Kazuko's mother.

   私は和子さんのお母さんに / からなしをいただきました。

   Watashi wa Kazuko(-san) no o-kā-san ni / kara nashi o itadakimashita.

3. Robin received a scholarship from the university.

   ロビンは大学から奨学金をもらった。

   Robin wa daigaku kara shōgakukin o moratta.

love letter	ラブレター	*raburetā*
classmate	クラスメート	*kurasumēto*
Paris	パリ	*pari*
manager	マネージャー	*manējā*
money	お金	*o-kane*

Say the following in Japanese:

1. Sarah received a love letter from her classmate.

2. I received a souvenir from Paris from the manager's wife.

3. Mr. Ogawa received some money from the company.

---

1. サラ（さん）はクラスメートに / からラブレターをもらった / もらいました。
   Sara(-san) wa kurasumēto ni / kara raburetā o moratta / moraimashita.

2. 私はマネージャーの奥さんに / からパリのお土産をいただいた / いただきました。
   Watashi wa manējā no oku-san ni / kara Pari no o-miyage o itadaita / ita-dakimashita.

3. 小川さんは会社からお金をもらった / もらいました。
   Ogawa-san wa kaisha kara o-kane o moratta / moraimashita.

119

I'll have Mr. Hara teach me golf.

原さんにゴルフを教え**てもらう** / 教え**てもらいます**。
*Hara-san ni gorufu o oshie**te morau** / oshie**te moraimasu**.*

The *te* form of a verb, followed by *morau* or *itadaku*, expresses someone's receiving a favorable action from someone else. *Morau* is used when the social status of the recipient of the action is about equal to or higher than that of the doer (Examples 1, 2), while *itadaku* is used when the recipient's status is lower than that of the doer (Example 3). *Morau* and *itadaku* are used as auxiliaries in this pattern.

The indirect object marked by the particle *ni* (the doer of the favorable action) cannot be the first person when the verb *morau* is used.

Examples

1. I'll have Ms. Toda come to help me.

戸田さんに手伝いに来てもらいます。

Toda-san ni tetsudai ni kite moraimasu.

2. Yuriko had her younger sister knit a sweater for her.

ゆり子さんは妹（さん）にセーターを編んでもらった。

Yuriko-san wa imōto(-san) ni sētā o ande moratta.

3. I had my teacher lend me a map of Japan.

先生に日本の地図を貸していただいた。

Sensei ni Nihon no chizu o kashite itadaita.

Practice

bookshelf	本棚	*hondana*
sign	サインする	*sain suru*
department head	部長	*buchō*

Say the following in Japanese:

1. I had my older brother make a bookshelf for me.
2. She had Mr. Sugi sell her car.
3. I'll have the department head sign these papers.

1. 兄に本棚を作ってもらった / 作ってもらいました。
   Ani ni hondana o tsukutte moratta / tsukutte moraimahita.

2. 彼女は杉さんに車を売ってもらった / 売ってもらいました。
   Kanojo wa Sugi-san ni kuruma o utte moratta / utte moraimashita.

3. 部長にこの書類にサインしていただく/ サインしていただきます。
   Buchō ni kono shorui ni sain shite itadaku / sain shite itadakimasu.

120

My mother gave me this ring.

母が (私に) この指輪を**くれた** / **くれました**。
*Haha ga (watashi ni) kono yubiwa o **kureta** / **kuremashita**.*

The verbs *kureru* and *kudasaru* (both meaning "give") indicate someone's giving something to the speaker, or to someone who is close, kinshipwise or otherwise, to him or her (Examples 2). *Kureru* is used when the giver's social status is about equal to or lower than that of the speaker or recipient, while the honorific *kudasaru* is reserved for situations where the status of the giver is decidedly higher than that of the speaker or recipient (Example 3).

The indirect object marked by the particle *ni* (the recipient) is usually omitted when it is clear from context.

Examples

1. Yoshiko often gives me delicious cookies.

   良子(さん) はよく(私に) おいしいクッキーをくれる。
   Yoshiko(-san) wa yoku (watashi ni) oishii kukkī o kureru.

2. Ms. Doi gave my daughter this doll.

土井さんが娘にこの人形をくれました。

Doi-san ga musume ni kono ningyō o kuremashita.

3. My teacher gave me a dictionary.

先生が (私に) 辞書をくださいました。

Sensei ga (watashi ni) jisho o kudasaimashita.

Practice

stranger	知らない人	*shiranai hito*
apple	りんご	*ringo*
scarf	マフラー	*mafurā*
two (tickets)	2枚	*ni-mai*

Say the following in Japanese:

1. A stranger gave me an apple.

2. Mr. Yamano gave my son a scarf.

3. My piano teacher gave me two concert tickets.

Answers

1. 知らない人が (私に) りんごをくれた / くれました。
   Shiranai hito ga (watashi ni) ringo o kureta / kuremashita.

2. 山野さんが息子にマフラーをくれた / くれました。
   Yamano-san ga musuko ni mafurā o kureta / kuremashita.

3. ピアノの先生が (私に) コンサートの切符を2枚くださった / くださいました。
   Piano no sensei ga (watashi ni) konsāto no kippu o ni-mai kudasatta / kudasaimashita.

121

Ms. Kubo cooked sukiyaki for us.

久保さんが（私達に）すき焼きを作って**くれた** / 作っ
て**くれました**。

*Kubo-san ga (watashi-tachi ni) sukiyaki o tsukutte **kureta** /
tsukutte **kuremashita**.*

The *te* form of a verb, followed by *kureru* or *kudasaru*, expresses someone's
doing a favorable action to or for the speaker, or to or for someone who is
close, kinshipwise or otherwise, to him or her (Example 2). *Kureru* is used
when the social status of the doer of the action is about equal to or lower
than that of the speaker or recipient of the action (Examples 1, 2), while
the honorific *kudasaru* is used when doer's status is higher than that of the
speaker or recipient (Example 3).

The indirect object marked by the particle *ni* (the recipient of the favorable action) is usually omitted when it is clear from context.

Examples

1. Sometimes Mr. Miki lends me his camera.

   時々三木さんが（私に）カメラを貸してくれます。

   *Tokidoki Miki-san ga (watashi ni) kamera o kashite kure-
   masu.*

2. My friend taught my mother how to use a computer.

   友達が母にコンピューターの使い方を教えてくれた。

   *Tomodachi ga (haha ni) konpyūtā no tsukaikata o oshiete
   kureta.*

3. Professor Miyata informed us of the news.

宮田先生が（私達に）そのニュースを知らせてくだ
さった。

Miyata-sensei ga (watashi-tachi ni) sono nyūsu o shirasete kudasatta.

Practice

girlfriend	ガールフレンド	*gārufurendo*
how to eat/way of eating	食べ方	*tabekata*
send	送る	*okuru*
tuition	授業料	*jugyōryō*

Say the following in Japanese:

1. My girlfriend taught me how to eat sushi.

2. My father sends me my tuition.

3. Professor Miyake showed us a movie.

Answers

1. ガールフレンドが（僕に）すしの食べ方を教えてくれた / 教えてくれました。
   Gārufurendo ga (boku ni) sushi no tabekata o oshiete kureta / oshiete kuremashita.

2. 父が（私に）授業料を送ってくれる / 送ってくれます。
   Chichi ga (watashi ni) jugyōryō o okutte kureru / okutte kuremasu.

3. 三宅先生が（私達に）映画を見せてくださった / 見せてくださいました。
   Miyake-sensei ga (watashi-tachi ni) eiga o misete kudasatta / misete kudasaimashita.

10 Expressing Conjecture and Hearsay, and Quoting People

122

> (a) Mr. Johnson will probably come today.
>
> (b) That hotel is probably expensive.
>
> (c) Ben is probably good at dancing.

(a) ジョンソンさんは今日来る**だろう** / **でしょう**。
*Jonson-san wa kyō kuru **darō** / **deshō**.*

(b) あのホテルは高い**だろう** / **でしょう**。
*Ano hoteru wa takai **darō** / **deshō**.*

(c) ベン（さん）はダンスが上手**だろう** / **でしょう**。
*Ben(-san) wa dansu ga jōzu **darō** / **deshō**.*

Darō, the presumptive form of the copula *da*, is used as an auxiliary to express conjecture. It is used with nouns and all forms of verbs and adjectives. *Deshō* is the polite form of *darō* and is used likewise.

The adverbs *tabun* ("perhaps") and *kitto* ("certainly") are sometimes used with *darō* or *deshō* to make a conjecture sound more certain (Examples 3, 4).

Examples

1. That young man is probably a foreigner.
   あの若い男の人は外国人でしょう。
   Ano wakai otoko no hito wa gaikokujin deshō.

2. The exam was probably difficult.

試験は難しかっただろう。

Shiken wa muzukashikatta darō.

3. She probably won't come to the reception.

彼女はたぶんレセプションに来ないだろう。

Kanojo wa tabun resepushon ni konai darō.

4. I'm sure the procedure will be simple.

その手続きはきっと簡単でしょう。

Sono tetsuzuki wa kitto kantan deshō.

Practice

lecture	講義	*kōgi*
end	終わる	*owaru*
(married) couple	夫婦	*fūfu*
get divorced	離婚する	*rikon suru*
class reunion	クラス会	*kurasukai*

Say the following in Japanese:

1. This is probably Mr. Hill's car.
2. The lecture probably won't end by 3 o'clock.
3. They (= the couple) will probably get divorced.
4. I'm sure the class reunion was fun.

1. これはヒルさんの車だろう / でしょう。
   Kore wa Hiru-san no kuruma darō / deshō.

2. 講義は3時までに終わらないだろう / でしょう。
   Kōgi wa san-ji made ni owaranai darō / deshō.

3. あの夫婦はたぶん離婚するだろう / でしょう。
   Ano fūfu wa tabun rikon suru darō / deshō.

4. クラス会はきっと楽しかっただろう / でしょう。
   Kurasukai wa kitto tanoshikatta darō / deshō.

123

(a) It might rain tomorrow.

(b) The movie might be boring.

(c) He might be bad at singing.

(a) 明日雨が降る**かもしれない / かもしれません**。
   *Ashita ame ga furu **kamoshirenai / kamoshiremasen**.*

(b) 映画はつまらない**かもしれない / かもしれません**。
   *Eiga wa tsumaranai **kamoshirenai / kamoshiremasen**.*

(c) 彼は歌が下手**かもしれない / かもしれません**。
   *Kare wa uta ga heta **kamoshirenai / kamoshiremasen**.*

The auxiliary *i*-adjective *kamoshirenai* ("might") expresses speculation or a guess on the part of the speaker. It is used with nouns and all forms of verbs and adjectives. *Kamoshiremasen*, the polite form, is used likewise.

1. The plane might arrive a little earlier.

飛行機は少し早く着くかもしれない。

Hikōki wa sukoshi hayaku tsuku kamoshirenai.

2. That musical might not be interesting, you know.

あのミュージカルはおもしろくないかもしれませんよ。

Ano myūjikaru wa omoshiroku nai kamoshiremasen yo.

3. That might have been Mr. Hunt from the embassy.

あれは大使館のハントさんだったかもしれない。

Are wa taishikan no Hanto-san datta kamoshirenai.

Practice

Chinese food	中国料理	*Chūgoku ryōri*
bring (someone somewhere)	連れて来る	*tsuretekuru*

Say the following in Japanese:

1. The rain might not stop by tomorrow.
2. Jim might have disliked Chinese food.
3. Yuriko might bring her friend to the picnic.

Answers

1. 雨は明日までに止まないかもしれない / かもしれません。
   Ame wa ashita made ni yamanai kamoshirenai / kamoshiremasen

2. ジム（さん）は中国料理が嫌いだったかもしれない / かもしれません。
   Jimu(-san) wa Chūgoku ryōri ga kirai datta kamoshirenai / kamoshire-masen.

3. ゆり子さんはピクニックに友達を連れて来るかもしれない / かもしれません。
   Yuriko-san wa pikunikku ni tomodachi o tsuretekuru kamoshirenai / kamoshiremasen.

(a) There is no doubt that he will succeed.

(b) This watch must be expensive.

(c) The ceremony must have been gorgeous.

(a) 彼は成功する**に違いない / 違いありません**。
*Kare wa seikō suru **ni chigainai** / **chigaiarimasen**.*

(b) この時計は高い**に違いない / 違いありません**。
*Kono tokei wa takai **ni chigainai** / **chigaiarimasen**.*

(c) 式は豪華だった**に違いない / 違いありません**。
*Shiki wa gōka datta **ni chigainai** / **chigaiarimasen**.*

The auxiliary *i*-adjective *chigainai* ("be no doubt"), preceded by the particle *ni*, expresses the speaker's conviction about a guess. It is used with nouns and all forms of verbs and adjectives. *Chigaiarimasen*, the polite from, is used likewise.

Examples

1. Mr. Kihara must have forgotten the appointment.
   木原さんは約束を忘れたに違いない。
   Kihara-san wa yakusoku o wasureta ni chigainai.

2. This fish must not be fresh.
   この魚は新しくないに違いありません。
   Kono sakana wa atarashiku nai ni chigaiarimasen.

3. Our new baseball coach must be strict.

今度の野球のコーチは厳格に違いない。

Kondo no yakyū no kōchi wa genkaku ni chigainai.

4. That building must be the city library.

あの建物は市の図書館に違いありません。

Ano tatemono wa shi no toshokan ni chigaiarimasen.

Practice

debate	討論会	*tōronkai*
look for	探す	*sagasu*

Say the following in Japanese:

1. There is no doubt that Mike will participate in the debate.
2. The lake water must be cold.
3. The cherry blossoms in the park must have been pretty.
4. He must be looking for a job.

Answers

1. マイク（さん）は討論会に参加するに違いない / 違いありません。
   Maiku(-san) wa tōronkai ni sanka suru ni chigainai / chigaiarimasen.

2. 湖の水は冷たいに違いない / 違いありません。
   Mizuumi no mizu wa tsumetai ni chigainai / chigaiarimasen.

3. 公園の桜の花はきれいだったに違いない / 違いありません。
   Kōen no sakura no hana wa kirei datta ni chigainai / chigaiarimasen.

4. 彼は仕事を探しているに違いない / 違いありません。
   Kare wa shigoto o sagashite iru ni chigainai / chigaiarimasen.

> (a) Sales will increase, I'm sure.
>
> (b) I'm quite sure that the meeting was short.
>
> (c) That inn is sure to be quiet.

(a) 売り上げは増える**はず**だ / です。
    *Uriage wa fueru **hazu** da / desu.*

(b) 会議は短かった**はず**だ / です。
    *Kaigi wa mijikakatta **hazu** da / desu.*

(c) あの旅館は静かな**はず**だ / です。
    *Ano ryokan wa shizukana **hazu** da / desu.*

Hazu, preceded by all forms of verbs and adjectives, expresses the speaker's firm expectation or belief that someone will do something or that something will happen or be the case. *Hazu* is a pseudo noun (a noun that cannot be used alone, without a modifier) and is usually accompanied by the copula *da* or *desu*.

Examples

1. Prices will (only) go up from now on.
   これから物価が上がるはずだ。
   Kore kara bukka ga agaru hazu da.

2. I'm quite sure that Bill didn't come to school yesterday.
   昨日ビルさんは学校へ来なかったはずです。
   Kinō Biru(-san) wa gakkō e konakatta hazu desu.

3. That restaurant is very expensive, I'm sure.

あのレストランはとても高いはずです。

Ano resutoran wa totemo takai hazu desu.

4. I'm quite sure that his secretary was competent.

彼の秘書は有能だったはずだ。

Kare no hisho wa yūnō datta hazu da.

last year	去年	*kyonen*
rope	ロープ	*rōpu*
durable	丈夫な	*jōbuna*

Say the following in Japanese:

1. I'm quite sure that he quit the company last year.
2. This rope is durable, I'm sure.
3. I'm quite sure that Anne didn't go to the exhibition.

Answers

1. 彼は去年会社を辞めたはずだ / です。
   Kare wa kyonen kaisha o yameta hazu da / desu.

2. このロープは丈夫なはずだ / です。
   Kono rōpu wa jōbuna hazu da / desu.

3. アン（さん）は展覧会に行かなかったはずだ / です。
   An(-san) wa tenrankai ni ikanakatta hazu da / desu.

126

(a) It looks like it will snow.

(b) This cake looks delicious.

(c) That child looks healthy.

(a) 雪が降り**そうだ** / **そうです**。
*Yuki ga furi **sō da** / **sō desu**.*

(b) このケーキはおいし**そうだ** / **そうです**。
*Kono kēki wa oishi **sō da** / **sō desu**.*

(c) あの子は元気**そうだ** / **そうです**。
*Ano ko wa genki **sō da** / **sō desu**.*

The auxiliary *na*-adjective *sō da* ("looks …," "appears to be …"), preceded by the stem of the *masu* form of a verb, as in (a), or by the stem of an adjective, as in (b) and (c), expresses the speaker's conjecture about the future, or about the current state or condition of someone or something, based on sensory evidence or general feeling, or both. In this pattern, the adjective *ii* ("good") and the negative *nai* ("not") change to *yosa* and *nasa*, respectively, before *sō da* (Example 3).

Examples

1. It looks like the flowers in the garden will bloom soon.
   庭の花はもうすぐ咲きそうだ。
   Niwa no hana wa mō sugu saki sō da.

2. She looked lonely at last night's party.
   彼女はゆうべのパーティーで寂しそうだった。
   Kanojo wa yūbe no pātī de sabishi sō datta.

3. He looks intelligent but doesn't look physically strong.

彼は頭はよさそうだが体は強くなさそうだ。

Kare wa atama wa yosa sō da ga karada wa tsuyokunasa sō da.

4. The young (married) couple looked happy.

若い夫婦は幸せそうだった。

Wakai fūfu wa shiawase sō datta.

Practice

typhoon	台風	*taifū*
all day (long)	一日中	*ichinichijū*
inconvenient	不便な	*fubenna*

Say the following in Japanese:

1. It looks like a typhoon is coming tonight.
2. The section chief looked busy all day long.
3. It sounds as though the hotel is inconvenient for shopping.

Answers

1. 今晩台風が来そうだ / そうです。
   Konban taifū ga ki sō da / sō desu.

2. 課長は一日中忙しそうだった / そうでした。
   Kachō wa ichinichijū isogashi sō datta / sō deshita.

3. そのホテルは買い物に不便そうだ / そうです。
   Sono hoteru wa kaimono ni fuben sō da / sō desu.

(a) It seems that Mr. Ross will return to America.

(b) It seems that the game was boring.

(c) That singer seems to be famous.

(a) ロスさんはアメリカに帰る**らしい** / **らしいです**。
*Rosu-san wa Amerika ni kaeru **rashii** / **rashii desu**.*

(b) 試合はつまらなかった**らしい** / **らしいです**。
*Shiai wa tsumaranakatta**rashii** / **rashii desu**.*

(c) あの歌手は有名**らしい** / **らしいです**。
*Ano kashu wa yūmei **rashii** / **rashii desu**.*

The auxiliary *i*-adjective *rashii* ("seems"), preceded by a noun or verb or an adjective in any form, expresses the speaker's conjecture based on what he or she considers to be reliable information.

Examples

1. He seems to have gone to bed already.
   彼はもう寝たらしい。
   Kare wa mō neta rashii.

2. It seems that region has much snow.
   あの地方は雪が多いらしいです。
   Ano chihō wa yuki ga ōi rashii desu.

3. It seems that she disliked mathematics.

彼女は数学が嫌いだったらしい。

Kanojo wa sūgaku ga kirai datta rashii.

4. This place seems to be a kindergarten.

ここは幼稚園らしい。

Koko wa yōchien rashii.

Practice

wild bird	野鳥	*yachō*
entrance exam	入学試験	*nyūgaku shiken*

Say the following in Japanese:

1. It seems that he liked wild birds.

2. That college's entrance exams seem to be difficult.

3. It seems that Ms. Noda won't go to the concert.

Answers

1. 彼は野鳥が好きだったらしい / らしいです。
   Kare wa yachō ga suki datta rashii / rashii desu.

2. あの大学の入学試験は難しいらしい / らしいです。
   Ano daigaku no nyūgaku shiken wa muzukashii rashii / rashii desu.

3. 野田さんはコンサートに行かないらしい / らしいです。
   Noda-san wa kansāto ni ikanai rashii / rashii desu.

> (a) It seems that a house will be built over there.
>
> (b) Mr. Ono's illness seems to be serious.
>
> (c) It seems that the negotiations were difficult.

(a) あそこに家が建つ**ようだ / ようです**。
*Asoko ni uchi ga tatsu **yō da** / **yō desu**.*

(b) 小野さんの病気は重い**ようだ / ようです**。
*Ono-san no byōki wa omoi **yō da** / **yō desu**.*

(c) 交渉は困難だった**ようだ / ようです**。
*Kōshō wa konnan datta **yō da** / **yō desu**.*

The auxiliary *na*-adjective *yō da* ("seems"), preceded by a verb or an adjective in any form, expresses the speaker's conjecture based on firsthand information.

NOTE: In casual conversation *mitai da* ("seems") may be used in place of *yō da* (Example 4).

Examples

1. It seems that this machine is broken.

   この機械は壊れたようだ。
   Kono kikai wa kowareta yō da.

2. It seems that the result of the experiment was good.

   実験の結果はよかったようです。
   Jikken no kekka wa yokatta yō desu.

3. He seems to be free (not busy) on Mondays.

月曜日は、彼はひまなようだ。

Getsuyōbi wa, kare wa himana yō da.

4. It seems that she won't marry him after all.

結局彼女は彼と結婚しないみたいだ。

Kekkyoku, kanojo wa kare to kekkon shinai mitai da.

Practice

| go bankrupt | 倒産する | *tōsan suru* |
| engine | エンジン | *enjin* |

Say the following in Japanese:

1. It seems that his company went bankrupt.

2. It seems that this car has a good engine.

3. It seems that Ms. Aoki's mother was strict.

Answers

1. 彼の会社は倒産したようだ / ようです。
   Kare no kaisha wa tōsan shita yō da / yō desu.

2. この車はエンジンがいいようだ / ようです。
   Kono kuruma wa enjin ga ii yō da / yō desu.

3. 青木さんのお母さんは厳格だったようだ / ようです。
   Aoki-san no o-kā-san wa genkaku datta yō da / yō desu.

129

I heard that there was a fire in Ginza.

銀座で火事があった**そうだ / そうです**。
*Ginza de kaji ga atta **sō da** / **sō desu**.*

The auxiliary *sō da* ("I heard"), placed at the end of a sentence, expresses hearsay—what the speaker heard or obtained indirectly. The predicates before *sō da* appear in the plain form and may be in any tense.

Examples

1. I heard that Mr. Oki is an instructor of judo.
   沖さんは柔道の先生だそうだ。
   Oki-san wa jūdo no sensei da sō da.

2. I heard that Toshiko is very good at cooking.
   敏子さんは料理がとても上手だそうです。
   Toshiko-san wa ryōri ga totemo jōzu da sō desu.

3. I hear that the bread at that store isn't good.
   あの店のパンはよくないそうだ。
   Ano mise no pan wa yoku nai sō da.

4. I heard that Mr. Sakai quit smoking.
   酒井さんはたばこを止めたそうです。
   Sakai-san wa tabako o yameta sō desu.

| composer | 作曲家 | *sakkyokuka* |
| alcohol | お酒 | *o-sake* |

Say the following in Japanese:

1. I heard that Sarah's father was a composer.

2. I heard that Mr. Tamura doesn't drink any alcohol.

3. I heard that a new auditorium is going to be built next year.

Answers

1. サラのお父さんは作曲家だったそうだ / そうです。
   Sara no o-tō-san wa sakkyokuka datta sō da / sō desu.

2. 田村さんはお酒を飲まないそうだ / そうです。
   Tamura-san wa o-sake o nomanai sō da / sō desu.

3. 来年新しい講堂が建つそうだ / そうです。
   Rainen atarashii kōdō ga tatsu sō da / sō desu.

130

(a) Helen said, "I'll come at 9 o'clock."

(b) Sam said that his trip was enjoyable.

(a) ヘレン (さん) は「9時に来ます」と言った / 言いました。

*Heren(-san) wa "Ku-ji ni kimasu" **to itta** / **iimashita**.*

(b) サム (さん) は旅行は楽しかったと言った / 言いました。

*Samu(-san) wa ryokō wa tanoshikatta **to itta** / **iimashita**.*

To quote someone, the phrase *to iu* is used. This phrase, a combination of the particle *to* and the verb *iu* ("say"), follows a quotation or sentence, indicating either a direct quote, as in (a), or an indirect one, as in (b).

NOTE: The quotation-marker *to* is used with other verbs, too, such as *omou* ("think") or *kiku* ("ask"), to mark their content.

Examples

1. Mr. Saeki said, "The president is making a phone call now."
   佐伯さんは「社長は今電話をかけています」と言った。
   Saeki-san wa "Shachō wa ima denwa o kakete imasu" to itta.

2. Masako said, "The opera was splendid, wasn't it?"
   正子 (さん) は「オペラはすばらしかったですね」と言いました。
   Masako (-san) wa "Opera wa subarashikatta desu ne" to iimashita.

3. A stranger asked me, "What time is it now?"
   知らない人が私に「今何時ですか」と聞きました。
   Shiranai hito ga watashi ni "Ima nanji desu ka" to kikimashita.

4. I think that he will most certainly succeed in his enterprise.
   彼は必ず事業に成功すると思う。
   Kare wa kanarazu jigyō ni seikō suru to omou.

Practice

know	知っている	*shitte iru*

Say the following in Japanese:

1. He asked me, "Do you know Professor Yamano?"
2. Kazuo says (= is saying) that he wants to learn English.
3. Ms. Tada said that her father would be hospitalized next week.
4. I think that she was kind.

/Answers/

1. 彼は私に「山野先生を知っていますか」と聞いた / 聞きました。
   Kare wa watashi ni "Yamano-sensei o shitte imasu ka" to kiita / kikimashita.

2. 和夫は英語を習いたいと言っている / います。
   Kazuo wa Eigo o naraitai to itte iru / imasu.

3. 多田さんはお父さんが来週入院すると言った / 言いました。
   Tada-san wa o-tō-san ga raishū nyūin suru to itta / iimashita.

4. 彼女は親切だったと思う / 思います。
   Kanojo wa shinsetsu datta to omou / omoimasu.

11 Using Conditional, Passive, Causative, and Causative-Passive Forms

131

> (a) When spring comes, the flowers bloom.
>
> (b) If the walls are white, the room will be bright.
>
> (c) If you are bad at Japanese, you can't work here.

(a) 春が来ると、花が咲く / 咲きます。
*Haru ga kuru **to**, hana ga saku / sakimasu.*

(b) 壁が白いと、部屋が明るい（です）。
*Kabe ga shiroi **to**, heya ga akarui (desu).*

(c) 日本語が下手だと、ここでは働けない / 働けません。
*Nihongo ga heta da **to**, koko de wa hatarakenai / hatarakemasen.*

The particle *to* is used as a conjunction to connect two clauses. The *to* clause (the subordinate clause) expresses a condition that brings about an uncontrollable or unavoidable result: when someone does something or something happens, or when some state or condition exists, another action, event, or state will inevitably follow. The main clause (the clause following *to*) cannot be a command, a request, a suggestion, an invitation, or a statement of volition. And the tense before *to* must be the present, regardless of the tense of the main clause.

1. When I blew the whistle, the birds flew away.
   笛を鳴らすと、鳥が飛んでいった。
   Fue o narasu to, tori ga tonde itta.

2. If the weather is bad, there won't be a game, right?
   天気が悪いと、試合はありませんね。
   Tenki ga warui to, shiai wa arimasen ne.

3. If the vegetables are fresh, they sell well.
   野菜は新鮮だと、よく売れる。
   Yasai wa shinsen da to, yoku ureru.

Practice

push	押す	*osu*
bell	ベル	*beru*
useless/no good	だめな	*damena*

Say the following in Japanese:

1. When you push that bell, the door will open.
2. As for the beer, if it isn't cold, it won't taste good (= it won't be delicious).
3. If this report is no good, I will have to rewrite it.

1. あのベルを押すと、ドアが開く / 開きます。
   Ano beru o osu to, doa ga aku / akimasu.

2. ビールは冷たくないと、おいしくない / おいしくありません。
   Bīru wa tsumetaku nai to, oishiku nai / oishiku arimasen.

3. このレポートがだめだと、書き直さなければならない / なりません。
   Kono repōto ga dame da to, kakinaosanakereba naranai / narimasen.

132

(a) If you exercise regularly, you'll get thin.

(b) If it is cheaper, I intend to buy it.

(c) If the waves are calm, let's (go for a) swim.

(a) きちんと運動すれ**ば** / 運動し**たら**やせる / やせ
ます。

*Kichin to undō sure**ba** / undō shi**tara** yaseru / yasemasu.*

(b) もっと安けれ**ば** / 安かっ**たら**買うつもりだ / です。

*Motto yasukere**ba** / yasukat**tara** kau tsumori da / desu.*

(c) 波が静かな**ら**（**ば**） / 静かだっ**たら**泳ごう / 泳ぎま
しょう。

*Nami ga shizuka **nara**(**ba**) / shizuka dat**tara** oyogō / oyogi-mashō.*

The *ba* or *tara* form (the conditional form) of a verb or an adjective is a kind of conjunction which creates a subordinate clause that expresses a condition. It means "if." The *tara* form is obtained by adding *ra* to the *ta* form of a verb (→ Appendix 4), or to the past tense of an adjective (→ Appendix 3). The rules for obtaining the *ba* form are as follows:

Regular I verbs: The final *ru* of the plain, potential form is replaced with *ba*:

dictionary form	potential form	*ba* form
au ("meet")	→ *aeru*	→ *aeba*
iku ("go")	→ *ikeru*	→ *ikeba*
oyogu ("swim")	→ *oyogeru*	→ *oyogeba*
hanasu ("speak")	→ *hanaseru*	→ *hanaseba*
matsu ("wait")	→ *materu*	→ *mateba*
asobu ("play")	→ *asoberu*	→ *asobeba*
yomu ("read")	→ *yomeru*	→ *yomeba*
kaeru ("return")	→ *kaereru*	→ *kaereba*

Regular II verbs: *Reba* is added to the *masu* stem:

dictionary form	*masu* stem	*ba* form
miru ("see")	→ *mi*	→ *mireba*
taberu ("eat")	→ *tabe*	→ *tabereba*

Irregular verbs:

kuru ("come")	→ *kureba*
suru ("do")	→ *sureba*

Adjectives: *Kereba* is added to the stems of *i*-adjectives, as in (b) above, and *nara*(*ba*) to the stems of *na*-adjectives, as in (c) above.

The *tara* form is more colloquial than the *ba* form. *Nara*, used with *na*-adjectives, is the simplified form of *naraba*, which is the conditional form of the copula *da*. *Ba* is usually optional after *nara*.

The main clause of a sentence with *ba* or *tara* is less restrictive than one with the conjunctive particle *to* (→ Pattern 131): the clause may express a desire, suggestion, command, hope, or even a statement of volition.

1. If I have time, I want to see (the sights in) Nara.

時間があれば / あったら奈良を見物したいです。

Jikan ga areba / attara Nara o kenbutsu shitai desu.

2. If it's cold, please turn on the heater.

寒ければ / 寒かったらヒーターをつけてください。

Samukereba / samukattara hītā o tsukete kudasai.

3. If the ocean is dangerous, you had better not swim (in it).

海が危険なら / 危険だったら泳がないほうがいい
ですよ。

Umi ga kiken nara / kiken dattara oyoganai hō ga ii desu yo.

Practice

about one hour	1時間ほど	*ichi-jikan hodo*
necessary	必要な	*hitsuyōna*
right away	すぐ	*sugu*

Say the following in Japanese:

1. If you go by bus, you can get there in about one hour.

2. If it's necessary, you had better buy it right away.

3. If the cakes are delicious, they will sell well.

1. バスで行けば / 行ったら (そこまで) 1時間ほどで行ける / 行けます。
   Basu de ikeba / ittara (soko made) ichi-jikan hodo de ikeru / ikemasu.

2. 必要なら / 必要だったらすぐ買ったほうがいいですよ。
   Hitsuyō nara / hitsuyō dattara sugu katta hō ga ii desu yo.

3. ケーキはおいしければ / おいしかったらよく売れる / 売れます。
   Kēki wa oishikereba / oishikattara yoku ureru / uremasu.

133

> (a) If you are going to buy stocks, now is a good time.
>
> (b) If it's that interesting, let's go to see it.
>
> (c) If you like Japanese food, I'll cook some for you.

(a) 株を買う **(の) なら**、今がいい時期だ / です。
   Kabu o kau (no) nara, ima ga ii jiki da / desu.

(b) そんなにおもしろい **(の) なら**、見に行こう / 行きましょう。
   Sonna ni omoshiroi (no) nara, mi ni ikō / ikimashō.

(c) 日本食が好き**なら**、作ってあげる / 作ってあげます。
   Nihonshoku ga suki nara, tsukutte ageru / tsukutte agemasu.

Nara is a kind of conjunction which creates a subordinate clause that expresses a condition. It means "if." Verbs and *i*-adjectives coming before *nara* are optionally followed by the particle *no* (which turns them into nouns), while *na*-adjectives—or rather their stems, which come before *nara*—do not require *no*.

Being a conditional form, *nara* is frequently interchangeable with *ba*: *iku* (*no*) *nara* or *ikeba* (both meaning "if one goes"), *takai* (*no*) *nara* or *takakereba* (both meaning "if it is expensive"), etc. However, the subject of the *nara* clause (the subordinate clause) is usually not the speaker.

The main clause of a sentence with *nara* may be a suggestion, command, or statement of volition.

Examples

1. If you are going to Japan, study Japanese.
   日本へ行く (の) なら、日本語を勉強しなさい。
   Nihon e iku (*no*) *nara, Nihongo o benkyō shinasai.*

2. If it's near here, how about walking (the distance)?
   ここから近い (の) なら、歩きませんか。
   Koko kara chikai (*no*) *nara, arukimasen ka.*

3. If you aren't going to use it, may I borrow it?
   使わない (の) なら、借りてもいいですか。
   Tsukawanai (*no*) *nara, karite mo ii desu ka.*

4. If you are healthy, you can go anywhere.
   健康ならどこへでも行けますよ。
   Kenkō nara doko e demo ikemasu yo.

Practice

calendar	カレンダー	*karendā*
get ready	支度する	*shitaku suru*
invite	誘う	*sasou*

Say the following in Japanese:

1. If you want this calendar, I'll give it to you.

2. If you are not going to read this book, please return it to me.

3. If you are coming with me, get ready right away.

4. If Jim is free (not busy), I'd like to invite him to the movie.

---

1. このカレンダーが欲しい (の) なら、あげる / あげますよ。
   Kono karendā ga hoshii (no) nara, ageru / agemasu yo.

2. この本を読まない (の) なら、返してください。
   Kono hon o yomanai (no) nara, kaeshite kudasai.

3. 一緒に来る (の) なら、すぐ支度しなさい。
   Issho ni kuru (no) nara, sugu shitaku shinasai.

4. ジム (さん) がひまなら、映画に誘いたい / 誘いたいです。
   Jimu(-san) ga hima nara, eiga ni sasoi tai / sasoi tai desu.

134

(a) He plays golf even if it rains.

(b) I want to continue studying even if it is difficult.

(c) Even though she is rich, she doesn't spend money.

(a) 彼は雨が降っても ゴルフをする / します。
   Kare wa ame ga futte mo gorufu o suru / shimasu.

(b) 難しくても勉強を続けたい / 続けたいです。
   Muzukashikute mo benkyō o tsuzuketai / tsuzuketai desu.

(c) 彼女は裕福でもお金を使わない / 使いません。
   Kanojo wa yūfuku demo o-kane o tsukawanai / tsu-kaimasen.

The *te* form of a verb or an adjective, followed by the particle *mo*, is used as a conjunction to express a condition. It means "even if/though."

Examples

1. Even though Jeff doesn't study, his grades are always good.

ジェフさんは勉強しなくてもいつも成績がいいです。

Jefu(-san) wa benkyō shinakute mo itsumo seiseki ga ii desu.

2. Even if it is hot, he doesn't use the air conditioner.

彼は暑くてもエアコンを使わない。

Kare wa atsukute mo eakon o tsukawanai.

3. Even if it's safe, you had better not go to such a place.

安全でもそんな所へ行かないほうがいいですよ。

Anzen demo sonna tokoro e ikanai hō ga ii desu yo.

Practice

climb	登る	*noboru*
Mt. Everest	エベレスト山	*Eberesuto-zan*
dangerous	危険な	*kikenna*
dress	ドレス	*doresu*
parent	両親	*ryōshin*
object to	反対する	*hantai suru*

Say the following in Japanese:

1. I want to climb Mt. Everest even if it is dangerous.

2. She doesn't wear dresses even if she buys them.

3. Even if my parents object, I intend to marry him.

1. 危険でもエベレスト山に登りたい / 登りたいです。
   Kiken demo Eberesuto-zan ni noboritai / noboritai desu.

2. 彼女はドレスを買っても着ない / 着ません。
   Kanojo wa doresu o katte mo kinai / kimasen.

3. 両親が反対しても彼と結婚するつもりだ / です。
   Ryōshin ga hantai shite mo kare to kekkon suru tsumori da / desu.

135

I was deceived by the salesman.

私はセールスマンに**だまされた** / **だまされました**。
*Watashi wa sērusuman ni **damasareta** / **damasaremashita**.*

The passive voice is expressed by the stem of the negative (*nai*) form of a verb, followed by the auxiliary *reru* or *rareru*. *Reru* is used with Regular I verbs, e.g., *yoma**reru*** ("be read"), and *rareru* with Regular II verbs, e.g., *tabe**rareru*** ("be eaten"). The Irregular verbs *kuru* and *suru* become **korareru** (→ Pattern 137) and **sareru** ("be done"), respectively. All passive verbs are Regular II verbs.

   In a passive Japanese sentence, the object of the active sentence becomes the subject (and is therefore marked by the particle *ga*), and the agent (the doer of the action) takes the particle *ni* ("by"). The agent may, however, be omitted when it is not important or is unknown (Example 2).

Examples

1. Kenji is sometimes scolded by his father.

   健二は時々お父さんにしかられる。

   Kenji wa tokidoki o-tō-san ni shikarareru.

2. This hospital was built ten years ago.

この病院は10年前に建てられた。

Kono byōin wa jū-nen mae ni taterareta.

3. Professor Kimura is respected by his students.

木村先生は学生に尊敬されています。

Kimura-sensei wa gakusei ni sonkei sarete imasu.

Practice

praise	ほめる	*homeru*
recital	リサイタル	*risaitaru*
hold (a recital)	行う	*okonau*
invite	招待する	*shōtai suru*
reception	レセプション	*resepushon*

Say the following in Japanese:

1. The secretary was praised by the department head.

2. A recital will be held in the auditorium this evening.

3. Mr. Benson will be invited to the reception.

Answers

1. 秘書は部長にほめられた / ほめられました。
   Hisho wa buchō ni homerareta / homeraremashita.

2. 今晩講堂でリサイタルが行われる / 行われます。
   Konban kōdō de risaitaru ga okonawareru / okonawaremasu.

3. ベンソンさんはレセプションに招待される / 招待されます。
   Benson-san wa resepushon ni shōtai sareru / shōtai saremasu.

136

Masaru had his bicycle stolen by a thief.

勝は泥棒に自転車を**盗まれた** / **盗まれました**。

*Masaru wa dorobō ni jitensha o **nusumareta** / **nusumare-mashita**.*

The passive voice is often used in Japanese to indicate that a person is adversely affected by the action of another, as in the above example. The person affected is usually presented as the topic and marked by the particle *wa*, and the agent (the doer of the action) is marked by the particle *ni*.

The *te* form of a passive verb followed by *shimau* (→ Pattern 63) implies a sense of regret or completion (Example 3).

Examples

1. I had my blouse soiled by a baby.

   私は赤ちゃんにブラウスを汚された。

   Watashi wa aka-chan ni burausu o yogosareta.

2. My son had his hand bitten by the neighbor's dog.

   息子は隣の犬に手をかまれた。

   Musuko wa tonari no inu ni te o kamareta.

3. I had a tooth pulled out by my dentist.

   私は歯医者に歯を抜かれてしまった。

   Watashi wa haisha ni ha o nukarete shimatta.

lover	恋人	*koibito*
take/steal	取る	*toru*
friend	友達	*tomodachi*
break	壊す	*kowasu*
tear up	破る	*yaburu*

Say the following in Japanese:

1. I had my lover stolen by a friend.

2. My daughter had her doll broken by the neighbor's child.

3. The letter was torn up by my teacher.

Answers

1. 私は友達に恋人を取られた / 取られました。
   Watashi wa tomodachi ni koibito o torareta / toraremashita.

2. 娘は隣の子供に人形を壊された / 壊されました。
   Musume wa tonari no kodomo ni ningyō o kowasareta / kowasare-mashita.

3. 私は手紙を先生に破られた / 破られました。
   Watashi wa tegami o sensei ni yaburareta / yaburaremashita.

137

My friend came to my house late at night (much to my inconvenience).

私は友達に夜遅く家に**来られた** / **来られました**。

*Watashi wa tomodachi ni yoru osoku uchi ni **korareta** / **koraremashita**.*

An intransitive verb in the passive form indicates that a person is adversely affected by someone else's action or by some unpleasant event.

1. We were rained on at our fishing spot.

   私達は釣り場で雨に降られた。

   Watashi-tachi wa tsuriba de ame ni furareta.

2. My wife died a year ago (to my great grief).

   私は1年前に家内に死なれました。

   Watashi wa ichi-nen mae ni kanai ni shinaremashita.

3. A big man sat in front of me at the theater (and I was unhappy).

   私は劇場で大きい男の人に前に座られた。

   Watashi wa gekijō de ōkii otoko no hito ni mae ni suwarareta.

Practice

baby	赤ちゃん	*aka-chan*
cry	泣く	*naku*
all night (long)	一晩中	*hitobanjū*
laugh	笑う	*warau*
leave	出て行く	*dete iku*

Say the following in Japanese:

1. Our baby cried all night long (to our annoyance).

2. Takashi was laughed at by everybody.

3. Mr. Kita's wife left him.

1. 私達は一晩中赤ちゃんに泣かれた / 泣かれました。
   Watashi-tachi wa hitobanjū aka-chan ni nakareta / nakaremashita.

2. 隆（さん）はみんなに笑われた / 笑われました。
   Takashi(-san) wa minna ni warawareta / warawaremashita.

3. 北さんは奥さんに出て行かれた / 出て行かれました。
   Kita-san wa oku-san ni dete ikareta / dete ikaremashita.

138

Mr. Sasaki made/let me write the report.

佐々木さんは私にレポートを書かせた / 書かせました。

*Sasaki-san wa watashi ni repōto o **kakaseta** / **kakase-mashita**.*

The stem of the negative (*nai*) form of a verb, followed by the auxiliary *seru* or *saseru*, expresses what is called the causative form—the form used to express the idea of someone's making or letting someone else do something. *Seru* is used with Regular I verbs, e.g., *ikaseru* ("make ... go"), and *saseru* with Regular II verbs, e.g., *misaseru* ("make ... see"). The Irregular verbs *kuru* and *suru* become **kosaseru** ("make ... come") and **saseru** ("make ... do"), respectively. All causative verbs are Regular II verbs.

In a causative sentence, the causer (the doer of the action) is usually presented as the topic and is marked by the particle *wa*, whereas the causee (the one being acted upon) is the object and is marked by either *ni* or *o*. If the causative verb is a transitive one (i.e., takes a direct object marked by the particle *o*), the causee will be marked by *ni* (Example 1). If the verb is intransitive, however, the causee is marked by *o* (Examples 2, 3).

The *te* form of a causative verb may be followed by the auxiliary verbs *yaru*, *ageru* (→ Pattern 117), or *kureru* (→ Pattern 121), to indicate someone's performing a favor for someone else (Examples 4, 5).

Finally, a shortened causative form may be obtained by changing the final *seru* to *su*, e.g., *ikaseru → ikasu*, *misaseru → misasu*, *kosaseru → kosasu*, *saseru → sasu*. All causative verbs of this type are Regular I verbs.

Examples

1. I intend to make/let my daughter learn the piano.
   私は娘にピアノを習わせるつもりです。
   Watashi wa musume ni piano o narawaseru tsumori desu.

2. The president let his secretary go home early.
   社長は秘書を早く家へ帰らせた。
   Shachō wa hisho o hayaku uchi e kaeraseta.

3. Mr. Yagi made/let his son work in the factory.
   八木さんは息子を工場で働かせた。
   Yagi-san wa musuko o kōjō de hatarakaseta.

4. I let Kazuo go camping.
   私は和夫をキャンプに行かせてやった。
   Watashi wa Kazuo o kyanpu ni ikasete yatta.

5. My father let me use his camera.
   父は私にカメラを使わせてくれた。
   Chichi wa watashi ni kamera o tsukawasete kureta.

Practice

clean (a room)	掃除する	*sōji suru*
coworker	同僚	*dōryō*
get angry	怒る	*okoru*

Say the following in Japanese:

1. I made Masako clean her room.

2. He sometimes makes his coworkers (get) angry.

3. The child made the dog swim.

4. The teacher let students watch TV in the classroom.

/Answers/

1. 私は正子（さん）に部屋を掃除させた / 掃除させました。
   Watashi wa Masako(-san) ni heya o sōji saseta / sōji sasemashita.

2. 彼は時々同僚を怒らせる / 怒らせます。
   Kare wa tokidoki dōryō o okoraseru / okorasemasu.

3. 子供は犬を泳がせた / 泳がせました。
   Kodomo wa inu o oyogaseta / oyogasemashita.

4. 先生は学生に教室でテレビを見させた / 見させました。
   Sensei wa gakusei ni kyōshitsu de terebi o misaseta / misasemashita.

139

I was made to walk to the station by my father.

私は父に駅まで**歩かせられた** / **歩かせられました**。
*Watashi wa chichi ni eki made **arukaserareta** / **arukaserare-mashita**.*

The stem of the negative (*nai*) form of a verb, followed by the auxiliary *serareru* or *saserareru*, expresses the causative-passive form: that is, the causative form made passive. *Serareru* is used with Regular I verbs, e.g., *ikaserareru* ("be made to go"), and *saserareru* with Regular II verbs, e.g., *tabesaserareru* ("be made to eat"). The Irregular verbs *kuru* and *suru* become **kosaserareru** ("be made to come") and **saserareru** ("be made to do"), respectively. All causative-passive verbs are Regular II verbs.

A causative-passive sentence indicates that a person is made, rather than allowed, to do something by someone. The person affected by the action is usually presented as the topic and is marked by the particle *wa*, and the person who forces the action upon him or her is marked by the particle *ni*.

A shortened causative-passive form, only for Regular I verbs, can be obtained from the verb's shortened causative form, in the following way: *kakasu* (shortend causative form of *kaku*) → *kakasa* (stem of the negative form of *kakasu*) + **reru** → *kaka**sareru*** ("be made to write").

Examples

1. Students are made to write compositions by their teachers.
   学生は先生に作文を書かせられる / 書かされる。
   Gakusei wa sensei ni sakubun o kakaserareru / kakasareru.

2. We were made to wait for a long time at the airport.
   私達は空港で長い間待たせられた / 待たされた。
   Watashi-tachi wa kūkō de nagai aida mataserareta / matasareta.

3. Mr. Ono was made to check the data by the section chief.
   小野さんは課長にデータを調べさせられた。
   Ono-san wa kachō ni dēta o shirabesaserareta.

4. The store clerks are made to come to the store by 8 o'clock.
   店員は8時までに店に来させられます。
   Ten'in wa hachi-ji made ni mise ni kosaseraremasu.

polish	磨く	*migaku*
silver	銀	*gin*
perfume	香水	*kōsui*

Say the following in Japanese:

1. Ben was made to eat sashimi by Akira.

2. I was made to polish a silver vase by my mother.

3. Masako was made to buy expensive perfume by her friend.

4. Sometime I am made to do someone else's work.

Answers

1. ベン（さん）は明（さん）に刺身を食べさせられた / 食べさせられました。
   Ben(-san) wa Akira(-san) ni sashimi o tabesaserareta / tabesaserare-mashita.

2. 私は母に銀の花瓶を磨かせられた / 磨かせられました / 磨かされた / 磨かされました。
   Watashi wa haha ni gin no kabin o migakaserareta / migakaseraremashita / migakasareta / migakasaremashita.

3. 正子（さん）は友達に高い香水を買わせられた / 買わせられました / 買わされた / 買わされました。
   Masako(-san) wa tomodachi ni takai kōsui o kawaserareta / kawaserare-mashita / kawasareta / kawasaremashita.

4. 時々私はほかの人の仕事をさせられる / させられます。
   Tokidoki watashi wa hoka no hito no shigoto o saserareru / saseraremasu.

12 Making Relative Clauses

140

The student (who is) talking with the teacher is John Miller.

先生と話している学生はジョン・ミラーさんだ / です。
Sensei to hanashite iru gakusei wa Jon Mirā-san da / desu.

A relative clause in Japanese is a modifying clause that comes before, rather than after, the noun it modifies. (Japanese does not have relative pronouns such as "who," "which," "that," nor relative adverbs like "when" or "where.") The predicate of a Japanese relative clause can be in any tense—present, past, or progressive—but it must be in the plain rather than the polite form.

Examples

1. Those who won't attend the banquet are Mr. Sada and Ms. Minami.

   宴会に出ない人は佐田さんと南さんです。
   Enkai ni denai hito wa Sada-san to Minami-san desu.

2. The person who has just gotten out of the car is our new department head.

   今、車を降りた人が新しい部長だ。
   Ima, kuruma o orita hito ga atarashii buchō da.

3. Which is the bus that goes to Harajuku?

原宿へ行くバスはどれですか。

Harajuku e iku basu wa dore desu ka.

4. The car (that's been) parked in front of the entrance is Mr. Benson's.

入り口の前に止めてある車はベンソンさんのです。

Iriguchi no mae ni tomete aru kuruma wa Benson-san no desu.

Practice

wear (skirt, pants, shoes)	はく	*haku*
invent	発明する	*hatsumei suru*

Say the following in Japanese:

1. That is the plane that came from Hong Kong.
2. The person who is wearing that white skirt is Mr. Okamura's wife.
3. The person who invented this machine is American.
4. The dictionary (that has been placed) on the desk is Mike's

---

Answers

1. あれは香港から来た飛行機だ / です。
   Are wa Honkon kara kita hikōki da / desu.

2. あの白いスカートをはいている人が岡村さんの奥さんだ / です。
   Ano shiroi sukāto o haite iru hito ga Okamura-san no oku-san da / desu.

3. この機械を発明した人はアメリカ人だ / です。
   Kono kikai o hatsumei shita hito wa Amerikajin da / desu.

4. 机の上に置いてある辞書はマイク（さん）のだ / です。
   Tsukue no ue ni oite aru jisho wa Maiku(-san) no da / desu.

141

The novels (that) he writes always sell well.

彼が / の書く小説はいつもよく売れる / 売れます。
Kare ga / no kaku shōsetsu wa itsumo yoku ureru / uremasu.

The relative (modifying) clause here is different form the one introduced in Pattern 140 above only in that it features a subject marked by the particle *ga*. In a relative (modifying) clause of this type, the particle *no* may replace *ga* as the subject-marker. However, the subject may be omitted entirely if it is understood from context (Example 2).

Examples

1. These are pictures that my husband took.
   これは主人が / の撮った写真です。
   Kore wa shujin ga / no totta shashin desu.

2. Let's go to buy the things we'll take to the picnic.
   ピクニックに持って行く物を買いに行きましょう。
   Pikunikku ni motte iku mono o kai ni ikimashō.

3. The company he worked at is in Kobe.
   彼が / の働いていた会社は神戸にある。
   Kare ga / no hataraite ita kaisha wa Kōbe ni aru.

4. On weekends when it doesn't rain, I play golf or tennis.
   雨が / の降らない週末にはゴルフかテニスをします。
   Ame ga / no furanai shūmatsu ni wa gorufu ka tenisu o shimasu.

be born	生まれる	*umareru*
things/items	物	*mono*
need	要る	*iru*

Say the following in Japanese:

1. This is the house where I was born.

2. The pie that Yuriko made was delicious.

3. Please write on this (piece of) paper the things we'll need for the party.

4. I took some pictures with the camera I got from my father.

Answers

1. これは私が / の生まれた家だ / です。
   Kore wa watashi ga / no umareta uchi da / desu.

2. ゆり子 (さん) が / の作ったパイはおいしかった / おいしかったです。
   Yuriko(-san) ga / no tsukutta pai wa oishikatta / oishikatta desu.

3. パーティーに要る物をこの紙に書いてください。
   Pātī ni iru mono o kono kami ni kaite kudasai.

   OR

   この紙にパーティーに要る物を書いてください。
   Kono kami ni pātī ni iru mono o kaite kudasai.

4. 父にもらったカメラで写真を撮った / 撮りました。
   Chichi ni moratta kamera de shashin o totta / torimashita.

142

The computers that were expensive have become cheaper.

高かったコンピューターが安くなった / 安くなりました。
Takakatta konpyūtā ga yasuku natta / yasuku narimashita.

Here the relative (modifying) clause features an adjective instead of a verb. The tense of this clause may be present or past, and may be either affirmative or negative. However, it must be in the present tense if the state presented in it is concurrent with the action or state presented in the main clause (Example 4).

Examples

1. Do you know someone who is good at English?
   英語が / の上手な人を知っていますか。
   Eigo ga / no jōzuna hito o shitte imasu ka.

2. The trip to Canada, which was great fun, ended.
   とても楽しかったカナダ旅行が終わりました。
   Totemo tanoshikatta Kanada ryokō ga owarimashita.

3. The room next door, which had been quiet, suddenly became noisy.
   静かだった隣の部屋が急に騒がしくなった。
   Shizuka datta tonari no heya ga kyū ni sawagashiku natta.

4. My daughter wanted a doll that had blue eyes.
   娘は目が / の青い人形を欲しがった。
   Musume wa me ga / no aoi ningyō o hoshigatta.

dance	踊る	*odoru*
healthy	元気な	*genkina*
suddenly	急に	*kyū ni*
pass away	亡くなる	*nakunaru*
become easy	やさしくなる	*yasashiku naru*
these days	近頃	*chikagoro*

Say the following in Japanese:

1. Dan came to like the sashimi that he had disliked.

2. Anne danced with Sam, who was good at dancing.

3. Mr. Hara, who had been healthy, suddenly passed away.

4. Japanese that was difficult has become easier these days.

Answers

1. ダン（さん）は嫌いだった刺身が好きになった / なりました。
   Dan(-san) wa kiraidatta sashimi ga suki ni natta / narimashita.

2. アン（さん）はダンスが / の上手なサム（さん）と踊った / 踊りました。
   An(-san) wa dansu ga / no jōzuna Samu(-san) to odotta / odorimashita.

3. 元気だった原さんが急に亡くなった / 亡くなりました。
   Genki datta Hara-san ga kyū ni nakunatta / nakunarimashita.

4. 難しかった日本語が近頃やさしくなった / やさしくなりました。
   Muzukashikatta Nihongo ga chikagoro yasashiku natta / yasashiku narimashita.

Appendixes

1. Numerals

Numbers in Japanese can be written with either Arabic numerals, as they are throughout this book, or with kanji numerals. Arabic numerals are usually used in horizontal text, whereas kanji numerals mostly appear in vertical text.

Cardinal Numbers

NATIVE-JAPANESE NUMERALS

1	*hito*(*tsu*) 一（つ）	3	*mit*(*tsu*) 三（つ）	5	*itsu*(*tsu*) 五（つ）	7	*nana*(*tsu*) 七（つ）	9	*kokono*(*tsu*) 九（つ）
2	*futa*(*tsu*) 二（つ）	4	*yot*(*tsu*) 四（つ）	6	*mut*(*tsu*) 六（つ）	8	*yat*(*tsu*) 八（つ）	10	*tō* 十

CHINESE-ORIGIN NUMERALS

1	*ichi* 一	10	*jū* 十	19	*jū-ku / jū-kyū* 十九
2	*ni* 二	11	*jū-ichi* 十一	20	*ni-jū* 二十
3	*san* 三	12	*jū-ni* 十二	21	*ni-jū-ichi* 二十一
4	*shi / yon* 四	13	*jū-san* 十三	24	*ni-jū-shi / ni-jū-yon* 二十四
5	*go* 五	14	*jū-shi / jū-yon* 十四	30	*san-jū* 三十
6	*roku* 六	15	*jū-go* 十五	40	*yon-jū / shi-jū* 四十
7	*shichi / nana* 七	16	*jū-roku* 十六	44	*yon-jū-shi / yon-jū-yon* 四十四
8	*hachi* 八	17	*jū-shichi / jū-nana* 十七	50	*go-jū* 五十
9	*ku / kyū* 九	18	*jū-hachi* 十八	60	*roku-jū* 六十

70	shichi-jū / nana-jū 七十	110	hyaku-jū 百十	400	yon-hyaku 四百
77	shichi-jū-shichi nana-jū-nana 七十七	114	hyaku-jū-yon hyaku-jū-shi 百十四	419	yon-hyaku-jū-ku yon-hyaku-jū-kyū 四百十九
80	hachi-jū 八十	140	hyaku-yon-jū 百四十	500	go-hyaku 五百
90	kyū-jū 九十	200	ni-hyaku 二百	600	rop-pyaku 六百
99	kyū-jū-kyū / ku-jū-ku 九十九	270	ni-hyaku-shichi-jū ni-hyaku nana-jū 二百七十	700	nana-hyaku 七百
100	hyaku* 百	300	san-byaku 三百	800	hap-pyaku 八百
101	hyaku-ichi 百一	390	san-byaku-kyū-jū 三百九十	900	kyū-hyaku 九百

1,000	sen / is-sen** 千 / 一千	10,000	ichi-man 一万
2,000	ni-sen 二千	100,000	jū-man 十万
3,000	san-zen 三千	1,000,000	hyaku-man 百万
4,000	yon-sen 四千	10,000,000	is-sen-man 一千万
5,000	go-sen 五千	100,000,000	ichi-oku 一億
6,000	roku-sen 六千	1,000,000,000	jū-oku 十億
7,000	nana-sen 七千	10,000,000,000	hyaku-oku 百億
8,000	has-sen 八千	100,000,000,000	sen-oku / is-sen-oku 千億 / 一千億
9,000	kyū-sen 九千	1,000,000,000,000	it-chō 一兆

* 100 is always hyaku, never ichi-hyaku.
** 1,000 is usually read sen but is-sen is also used.

Ordinal Numbers

	-ban -番	*dai-* 第-	*-me* - 目	*-banme* - 番目
1st	*ichi-ban* 一番	*dai-ichi* 第一	*hitotsu-me* 一つ目	*ichi-banme* 一番目
2nd	*ni-ban* 二番	*dai-ni* 第二	*futatsu-me* 二つ目	*ni-banme* 二番目
3rd	*san-ban* 三番	*dai-san* 第三	*mittsu-me* 三つ目	*san-banme* 三番目
4th	*yon-ban* *yo-ban* 四番	*dai-yon* 第四	*yottsu-me* 四つ目	*yon-banme* *yo-banme* 四番目
5th	*go-ban* 五番	*dai-go* 第五	*itsutsu-me* 五つ目	*go-banme* 五番目
6th	*roku-ban* 六番	*dai-roku* 第六	*muttsu-me* 六つ目	*roku-banme* 六番目
7th	*nana-ban* *shichi-ban* 七番	*dai-nana* *dai-shichi* 第七	*nanatsu-me* 七つ目	*nana-banme* *shichi-banme* 七番目
8th	*hachi-ban* 八番	*dai-hachi* 第八	*yattsu-me* 八つ目	*hachi-banme* 八番目
9th	*kyū-ban* *ku-ban* 九番	*dai-kyū* *dai-ku* 第九	*kokonotsu-me* 九つ目	*kyū-banme* 九番目
10th	*jū-ban* 十番	*dai-jū* 第十	——	*jū-banme* 十番目

2. Counters

The following is a list of commonly used counters (→ Pattern 26). The changes in the pronunciations of the numbers and/or counters are shown in bold.

	mai 枚 paper ticket shirt	*dai* 台 car bicycle TV set	*do* 度 time degree C/F	*ryō* 両 car	*wa* 羽 bird
1	*ichi-mai* 一枚	*ichi-dai* 一台	*ichi-do* 一度	*ichi-ryō* 一両	*ichi-wa* 一羽
2	*ni-mai* 二枚	*ni-dai* 二台	*ni-do* 二度	*ni-ryō* 二両	*ni-wa* 二羽
3	*san-mai* 三枚	*san-dai* 三台	*san-do* 三度	*san-ryō* 三両	*san-**ba*** *san-wa* 三羽
4	*yon-mai* *yo-mai* 四枚	*yon-dai* *yo-dai* 四台	*yon-do* 四度	*yon-ryō* 四両	*yon-wa* 四羽
5	*go-mai* 五枚	*go-dai* 五台	*go-do* 五度	*go-ryō* 五両	*go-wa* 五羽
6	*roku-mai* 六枚	*roku-dai* 六台	*roku-do* 六度	*roku-ryō* 六両	*roku-wa* *ro**p-pa*** 六羽
7	*shichi-mai* *nana-mai* 七枚	*shichi-dai* *nana-dai* 七台	*shichi-do* *nana-do* 七度	*shichi-ryō* *nana-ryō* 七両	*nana-wa* *shichi-wa* 七羽
8	*hachi-mai* 八枚	*hachi-dai* 八台	*hachi-do* 八度	*hachi-ryō* 八両	*hachi-wa* *ha**p-pa*** 八羽
9	*kyū-mai* *ku-mai* 九枚	*ku-dai* *kyū-dai* 九台	*ku-do* *kyū-do* 九度	*kyū-ryō* 九両	*kyū-wa* 九羽
10	*jū-mai* 十枚	*jū-dai* 十台	*jū-do* 十度	*jū-ryō* 十両	*jū-wa* *ji**p-pa*** 十羽
How many ...?	*nan-mai* 何枚	*nan-dai* 何台	*nan-do* 何度	*nan-ryō* 何両	*nan-**ba*** 何羽

	satsu 冊 book notebook	*ten* 点 point grade	*sai* 歳 years old	*seki* 隻 large ship	*tō* 頭 horse cow whale
1	*is-satsu* 一冊	*it-ten* 一点	*is-sai* 一歳	*is-seki* 一隻	*it-tō* 一頭
2	*ni-satsu* 二冊	*ni-ten* 二点	*ni-sai* 二歳	*ni-seki* 二隻	*ni-tō* 二頭
3	*san-satsu* 三冊	*san-ten* 三点	*san-sai* 三歳	*san-seki* 三隻	*san-tō* 三頭
4	*yon-satsu* 四冊	*yon-ten* 四点	*yon-sai* 四歳	*yon-seki* 四隻	*yon-tō* 四頭
5	*go-satsu* 五冊	*go-ten* 五点	*go-sai* 五歳	*go-seki* 五隻	*go-tō* 五頭
6	*roku-satsu* 六冊	*roku-ten* 六点	*roku-sai* 六歳	*roku-seki* 六隻	*roku-tō* 六頭
7	*nana-satsu* 七冊	*nana-ten* *shichi-ten* 七点	*nana-sai* *shichi-sai* 七歳	*nana-seki* *shichi-seki* 七隻	*nana-tō* *shichi-tō* 七頭
8	*hachi-satsu* *has-satsu* 八冊	*hachi-ten* *hat-ten* 八点	*hachi-sai* *has-sai* 八歳	*hachi-seki* *has-seki* 八隻	*hachi-tō* *hat-tō* 八頭
9	*kyū-satsu* 九冊	*kyū-ten* 九点	*kyū-sai* 九歳	*kyū-seki* 九隻	*kyū-tō* 九頭
10	*jus-satsu* *jis-satsu* 十冊	*jut-ten* *jit-ten* 十点	*jus-sai* *jis-sai* 十歳	*jus-seki* *jis-seki* 十隻	*jut-tō* *jit-tō* 十頭
How many…?	*nan-satsu* 何冊	*nan-ten* 何点	*nan-sai* 何歳	*nan-seki* 何隻	*nan-tō* 何頭

	tsū 通 letter form	*chaku* 着 suit dress pair of pants	*soku* 足 pair of shoes pair of socks	*shō* 章 chapter	*ka* 課 lesson
1	*it-tsū* 一通	*it-chaku* 一着	*is-soku* 一足	*is-shō* 一章	*ik-ka* 一課
2	*ni-tsū* 二通	*ni-chaku* 二着	*ni-soku* 二足	*ni-shō* 二章	*ni-ka* 二課
3	*san-tsū* 三通	*san-chaku* 三着	*san-zoku* 三足	*san-shō* 三章	*san-ka* 三課
4	*yon-tsū* 四通	*yon-chaku* 四着	*yon-soku* 四足	*yon-shō* 四章	*yon-ka* 四課
5	*go-tsū* 五通	*go-chaku* 五着	*go-soku* 五足	*go-shō* 五章	*go-ka* 五課
6	*roku-tsū* 六通	*roku-chaku* 六着	*roku-soku* 六足	*roku-shō* 六章	*rok-ka* 六課
7	*nana-tsū* 七通	*nana-chaku* 七着	*nana-soku* 七足	*nana-shō* 七章	*nana-ka* 七課
8	*hat-tsū* 八通	*hat-chaku* 八着	*has-soku* 八足	*has-shō* 八章	*hak-ka* 八課
9	*kyū-tsū* 九通	*kyū-chaku* 九着	*kyū-soku* 九足	*kyū-shō* 九章	*kyū-ka* 九課
10	*jut-tsū* *jit-tsū* 十通	*jut-chaku* *jit-chaku* 十着	*jus-soku* *jis-soku* 十足	*jus-shō* *jis-shō* 十章	*juk-ka* *jik-ka* 十課
How many…?	*nan-tsū* 何通	*nan-chaku* 何着	*nan-zoku* 何足	*nan-shō* 何章	*nan-ka* 何課

	kai 階 floor/story	*ki* 機 airplane	*ken* 軒 house	*hiki* 匹 dog cat insect	*hon* 本 pen bottle umbrella
1	*ik-kai* 一階	*ik-ki* 一機	*ik-ken* 一軒	*ip-piki* 一匹	*ip-pon* 一本
2	*ni-kai* 二階	*ni-ki* 二機	*ni-ken* 二軒	*ni-hiki* 二匹	*ni-hon* 二本
3	*san-gai* *san-kai* 三階	*san-ki* 三機	*san-gen* 三軒	*san-biki* 三匹	*san-bon* 三本
4	*yon-kai* 四階	*yon-ki* 四機	*yon-ken* 四軒	*yon-hiki* 四匹	*yon-hon* 四本
5	*go-kai* 五階	*go-ki* 五機	*go-ken* 五軒	*go-hiki* 五匹	*go-hon* 五本
6	*rok-kai* 六階	*rok-ki* 六機	*rok-ken* 六軒	*rop-piki* 六匹	*rop-pon* 六本
7	*nana-kai* *shichi-kai* 七階	*nana-ki* 七機	*nana-ken* *shichi-ken* 七軒	*nana-hiki* 七匹	*nana-hon* *shichi-hon* 七本
8	*hachi-kai* *hak-kai* 八階	*hachi-ki* *hak-ki* 八機	*hachi-ken* *hak-ken* 八軒	*hachi-hiki* *hap-piki* 八匹	*hachi-hon* *hap-pon* 八本
9	*kyū-kai* 九階	*kyū-ki* 九機	*kyū-ken* 九軒	*kyū-hiki* 九匹	*kyū-hon* 九本
10	*juk-kai* *jik-kai* 十階	*juk-ki* *jik-ki* 十機	*juk-ken* *jik-ken* 十軒	*jup-piki* *jip-piki* 十匹	*jup-pon* *jip-pon* 十本
How many…?	*nan-kai* *nan-gai* 何階	*nan-ki* 何機	*nan-gen* 何軒	*nan-biki* 何匹	*nan-bon* 何本

266

	hai 杯 cup/glass	*tsu* つ apple orange egg	*ko* 個 apple orange egg	*nin* 人 person	*mei* 名 person (*formal*)
1	*ip-pai* 一杯	*hito-tsu* 一つ	*ik-ko* 一個	*hitori* 一人	*ichi-mei* 一名
2	*ni-hai* 二杯	*futa-tsu* 二つ	*ni-ko* 二個	*futari* 二人	*ni-mei* 二名
3	*san-bai* 三杯	*mit-tsu* 三つ	*san-ko* 三個	*san-nin* 三人	*san-mei* 三名
4	*yon-hai* 四杯	*yot-tsu* 四つ	*yon-ko* 四個	*yo-nin* 四人	*yon-mei* 四名
5	*go-hai* 五杯	*itsu-tsu* 五つ	*go-ko* 五個	*go-nin* 五人	*go-mei* 五名
6	*rop-pai* 六杯	*mut-tsu* 六つ	*rok-ko* 六個	*roku-nin* 六人	*roku-mei* 六名
7	*nana-hai* 七杯	*nana-tsu* 七つ	*nana-ko* 七個	*shichi-nin* *nana-nin* 七人	*shichi-mei* *nana-mei* 七名
8	*hachi-hai* *hap-pai* 八杯	*yat-tsu* 八つ	*hachi-ko* *hak-ko* 八個	*hachi-nin* 八人	*hachi-mei* 八名
9	*kyū-hai* 九杯	*kokono-tsu* 九つ	*kyū-ko* 九個	*kyū-nin* *ku-nin* 九人	*kyū-mei* 九名
10	*jup-pai* *jip-pai* 十杯	*tō* 十	*juk-ko* *jik-ko* 十個	*jū-nin* 十人	*jū-mei* 十名
How many …?	*nan-bai* 何杯	*iku-tsu* いくつ	*nan-ko* 何個	*nan-nin* 何人	*nan-mei* 何名

3. Adjective Inflection Chart

I-Adjectives

	PLAIN FORM	STEM	POLITE FORM	*TE* FORM
bad	悪い *warui*	悪 *waru*	悪いです *warui desu*	悪くて *warukute*
beautiful	美しい *utsukushii*	美し *utsukushi*	美しいです *utsukushii desu*	美しくて *utsukushikute*
big/large	大きい *ōkii*	大き *ōki*	大きいです *ōkii desu*	大きくて *ōkikute*
black	黒い *kuroi*	黒 *kuro*	黒いです *kuroi desu*	黒くて *kurokute*
blue	青い *aoi*	青 *ao*	青いです *aoi desu*	青くて *aokute*
busy	忙しい *isogashii*	忙し *isogashi*	忙しいです *isogashii desu*	忙しくて *isogashikute*
cheap/inexpensive	安い *yasui*	安 *yasu*	安いです *yasui desu*	安くて *yasukute*
cold	寒い *samui*	寒 *samu*	寒いです *samui desu*	寒くて *samukute*
cold (to touch)	冷たい *taumetai*	冷た *tsumeta*	冷たいです *tsumetai desu*	冷たくて *tsumetakute*
cute	かわいい *kawaii*	かわい *kawai*	かわいいです *kawaii desu*	かわいくて *kawaikute*
dark	暗い *kurai*	暗 *kura*	暗いです *kurai desu*	暗くて *kurakute*
delicious	おいしい *oishii*	おいし *oishi*	おいしいです *oishii desu*	おいしくて *oishikute*
detailed	詳しい *kuwashii*	詳し *kuwashi*	詳しいです *kuwashii desu*	詳しくて *kuwashikute*

NEGATIVE FORM	PAST TENSE	NEGATIVE PAST TENSE	CONDITIONAL (*TARA* / *BA*) FORM
悪くない *waruku nai*	悪かった *warukatta*	悪くなかった *waruku nakatta*	悪かったら / 悪ければ *warukattara / warukereba*
美しくない *utsukushiku nai*	美しかった *utsukushikatta*	美しくなかった *utsukushiku nakatta*	美しかったら / 美しければ *utsukushikattara / utsukushikereba*
大きくない *ōkiku nai*	大きかった *ōkikatta*	大きくなかった *ōkiku nakatta*	大きかったら / 大きければ *ōkikattara / ōkikereba*
黒くない *kuroku nai*	黒かった *kurokatta*	黒くなかった *kuroku nakatta*	黒かったら / 黒ければ *kurokattara / kurokereba*
青くない *aoku nai*	青かった *aokatta*	青くなかった *aoku nakatta*	青かったら / 青ければ *aokattara / aokereba*
忙しくない *isogashiku nai*	忙しかった *isogashikatta*	忙しくなかった *isogashiku nakatta*	忙しかったら / 忙しければ *isogashikattara / isogashikereba*
安くない *yasuku nai*	安かった *yasukatta*	安くなかった *yasuku nakatta*	安かったら / 安ければ *yasukattara / yasukereba*
寒くない *samuku nai*	寒かった *samukatta*	寒くなかった *samuku nakatta*	寒かったら / 寒ければ *samukattara / samukereba*
冷たくない *tsumetaku nai*	冷たかった *tsumetakatta*	冷たくなかった *tsumetaku nakatta*	冷たかったら / 冷たければ *tsumetakattara / tsumetakereba*
かわいくない *kawaiku nai*	かわいかった *kawaikatta*	かわいくなかった *kawaiku nakatta*	かわいかったら / かわいければ *kawaikattara / kawaikereba*
暗くない *kuraku nai*	暗かった *kurakatta*	暗くなかった *kuraku nakatta*	暗かったら / 暗ければ *kurakattara / kurakereba*
おいしくない *oishiku nai*	おいしかった *oishikatta*	おいしくなかった *oishiku nakatta*	おいしかったら / おいしければ *oishikattara / oishikereba*
詳しくない *kuwashiku nai*	詳しかった *kuwashikatta*	詳しくなかった *kuwashiku nakatta*	詳しかったら / 詳しければ *kuwashikattara / kuwashikereba*

	PLAIN FORM	STEM	POLITE FORM	*TE* FORM
difficult	難しい *muzukashii*	難し *muzukashi*	難しいです *muzukashii desu*	難しくて *muzukashikute*
dirty	汚い *kitanai*	汚 *kitana*	汚いです *kitanai desu*	汚くて *kitanakute*
early	早い *hayai*	早 *haya*	早いです *hayai desu*	早くて *hayakute*
easy	やさしい *yasashii*	やさし *yasashi*	やさしいです *yasashii desu*	やさしくて *yasashikute*
expensive/high	高い *takai*	高 *taka*	高いです *takai desu*	高くて *takakute*
far	遠い *tōi*	遠 *tō*	遠いです *tōi desu*	遠くて *tōkute*
fun	楽しい *tanoshii*	楽し *tanoshi*	楽しいです *tanoshii desu*	楽しくて *tanoshikute*
fresh/new	新しい *atarashii*	新し *atarashi*	新しいです *atarashii desu*	新しくて *atarashikute*
good	いい *ii*	——	いいです *ii desu*	よくて *yokute*
heavy/serious	重い *omoi*	重 *omo*	重いです *omoi desu*	重くて *omokute*
hot	暑い *atsui*	暑 *atsu*	暑いです *atsui desu*	暑くて *atsukute*
interesting	おもしろい *omoshiroi*	おもしろ *omoshiro*	おもしろいです *omoshiroi desu*	おもしろくて *omoshirokute*
kind	優しい *yasashii*	優し *yasashi*	優しいです *yasashii desu*	優しくて *yasashikute*
large/spacious	広い *hiroi*	広 *hiro*	広いです *hiroi desu*	広くて *hirokute*

NEGATIVE FORM	PAST TENSE	NEGATIVE PAST TENSE	CONDITIONAL (*TARA* / *BA*) FORM
難しくない *muzukashiku nai*	難しかった *muzukashikatta*	難しくなかった *muzukashiku nakatta*	難しかったら / 難しければ *muzukashikattra / muzukashikereba*
汚くない *kitanaku nai*	汚かった *kitanakatta*	汚くなかった *kitanaku nakatta*	汚かったら / 汚ければ *kitanakattara / kitanakereba*
早くない *hayaku nai*	早かった *hayakatta*	早くなかった *hayaku nakatta*	早かったら / 早ければ *hayakattara / hayakereba*
やさしくない *yasashiku nai*	やさしかった *yasashikatta*	やさしくなかった *yasashiku nakatta*	やさしかったら / やさしければ *yasashikattara / yasashikereba*
高くない *takaku nai*	高かった *takakatta*	高くなかった *takaku nakatta*	高かったら / 高ければ *takakattara / takakereba*
遠くない *tōku nai*	遠かった *tōkatta*	遠くなかった *tōku nakatta*	遠かったら / 遠ければ *tōkattara / tōkereba*
楽しくない *tanoshiku nai*	楽しかった *tanoshikatta*	楽しくなかった *tanoshiku nakatta*	楽しかったら / 楽しければ *tanoshikattara / tanoshikereba*
新しくない *atarashiku nai*	新しかった *atarashikatta*	新しくなかった *atarashiku nakatta*	新しかったら / 新しければ *atarashikattara / atarashikereba*
よくない *yoku nai*	よかった *yokatta*	よくなかった *yoku nakatta*	よかったら / よければ *yokattara / yokereba*
重くない *omoku nai*	重かった *omokatta*	重くなかった *omoku nakatta*	重かったら / 重ければ *omokattara / omokereba*
暑くない *atsuku nai*	暑かった *atsukatta*	暑くなかった *atsuku nakatta*	暑かったら / 暑ければ *atsukattara / atsukereba*
おもしろくない *omoshiroku nai*	おもしろかった *omoshirokatta*	おもしろくなかった *omoshiroku nakatta*	おもしろかったら / おもしろければ *omoshirokattara / omoshirokereba*
優しくない *yasashiku nai*	優しかった *yasashikatta*	優しくなかった *yasashiku nakatta*	優しかったら / 優しければ *yasashikattara / yasashikereba*
広くない *hiroku nai*	広かった *hirokatta*	広くなかった *hiroku nakatta*	広かったら / 広ければ *hirokattara / hirokereba*

	PLAIN FORM	STEM	POLITE FORM	TE FORM
late	遅い *osoi*	遅 *oso*	遅いです *osoi desu*	遅くて *osokute*
light	軽い *karui*	軽 *karu*	軽いです *karui desu*	軽くて *karukute*
lonely	寂しい *sabishii*	寂し *sabishi*	寂しいです *sabishii desu*	寂しくて *sabishikute*
long	長い *nagai*	長 *naga*	長いです *nagai desu*	長くて *nagakute*
many/much	多い *ōi*	多 *ō*	多いです *ōi desu*	多くて *ōkute*
narrow	狭い *semai*	狭 *sema*	狭いです *semai desu*	狭くて *semakute*
old	古い *furui*	古 *furu*	古いです *furui desu*	古くて *furukute*
painful	痛い *itai*	痛 *ita*	痛いです *itai desu*	痛くて *itakute*
rare	珍しい *mezurashii*	珍し *mezurashi*	珍しいです *mezurashii desu*	珍しくて *mezurashikute*
red	赤い *akai*	赤 *aka*	赤いです *akai desu*	赤くて *akakute*
short	短い *mijikai*	短 *mijika*	短いです *mijikai desu*	短くて *mijikakute*
small	小さい *chiisai*	小さ *chiisa*	小さいです *chiisai desu*	小さくて *chiisakute*
soft/tender	柔らかい *yawarakai*	柔らか *yawaraka*	柔らかいです *yawarakai desu*	柔らかくて *yawarakakute*
steep	険しい *kewashii*	険し *kewashi*	険しいです *kewashii desu*	険しくて *kewashikute*

NEGATIVE FORM	PAST TENSE	NEGATIVE PAST TENSE	CONDITIONAL (*TARA* / *BA*) FORM
遅くない *osoku nai*	遅かった *osokatta*	遅くなかった *osoku nakatta*	遅かったら / 遅ければ *osokattara / osokereba*
軽くない *karuku nai*	軽かった *karukatta*	軽くなかった *karuku nakatta*	軽かったら / 軽ければ *karukattara / karukereba*
寂しくない *sabishiku nai*	寂しかった *sabishikatta*	寂しくなかった *sabishiku nakatta*	寂しかったら / 寂しければ *sabishikattara / sabishikereba*
長くない *nagaku nai*	長かった *nagakatta*	長くなかった *nagaku nakatta*	長かったら / 長ければ *nagakattara / nagakereba*
多くない *ōku nai*	多かった *ōkatta*	多くなかった *ōku nakatta*	多かったら / 多ければ *ōkattara / ōkereba*
狭くない *semaku nai*	狭かった *semakatta*	狭くなかった *semaku nakatta*	狭かったら / 狭ければ *semakattara / semakereba*
古くない *furuku nai*	古かった *furukatta*	古くなかった *furuku nakatta*	古かったら / 古ければ *furukattara / furukereba*
痛くない *itaku nai*	痛かった *itakatta*	痛くなかった *itaku nakatta*	痛かったら / 痛ければ *itakattara / itakereba*
珍しくない *mezurashiku nai*	珍しかった *mezurashikatta*	珍しくなかった *mezurashiku nakatta*	珍しかったら / 珍しければ *mezurashikattara / mezurashikereba*
赤くない *akaku nai*	赤かった *akakatta*	赤くなかった *akaku nakatta*	赤かったら / 赤ければ *akakattara / akakereba*
短くない *mijikaku nai*	短かった *mijikakatta*	短くなかった *mijikaku nakatta*	短かったら / 短ければ *mijikakattara / mijikakereba*
小さくない *chiisaku nai*	小さかった *chiisakatta*	小さくなかった *chiisaku nakatta*	小さかったら / 小さければ *chiisakattara / chiisakereba*
柔らかくない *yawarakaku nai*	柔らかかった *yawarakakatta*	柔らかくなかった *yawarakaku nakatta*	柔らかかったら / 柔らかければ *yawarakakattara / yawarakakereba*
険しくない *kewashiku nai*	険しかった *kewashikatta*	険しくなかった *kewashiku nakatta*	険しかったら / 険しければ *kewashikattara / kewashikereba*

	PLAIN FORM	STEM	POLITE FORM	*TE* FORM
strict	厳しい *kibishii*	厳し *kibishi*	厳しいです *kibishii desu*	厳しくて *kibishikute*
strong	強い *tsuyoi*	強 *tsuyo*	強いです *tsuyoi desu*	強くて *tsuyokute*
sweet	甘い *amai*	甘 *ama*	甘いです *amai desu*	甘くて *amakute*
thick	厚い *atsui*	厚 *atsu*	厚いです *atsui desu*	厚くて *atsukute*
thin	細い *hosoi*	細 *hoso*	細いです *hosoi desu*	細くて *hosokute*
warm	暖かい *atatakai*	暖か *atataka*	暖かいです *atatakai desu*	暖かくて *atatakakute*
white	白い *shiroi*	白 *shiro*	白いです *shiroi desu*	白くて *shirokute*
young	若い *wakai*	若 *waka*	若いです *wakai desu*	若くて *wakakute*

Na-Adjectives

NOTE: For simplicity, the attributive form (the form with *na*) has been omitted from this list.

	PLAIN FORM*	STEM	POLITE FORM	*TE* FORM
accurate	正確だ *seikaku da*	正確 *seikaku*	正確です *seikaku desu*	正確で *seikaku de*
bad/lousy (at some activity)	下手だ *heta da*	下手 *heta*	下手です *heta desu*	下手で *heta de*
bold	大胆だ *daitan da*	大胆 *daitan*	大胆です *daitan desu*	大胆で *daitan de*

* The "plain form" and the "dictionary form" are different for *na*-adjectives: the stem (the form without *na*) is the form found in most dictionaries.

NEGATIVE FORM	PAST TENSE	NEGATIVE PAST TENSE	CONDITIONAL (*TARA* / *BA*) FORM
厳しくない *kibishiku nai*	厳しかった *kibishikatta*	厳しくなかった *kibishiku nakatta*	厳しかったら / 厳しければ *kibishikattara / kibishikereba*
強くない *tsuyoku nai*	強かった *tsuyokatta*	強くなかった *tsuyoku nakatta*	強かったら / 強ければ *tsuyokattara / tsuyokereba*
甘くない *amaku nai*	甘かった *amakatta*	甘くなかった *amaku nakatta*	甘かったら / 甘ければ *amakattara / amakereba*
厚くない *atsuku nai*	厚かった *atsukatta*	厚くなかった *atsuku nakatta*	厚かったら / 厚ければ *atsukattara / atsukereba*
細くない *hosoku nai*	細かった *hosokatta*	細くなかった *hosoku nakatta*	細かったら / 細ければ *hosokattara / hosokereba*
暖かくない *atatakaku nai*	暖かかった *atatakakatta*	暖かくなかった *atatakaku nakatta*	暖かかったら / 暖かければ *atatakakattara / atatakakereba*
白くない *shiroku nai*	白かった *shirokatta*	白くなかった *shiroku nakatta*	白かったら / 白ければ *shirokattara / shirokereba*
若くない *wakaku nai*	若かった *wakakatta*	若くなかった *wakaku nakatta*	若かったら / 若ければ *wakakattara / wakakereba*

NEGATIVE FORM	PAST TENSE	NEGATIVE PAST TENSE	CONDITIONAL (*TARA* / *BA*) FORM
正確ではない *seikaku de wa nai*	正確だった *seikaku datta*	正確ではなかった *seikaku de wa nakatta*	正確だったら / 正確なら *seikaku dattara / seikaku nara*
下手ではない *heta de wa nai*	下手だった *heta datta*	下手ではなかった *heta de wa nakatta*	下手だったら / 下手なら *heta dattara / heta nara*
大胆ではない *daitan de wa nai*	大胆だった *daitan datta*	大胆ではなかった *daitan de wa nakatta*	大胆だったら / 大胆なら *daitan dattara / daitan nara*

	PLAIN FORM	STEM	POLITE FORM	TE FORM
bright	鮮やかだ *azayaka da*	鮮やか *azayaka*	鮮やかです *azayaka desu*	鮮やかで *azayaka de*
careful	慎重だ *shinchō da*	慎重 *shinchō*	慎重です *shinchō desu*	慎重で *shinchō de*
competent	有能だ *yūnō da*	有能 *yūnō*	有能です *yūnō desu*	有能で *yūnō de*
complicated	複雑だ *fukuzatsu da*	複雑 *fukuzatsu*	複雑です *fukuzatsu desu*	複雑で *fukuzatsu de*
convenient	便利だ *benri da*	便利 *benri*	便利です *benri desu*	便利で *benri de*
dangerous	危険だ *kiken da*	危険 *kiken*	危険です *kiken desu*	危険で *kiken de*
difficult	困難だ *konnan da*	困難 *konnan*	困難です *konnan desu*	困難で *konnan de*
diligent	勤勉だ *kinben da*	勤勉 *kinben*	勤勉です *kinben desu*	勤勉で *kinben de*
disliked	嫌いだ *kirai da*	嫌い *kirai*	嫌いです *kirai desu*	嫌いで *kirai de*
durable	丈夫だ *jōbu da*	丈夫 *jōbu*	丈夫です *jōbu desu*	丈夫で *jōbu de*
favorite	好きだ *suki da*	好き *suki*	好きです *suki desu*	好きで *suki de*
famous	有名だ *yūmei da*	有名 *yūmei*	有名です *yūmei desu*	有名で *yūmei de*
free (not busy)	ひまだ *hima da*	ひま *hima*	ひまです *hima desu*	ひまで *hima de*
fresh	新鮮だ *shinsen da*	新鮮 *shinsen*	新鮮です *shinsen desu*	新鮮で *shinsen de*

NEGATIVE FORM	PAST TENSE	NEGATIVE PAST TENSE	CONDITIONAL (*TARA* / *BA*) FORM
鮮やかではない *azayaka de wa nai*	鮮やかだった *azayaka datta*	鮮やかではなかった *azayaka de wa nakatta*	鮮やかだったら / 鮮やかなら *azayaka dattara / azayaka nara*
慎重ではない *shinchō de wa nai*	慎重だった *shinchō datta*	慎重ではなかった *shinchō de wa nakatta*	慎重だったら / 慎重なら *shinchō dattara / shinchō nara*
有能ではない *yūnō de wa nai*	有能だった *yūnō datta*	有能ではなかった *yūnō de wa nakatta*	有能だったら / 有能なら *yūnō dattara / yūnō nara*
複雑ではない *fukuzatsu de wa nai*	複雑だった *fukuzatsu datta*	複雑ではなかった *fukuzatsu de wa nakatta*	複雑だったら / 複雑なら *fukuzatsu dattara / fukuzatsu nara*
便利ではない *benri de wa nai*	便利だった *benri datta*	便利ではなかった *benri de wa nakatta*	便利だったら / 便利なら *benri dattara / benri nara*
危険ではない *kiken de wa nai*	危険だった *kiken datta*	危険ではなかった *kiken de wa nakatta*	危険だったら / 危険なら *kiken dattara / kiken nara*
困難ではない *konnan de wa nai*	困難だった *konnan datta*	困難ではなかった *konnan de wa nakatta*	困難だったら / 困難なら *konnan dattara / konnan nara*
勤勉ではない *kinben de wa nai*	勤勉だった *kinben datta*	勤勉ではなかった *kinben de wa nakatta*	勤勉だったら / 勤勉なら *kinben dattara / kinben nara*
嫌いではない *kirai de wa nai*	嫌いだった *kirai datta*	嫌いではなかった *kirai de wa nakatta*	嫌いだったら / 嫌いなら *kirai dattara / kirai nara*
丈夫ではない *jōbu de wa nai*	丈夫だった *jōbu datta*	丈夫ではなかった *jōbu de wa nakatta*	丈夫だったら / 丈夫なら *jōbu dattara / jōbu nara*
好きではない *suki de wa nai*	好きだった *suki datta*	好きではなかった *suki de wa nakatta*	好きだったら / 好きなら *suki dattara / suki nara*
有名ではない *yūmei de wa nai*	有名だった *yūmei datta*	有名ではなかった *yūmei de wa nakatta*	有名だったら / 有名なら *yūmei dattara / yūmei nara*
ひまではない *hima de wa nai*	ひまだった *hima datta*	ひまではなかった *hima de wa nakatta*	ひまだったら / ひまなら *hima dattara / hima nara*
新鮮ではない *shinsen de wa nai*	新鮮だった *shinsen datta*	新鮮ではなかった *shinsen de wa nakatta*	新鮮だったら / 新鮮なら *shinsen dattara / shinsen nara*

	PLAIN FORM	STEM	POLITE FORM	*TE* FORM
generous/lenient	寛大だ *kandai da*	寛大 *kandai*	寛大です *kandai desu*	寛大で *kandai de*
good/skillful	上手だ *jōzu da*	上手 *jōzu*	上手です *jōzu desu*	上手で *jōzu de*
gorgeous/lavish	豪華だ *gōka da*	豪華 *gōka*	豪華です *gōka desu*	豪華で *gōka de*
happy	幸せだ *shiawase da*	幸せ *shiawase*	幸せです *shiawase desu*	幸せで *shiawase de*
healthy	元気だ *genki da*	元気 *genki*	元気です *genki desu*	元気で *genki de*
honest	正直だ *shōjiki da*	正直 *shōjiki*	正直です *shōjiki desu*	正直で *shōjiki de*
important	大切だ *taisetsu da*	大切 *taiseteu*	大切です *taisetsu desu*	大切で *taisetsu de*
inconvenient	不便だ *fuben da*	不便 *fuben*	不便です *fuben desu*	不便で *fuben de*
kind	親切だ *shinsetsu da*	親切 *shinsetsu*	親切です *shinsetsu desu*	親切で *shinsetsu de*
luxurious	ぜいたくだ *zeitaku da*	ぜいたく *zeitaku*	ぜいたくです *zeitaku desu*	ぜいたくで *zeitaku de*
magnificent	立派だ *rippa da*	立派 *rippa*	立派です *rippa desu*	立派で *rippa de*
mild	温暖だ *ondan da*	温暖 *ondan*	温暖です *ondan desu*	温暖で *ondan de*
necessary	必要だ *hitsuyō da*	必要 *hitsuyō*	必要です *hitsuyō desu*	必要で *hitsuyō de*
perfect	完全だ *kanzen da*	完全 *kanzen*	完全です *kanzen desu*	完全で *kanzen de*

NEGATIVE FORM	PAST TENSE	NEGATIVE PAST TENSE	CONDITIONAL (*TARA* / *BA*) FORM
寛大ではない *kandai de wa nai*	寛大だった *kandai datta*	寛大ではなかった *kandai de wa nakatta*	寛大だったら / 寛大なら *kandai dattara / kandai nara*
上手ではない *jōzu de wa nai*	上手だった *jōzu datta*	上手ではなかった *jōzu de wa nakatta*	上手だったら / 上手なら *jōzu dattara / jōzu nara*
豪華ではない *gōka de wa nai*	豪華だった *gōka datta*	豪華ではなかった *gōka de wa nakatta*	豪華だったら / 豪華なら *gōka dattara / gōka nara*
幸せではない *shiawase de wa nai*	幸せだった *shiawase datta*	幸せではなかった *shiawase de wa nakatta*	幸せだったら / 幸せなら *shiawase dattara / shiawase nara*
元気ではない *genki de wa nai*	元気だった *genki datta*	元気ではなかった *genki de wa nakatta*	元気だったら / 元気なら *genki dattara / genki nara*
正直ではない *shōjiki de wa nai*	正直だった *shōjiki datta*	正直ではなかった *shōjiki de wa nakatta*	正直だったら / 正直なら *shōjiki dattara / shōjiki nara*
大切ではない *taisetsu de wa nai*	大切だった *taisetsu datta*	大切ではなかった *taisetsu de wa nakatta*	大切だったら / 大切なら *taisetsu dattara / taisetsu nara*
不便ではない *fuben de wa nai*	不便だった *fuben datta*	不便ではなかった *fuben de wa nakatta*	不便だったら / 不便なら *fuben dattara / fuben nara*
親切ではない *shinsetsu de wa nai*	親切だった *shinsetsu datta*	親切ではなかった *shinsetsu de wa nakatta*	親切だったら / 親切なら *shinsetsu dattara / shinsetsu nara*
ぜいたくではない *zeitaku de wa nai*	ぜいたくだった *zeitaku datta*	ぜいたくではなかった *zeitaku de wa nakatta*	ぜいたくだったら / ぜいたくなら *zeitaku dattara / zeitaku nara*
立派ではない *rippa de wa nai*	立派だった *rippa datta*	立派ではなかった *rippa de wa nakatta*	立派だったら / 立派なら *rippa dattara / rippa nara*
温暖ではない *ondan de wa nai*	温暖だった *ondan datta*	温暖ではなかった *ondan de wa nakatta*	温暖だったら / 温暖なら *ondan dattara / ondan nara*
必要ではない *hitsuyō de wa nai*	必要だった *hitsuyō datta*	必要ではなかった *hitsuyō de wa nakatta*	必要だったら / 必要なら *hitsuyō dattara / hitsuyō nara*
完全ではない *kanzen de wa nai*	完全だった *kanzen datta*	完全ではなかった *kanzen de wa nakatta*	完全だったら / 完全なら *kanzen dattara / kanzen nara*

	PLAIN FORM	STEM	POLITE FORM	_TE_ FORM
polite	丁寧だ _teinei da_	丁寧 _teinei_	丁寧です _teinei desu_	丁寧で _teinei de_
pretty/clean	きれいだ _kirei da_	きれい _kirei_	きれいです _kirei desu_	きれいで _kirei de_
promising	有望だ _yūbō da_	有望 _yūbō_	有望です _yūbō desu_	有望で _yūbō de_
rich	裕福だ _yūfuku da_	裕福 _yūfuku_	裕福です _yūfuku desu_	裕福で _yūfuku de_
safe	安全だ _anzen da_	安全 _anzen_	安全です _anzen desu_	安全で _anzen de_
simple	簡単だ _kantan da_	簡単 _kantan_	簡単です _kantan desu_	簡単で _kantan de_
strict	厳格だ _genkaku da_	厳格 _genkaku_	厳格です _genkaku desu_	厳格で _genkaku de_
useless/no good	だめだ _dame da_	だめ _dame_	だめです _dame desu_	だめで _dame de_
various	色々だ _iroiro da_	色々 _iroiro_	色々です _iroiro desu_	色々で _iroiro de_

NEGATIVE FORM	PAST TENSE	NEGATIVE PAST TENSE	CONDITIONAL (*TARA / BA*) FORM
丁寧ではない *teinei de wa nai*	丁寧だった *teinei datta*	丁寧ではなかった *teinei de wa nakatta*	丁寧だったら / 丁寧なら *teinei dattara / teinei nara*
きれいではない *kirei de wa nai*	きれいだった *kirei datta*	きれいではなかった *kirei de wa nakatta*	きれいだったら / きれいなら *kirei dattara / kirei nara*
有望ではない *yūbō de wa nai*	有望だった *yūbō datta*	有望ではなかった *yūbō de wa nakatta*	有望だったら / 有望なら *yūbō dattara / yūbō nara*
裕福ではない *yūfuku de wa nai*	裕福だった *yūfuku datta*	裕福ではなかった *yūfuku de wa nakatta*	裕福だったら / 裕福なら *yūfuku dattara / yūfuku nara*
安全ではない *anzen de wa nai*	安全だった *anzen datta*	安全ではなかった *anzen de wa nakatta*	安全だったら / 安全なら *anzen dattara / anzen nara*
簡単ではない *kantan de wa nai*	簡単だった *kantan datta*	簡単ではなかった *kantan de wa nakatta*	簡単だったら / 簡単なら *kantan dattara / kantan nara*
厳格ではない *genkaku de wa nai*	厳格だった *genkaku datta*	厳格ではなかった *genkaku de wa nakatta*	厳格だったら / 厳格なら *genkaku dattara / genkaku nara*
だめではない *dame de wa nai*	だめだった *dame datta*	だめではなかった *dame de wa nakatta*	だめだったら / だめなら *dame dattara / dame nara*
色々ではない *iroiro de wa nai*	色々だった *iroiro datta*	色々ではなかった *iroiro de wa nakatta*	色々だったら / 色々なら *iroiro dattara / iroiro nara*

4. Verb Conjugation Chart

Regular I Verbs

	PLAIN FORM	*MASU* FORM	*TE* FORM	*NAI* FORM	*TA* FORM
angry, get	怒る *okoru*	怒ります *okorimasu*	怒って *okotte*	怒らない *okoranai*	怒った *okotta*
arrive	着く *tsuku*	着きます *tsukimasu*	着いて *tsuite*	着かない *tsukanai*	着いた *tsuita*
ask	聞く *kiku*	聞きます *kikimasu*	聞いて *kiite*	聞かない *kikanai*	聞いた *kiita*
be/exist	ある *aru*	あります *arimasu*	あって *atte*	ない *nai*	あった *atta*
bake	焼く *yaku*	焼きます *yakimasu*	焼いて *yaite*	焼かない *yakanai*	焼いた *yaita*
beat	負かす *makasu*	負かします *makashimasu*	負かして *makashite*	負かさない *makasanai*	負かした *makashita*
become	なる *naru*	なります *narimasu*	なって *natte*	ならない *naranai*	なった *natta*
begin	始まる *hajimaru*	始まります *hajimarimasu*	始まって *hajimatte*	始まらない *hajimaranai*	始まった *hajimatta*
bloom	咲く *saku*	咲きます *sakimasu*	咲いて *saite*	咲かない *sakanai*	咲いた *saita*
blow	吹く *fuku*	吹きます *fukimasu*	吹いて *fuite*	吹かない *fukanai*	吹いた *fuita*
break	壊す *kowasu*	壊します *kowashimasu*	壊して *kowashite*	壊さない *kowasanai*	壊した *kowashita*
brush/polish	磨く *migaku*	磨きます *migakimasu*	磨いて *migaite*	磨かない *migakanai*	磨いた *migaita*
built, be	建つ *tatsu*	建ちます *tachimasu*	建って *tatte*	建たない *tatanai*	建った *tatta*

BA FORM	TARA FORM	POTENTIAL FORM	VOLITIONAL FORM	PASSIVE FORM	CAUSATIVE FORM
怒れば okoreba	怒ったら okottara	怒れる okoreru	怒ろう okorō	怒られる okorareru	怒らせる okoraseru
着けば tsukeba	着いたら tsuitara	着ける tsukeru	着こう tsukō	着かれる tsukareru	着かせる tsukaseru
聞けば kikeba	聞いたら kiitara	聞ける kikeru	聞こう kikō	聞かれる kikareru	聞かせる kikaseru
あれば areba	あったら attara	——	あろう arō	——	——
焼けば yakeba	焼いたら yaitara	焼ける yakeru	焼こう yakō	焼かれる yakareru	焼かせる yakaseru
負かせば makaseba	負かしたら makashitara	負かせる makaseru	負かそう makasō	負かされる makasareru	負かさせる makasaseru
なれば nareba	なったら nattara	なれる nareru	なろう narō	——	ならせる naraseru
始まれば hajimareba	始まったら hajimattara	——	——	——	——
咲けば sakeba	咲いたら saitara	——	——	——	咲かせる sakaseru
吹けば fukeba	吹いたら fuitara	吹ける fukeru	吹こう fukō	——	——
壊せば kowasebe	壊したら kowashitara	壊せる kowaseru	壊そう kowasō	壊される kowasareru	壊させる kowasaseru
磨けば migakeba	磨いたら migaitara	磨ける migakeru	磨こう migakō	磨かれる migakareru	磨かせる migakaseru
建てば tateba	建ったら tattara	——	——	——	——

	PLAIN FORM	*MASU* **FORM**	*TE* **FORM**	*NAI* **FORM**	*TA* **FORM**
buy	買う *kau*	買います *kaimasu*	買って *katte*	買わない *kawanai*	買った *katta*
catch/pull	引く *hiku*	引きます *hikimasu*	引いて *hiite*	引かない *hikanai*	引いた *hiita*
cause	起こす *okosu*	起こします *okoshimasu*	起こして *okoshite*	起こさない *okosanai*	起こした *okoshita*
carry	運ぶ *hakobu*	運びます *hakobimasu*	運んで *hakonde*	運ばない *hakobanai*	運んだ *hakonda*
clear up	晴れる *hareru*	晴れます *haremasu*	晴れて *harete*	晴れない *harenai*	晴れた *hareta*
climb	登る *noboru*	登ります *noborimasu*	登って *nobotte*	登らない *noboranai*	登った *nobotta*
closed, be	閉まる *shimaru*	閉まります *shimarimasu*	閉まって *shimatte*	閉まらない *shimaranai*	閉まった *shimatta*
commute	通う *kayou*	通います *kayoimasu*	通って *kayotte*	通わない *kayowanai*	通った *kayotta*
correct/fix	直す *naosu*	直します *naoshimasu*	直して *naoshite*	直さない *naosanai*	直した *naoshita*
cry	泣く *naku*	泣きます *nakimasu*	泣いて *naite*	泣かない *nakanai*	泣いた *naita*
cut	切る *kiru*	切ります *kirimasu*	切って *kitte*	切らない *kiranai*	切った *kitta*
deceive	だます *damasu*	だまします *damashimasu*	だまして *damashite*	だまさない *damasanai*	だました *damashita*
decorate	飾る *kazaru*	飾ります *kazarimasu*	飾って *kazatte*	飾らない *kazaranai*	飾った *kazatte*
decrease (*intransitive verb*)	減る *heru*	減ります *herimasu*	減って *hette*	減らない *heranai*	減った *hetta*

BA FORM	*TARA* FORM	POTENTIAL FORM	VOLITIONAL FORM	PASSIVE FORM	CAUSATIVE FORM
買えば *kaeba*	買ったら *kattara*	買える *kaeru*	買おう *kaō*	買われる *kawareru*	買わせる *kawaseru*
引けば *hikeba*	引いたら *hiitara*	引ける *hikeru*	引こう *hikō*	引かれる *hikareru*	引かせる *hikaseru*
起こせば *okoseba*	起こしたら *okoshitara*	起こせる *okoseru*	起こそう *okosō*	起こされる *okosareru*	起こさせる *okosaseru*
運べば *hakobeba*	運んだら *hakondara*	運べる *hakoberu*	運ぼう *hakobō*	運ばれる *hakobareru*	運ばせる *hakobaseru*
晴れれば *harereba*	晴れたら *haretara*	——	——	——	——
登れば *noboreba*	登ったら *nobottara*	登れる *noboreru*	登ろう *noborō*	登られる *noborareru*	登らせる *noboraseru*
閉まれば *shimareba*	閉まったら *shimattara*	——	——	——	——
通えば *kayoeba*	通ったら *kayottara*	通える *kayoeru*	通おう *kayoō*	通われる *kayowareru*	通わせる *kayowaseru*
直せば *naoseba*	直したら *naoshitara*	直せる *naoseru*	直そう *naosō*	直される *naosareru*	直させる *naosaseru*
泣けば *nakeba*	泣いたら *naitara*	泣ける *nakeru*	泣こう *nakō*	泣かれる *nakareru*	泣かせる *nakaseru*
切れば *kireba*	切ったら *kittara*	切れる *kireru*	切ろう *kirō*	切られる *kirareru*	切らせる *kiraseru*
だませば *damaseba*	だましたら *damashitara*	だませる *damaseru*	だまそう *damasō*	だまされる *damasareru*	だまさせる *damasaseru*
飾れば *kazareba*	飾ったら *kazattara*	飾れる *kazareru*	飾ろう *kazarō*	飾られる *kazarareru*	飾らせる *kazaraseru*
減れば *hereba*	減ったら *hettara*	——	——	——	——

	PLAIN FORM	*MASU* FORM	*TE* FORM	*NAI* FORM	*TA* FORM
decrease (*transitive verb*)	減らす *herasu*	減らします *herashimasu*	減らして *herashite*	減らさない *herasanai*	減らした *herashita*
die	死ぬ *shinu*	死にます *shinimasu*	死んで *shinde*	死なない *shinanai*	死んだ *shinda*
do one's best	がんばる *ganbaru*	がんばります *ganbarimasu*	がんばって *ganbatte*	がんばらない *ganbaranai*	がんばった *ganbatta*
drink	飲む *nomu*	飲みます *nomimasu*	飲んで *nonde*	飲まない *nomanai*	飲んだ *nonda*
end/finish (*intransitive verb*)	終わる *owaru*	終わります *owarimasu*	終わって *owatte*	終わらない *owaranai*	終わった *owatta*
enter	入る *hairu*	入ります *hairimasu*	入って *haitte*	入らない *hairanai*	入った *haitta*
fixed, get	直る *naoru*	直ります *naorimasu*	直って *naotte*	直らない *naoranai*	直った *naotta*
fly	飛ぶ *tobu*	飛びます *tobimasu*	飛んで *tonde*	飛ばない *tobanai*	飛んだ *tonda*
get on/ride	乗る *noru*	乗ります *norimasu*	乗って *notte*	乗らない *noranai*	乗った *notta*
go down	下がる *sagaru*	下がります *sagarimasu*	下がって *sagatte*	下がらない *sagaranai*	下がった *sagatta*
go up	上がる *agaru*	上がります *agarimasu*	上がって *agatte*	上がらない *agaranai*	上がった *agatta*
grow	育つ *sodatsu*	育ちます *sodachimasu*	育って *sodatte*	育たない *sodatanai*	育った *sodatta*
hear/listen	聞く *kiku*	聞きます *kikimasu*	聞いて *kiite*	聞かない *kikanai*	聞いた *kiita*
help	手伝う *tetsudau*	手伝います *tetsudaimasu*	手伝って *tetsudatte*	手伝わない *tetsudawanai*	手伝った *tetsudatta*

BA FORM	*TARA* FORM	POTENTIAL FORM	VOLITIONAL FORM	PASSIVE FORM	CAUSATIVE FORM
減らせば *heraseba*	減らしたら *herashitara*	減らせる *heraseru*	減らそう *herasō*	減らされる *herasareru*	減らさせる *herasaseru*
死ねば *shineba*	死んだら *shindara*	死ねる *shineru*	死のう *shinō*	死なれる *shinareru*	死なせる *shinaseru*
がんばれば *ganbareba*	がんばったら *ganbattara*	がんばれる *ganbareru*	がんばろう *ganbarō*	がんばられる *ganbarareru*	がんばらせる *ganbaraseru*
飲めば *nomeba*	飲んだら *nondara*	飲める *nomeru*	飲もう *nomō*	飲まれる *nomareru*	飲ませる *nomaseru*
終われば *owareba*	終わったら *owattara*	終われる *owareru*	終わろう *owarō*	終わられる *owarareru*	終わらせる *owaraseru*
入れば *haireba*	入ったら *haittara*	入れる *haireru*	入ろう *hairō*	入られる *hairareru*	入らせる *hairaseru*
直れば *naoreba*	直ったら *naottara*	——	——	——	——
飛べば *tobeba*	飛んだら *tondara*	飛べる *toberu*	飛ぼう *tobō*	飛ばれる *tobareru*	飛ばせる *tobaseru*
乗れば *noreba*	乗ったら *nottara*	乗れる *noreru*	乗ろう *norō*	乗られる *norareru*	乗らせる *noraseru*
下がれば *sagareba*	下がったら *sagattara*	下がれる *sagareru*	下がろう *sagarō*	下がられる *sagarareru*	下がらせる *sagarasery*
上がれば *agareba*	上がったら *agattara*	上がれる *agareru*	上がろう *agarō*	上がられる *agarareru*	上がらせる *agaraseru*
育てば *sodateba*	育ったら *sodattara*	——	育とう *sodatō*	——	育たせる *sodataseru*
聞けば *kikeba*	聞いたら *kiitara*	聞ける *kikeru*	聞こう *kikō*	聞かれる *kikareru*	聞かせる *kikaseru*
手伝えば *tetsudaeba*	手伝ったら *tetsudattara*	手伝える *tetsudaeru*	手伝おう *tetsudaō*	手伝われる *tetsudawareru*	手伝わせる *tetsudawaseru*

	PLAIN FORM	MASU FORM	TE FORM	NAI FORM	TA FORM
hire	雇う *yatou*	雇います *yatoimasu*	雇って *yatotte*	雇わない *yatowanai*	雇った *yatotta*
hold/organize	行う *okonau*	行います *okonaimasu*	行って *okonatte*	行わない *okonawanai*	行った *okonatta*
hurry	急ぐ *isogu*	急ぎます *isogimasu*	急いで *isoide*	急がない *isoganai*	急いだ *isoida*
invite	誘う *sasou*	誘います *sasoimasu*	誘って *sasotte*	誘わない *sasowanai*	誘った *sasotta*
know	知る *shiru*	知ります *shirimasu*	知って *shitte*	知らない *shiranai*	知った *shitta*
laugh	笑う *warau*	笑います *waraimasu*	笑って *waratte*	笑わない *warawanai*	笑った *waratta*
learn	習う *narau*	習います *naraimasu*	習って *naratte*	習わない *narawanai*	習った *naratta*
lend	貸す *kasu*	貸します *kashimasu*	貸して *kashite*	貸さない *kasanai*	貸した *kashita*
live	住む *sumu*	住みます *sumimasu*	住んで *sunde*	住まない *sumanai*	住んだ *sunda*
look for	探す *sagasu*	探します *sagashimasu*	探して *sagashite*	探さない *sagasanai*	探した *sagashita*
make	作る *tsukuru*	作ります *tsukurimasu*	作って *tsukutte*	作らない *tsukuranai*	作った *tsukutta*
meet	会う *au*	会います *aimasu*	会って *atte*	会わない *awanai*	会った *atta*
move (*intransitive verb*)	動く *ugoku*	動きます *ugokimasu*	動いて *ugoite*	動かない *ugokanai*	動いた *ugoita*
move (*transitive verb*)	動かす *ugokasu*	動かします *ugokashimasu*	動かして *ugokashite*	動かさない *ugokasanai*	動かした *ugokashita*

BA FORM	TARA FORM	POTENTIAL FORM	VOLITIONAL FORM	PASSIVE FORM	CAUSATIVE FORM
雇えば *yatoeba*	雇ったら *yatottara*	雇える *yatoeru*	雇おう *yatoō*	雇われる *yatowareru*	雇わせる *yatowaseru*
行えば *okonaeba*	行ったら *okonattara*	行える *okonaeru*	行おう *okonaō*	行われる *okonawareru*	行わせる *okonawaseru*
急げば *isogeba*	急いだら *isoidara*	急げる *isogeru*	急ごう *isogō*	急がれる *isogareru*	急がせる *isogaseru*
誘えば *sasoeba*	誘ったら *sasottara*	誘える *sasoeru*	誘おう *sasoō*	誘われる *sasowareru*	誘わせる *sasowaseru*
知れば *shireba*	知ったら *shittara*	知れる *shireru*	知ろう *shirō*	知られる *shirareru*	知らせる *shiraseru*
笑えば *waraeba*	笑ったら *warattara*	笑える *waraeru*	笑おう *waraō*	笑われる *warawareru*	笑わせる *warawaseru*
習えば *naraeba*	習ったら *narattara*	習える *naraeru*	習おう *naraō*	——	習わせる *narawaseru*
貸せば *kaseba*	貸したら *kashitara*	貸せる *kaseru*	貸そう *kasō*	——	貸させる *kasaseru*
住めば *sumeba*	住んだら *sundara*	住める *sumeru*	住もう *sumō*	住まれる *sumareru*	住ませる *sumaseru*
探せば *sagaseba*	探したら *sagashitara*	探せる *sagaseru*	探そう *sagasō*	探される *sagasareru*	探させる *sagasaseru*
作れば *tsukureba*	作ったら *tsukuttara*	作れる *tsukureru*	作ろう *tsukurō*	作られる *tsukurareru*	作らせる *tsukuraseru*
会えば *aeba*	会ったら *attara*	会える *aeru*	会おう *aō*	会われる *awareru*	会わせる *awaseru*
動けば *ugokeba*	動いたら *ugoitara*	動ける *ugokeru*	動こう *ugokō*	動かれる *ugokareru*	動かせる *ugokaseru*
動かせば *ugokaseba*	動かしたら *ugokashitara*	動かせる *ugokaseru*	動かそう *ugokasō*	動かされる *ugokasareru*	動かさせる *ugokasaseru*

	PLAIN FORM	MASU FORM	TE FORM	NAI FORM	TA FORM
mow	刈る *karu*	刈ります *karimasu*	刈って *katte*	刈らない *karanai*	刈った *katta*
need	要る *iru*	要ります *irimasu*	要って *itte*	要らない *iranai*	要った *itta*
open	開く *aku*	開きます *akimasu*	開いて *aite*	開かない *akanai*	開いた *aita*
paint	塗る *nuru*	塗ります *nurimasu*	塗って *nutte*	塗らない *nuranai*	塗った *nutta*
pass (by)	通る *tōru*	通ります *tōrimasu*	通って *tōtte*	通らない *tōranai*	通った *tōtta*
pass around	回す *mawasu*	回します *mawashimasu*	回して *mawashite*	回さない *mawasanai*	回した *mawashita*
pay	払う *harau*	払います *haraimasu*	払って *haratte*	払わない *harawanai*	払った *haratta*
play	遊ぶ *asobu*	遊びます *asobimasu*	遊んで *asonde*	遊ばない *asobanai*	遊んだ *asonda*
play (musical instrument)	弾く *hiku*	弾きます *hikimasu*	弾いて *hiite*	弾かない *hikanai*	弾いた *hiita*
push	押す *osu*	押します *oshimasu*	押して *oshite*	押さない *osanai*	押した *oshita*
put	置く *oku*	置きます *okimasu*	置いて *oite*	置かない *okanai*	置いた *oita*
put on (hat)	かぶる *kaburu*	かぶります *kaburimasu*	かぶって *kabutte*	かぶらない *kaburanai*	かぶった *kabutta*
rain/snow	降る *furu*	降ります *furimasu*	降って *futte*	降らない *furanai*	降った *futta*
read	読む *yomu*	読みます *yomimasu*	読んで *yonde*	読まない *yomanai*	読んだ *yonda*

BA FORM	*TARA* FORM	POTENTIAL FORM	VOLITIONAL FORM	PASSIVE FORM	CAUSATIVE FORM
刈れば *kareba*	刈ったら *kattara*	刈れる *kareru*	刈ろう *karō*	刈られる *karareru*	刈らせる *karaseru*
要れば *ireba*	要ったら *ittara*	——	——	——	——
開けば *akeba*	開いたら *aitara*	——	——	——	——
塗れば *nureba*	塗ったら *nuttara*	塗れる *nureru*	塗ろう *nurō*	塗られる *nurareru*	塗らせる *nuraseru*
通れば *tōreba*	通ったら *tōttara*	通れる *tōreru*	通ろう *tōrō*	通られる *tōrareru*	通らせる *tōraseru*
回せば *mawaseba*	回したら *mawashitara*	回せる *mawaseru*	回そう *mawasō*	回される *mawasareru*	回させる *mawasaseru*
払えば *haraeba*	払ったら *harattara*	払える *haraeru*	払おう *haraō*	払われる *harawareru*	払わせる *harawaseru*
遊べば *asobeba*	遊んだら *asondara*	遊べる *asoberu*	遊ぼう *asobō*	遊ばれる *asobareru*	遊ばせる *asobaseru*
弾けば *hikeba*	弾いたら *hiitara*	弾ける *hikeru*	弾こう *hikō*	弾かれる *hikareru*	弾かせる *hikaseru*
押せば *oseba*	押したら *oshitara*	押せる *oseru*	押そう *osō*	押される *osareru*	押させる *osaseru*
置けば *okeba*	置いたら *oitara*	置ける *okeru*	置こう *okō*	置かれる *okareru*	置かせる *okaseru*
かぶれば *kabureba*	かぶったら *kabuttara*	かぶれる *kabureru*	かぶろう *kaburō*	かぶられる *kaburareru*	かぶらせる *kaburaseru*
降れば *fureba*	降ったら *futtara*	——	——	降られる *furareru*	降らせる *furaseru*
読めば *yomeba*	読んだら *yondara*	読める *yomeru*	読もう *yomō*	読まれる *yomareru*	読ませる *yomaseru*

	PLAIN FORM	MASU FORM	TE FORM	NAI FORM	TA FORM
receive	もらう *morau*	もらいます *moraimasu*	もらって *moratte*	もらわない *morawanai*	もらった *moratta*
rest	休む *yasumu*	休みます *yasumimasu*	休んで *yasunde*	休まない *yasumanai*	休んだ *yasunda*
return (*intransitive verb*)	帰る *kaeru*	帰ります *kaerimasu*	帰って *kaette*	帰らない *kaeranai*	帰った *kaetta*
return (*transitive verb*)	返す *kaesu*	返します *kaeshimasu*	返して *kaeshite*	返さない *kaesanai*	返した *kaeshita*
ring	鳴る *naru*	鳴ります *narimasu*	鳴って *natte*	鳴らない *naranai*	鳴った *natta*
run	走る *hashiru*	走ります *hashirimasu*	走って *hashitte*	走らない *hashiranai*	走った *hashitta*
say	言う *iu*	言います *iimasu*	言って *itte*	言わない *iwanai*	言った *itta*
scold	しかる *shikaru*	しかります *shikarimasu*	しかって *shikatte*	しからない *shikaranai*	しかった *shikatta*
sell	売る *uru*	売ります *urimasu*	売って *utte*	売らない *uranai*	売った *utta*
send	送る *okuru*	送ります *okurimasu*	送って *okutte*	送らない *okuranai*	送った *okutta*
sing	歌う *utau*	歌います *utaimasu*	歌って *utatte*	歌わない *utawanai*	歌った *utatta*
sit	座る *suwaru*	座ります *suwarimasu*	座って *suwatte*	座らない *suwaranai*	座った *suwatta*
smoke	吸う *suu*	吸います *suimasu*	吸って *sutte*	吸わない *suwanai*	吸った *sutta*
soil	汚す *yogosu*	汚します *yogoshimasu*	汚して *yogoshite*	汚さない *yogosanai*	汚した *yogoshita*

BA FORM	*TARA* FORM	POTENTIAL FORM	VOLITIONAL FORM	PASSIVE FORM	CAUSATIVE FORM
もらえば *moraeba*	もらったら *morattara*	もらえる *moraeru*	もらおう *moraō*	もらわれる *morawareru*	もらわせる *morawaseru*
休めば *yasumeba*	休んだら *yasundara*	休める *yasumeru*	休もう *yasumō*	休まれる *yasumareru*	休ませる *yasumaseru*
帰れば *kaereba*	帰ったら *kaettara*	帰れる *kaereru*	帰ろう *kaerō*	帰られる *kaerareru*	帰らせる *kaeraseru*
返せば *kaeseba*	返したら *kaeshitara*	返せる *kaeseru*	返そう *kaesō*	返される *kaesareru*	返させる *kaesaseru*
鳴れば *nareba*	鳴ったら *nattara*	——	——	鳴られる *narareru*	——
走れば *hashireba*	走ったら *hashittara*	走れる *hashireru*	走ろう *hashirō*	走られる *hashirareru*	走らせる *hashiraseru*
言えば *ieba*	言ったら *ittara*	言える *ieru*	言おう *iō*	言われる *iwareru*	言わせる *iwaseru*
しかれば *shikareba*	しかったら *shikattara*	しかれる *shikareru*	しかろう *shikarō*	しかられる *shikarareru*	しからせる *shikaraseru*
売れば *ureba*	売ったら *uttara*	売れる *ureru*	売ろう *urō*	売られる *urareru*	売らせる *uraseru*
送れば *okureba*	送ったら *okuttara*	送れる *okureru*	送ろう *okurō*	送られる *okurareru*	送らせる *okuraseru*
歌えば *utaeba*	歌ったら *utattara*	歌える *utaeru*	歌おう *utaō*	歌われる *utawareru*	歌わせる *utawaseru*
座れば *suwareba*	座ったら *suwattra*	座れる *suwareru*	座ろう *suwarō*	座られる *suwarareru*	座らせる *suwaraseru*
吸えば *sueba*	吸ったら *suttara*	吸える *sueru*	吸おう *suō*	吸われる *suwareru*	吸わせる *suwaseru*
汚せば *yogoseba*	汚したら *yogoshitara*	汚せる *yogoseru*	汚そう *yogosō*	汚される *yogosareru*	汚させる *yogosaseru*

	PLAIN FORM	*MASU* FORM	*TE* FORM	*NAI* FORM	*TA* FORM
spend (time)	過ごす *sugosu*	過ごします *sugoshimasu*	過ごして *sugoshite*	過ごさない *sugosanai*	過ごした *sugoshita*
speak/talk	話す *hanasu*	話します *hanashimasu*	話して *hanashite*	話さない *hanasanai*	話した *hanashita*
stand	立つ *tatsu*	立ちます *tachimasu*	立って *tatte*	立たない *tatanai*	立った *tatta*
stay/remain	残る *nokoru*	残ります *nokorimasu*	残って *nokotte*	残らない *nokoranai*	残った *nokotta*
stay the night	泊まる *tomaru*	泊まります *tomarimasu*	泊まって *tomatte*	泊まらない *tomaranai*	泊まった *tomatta*
steal	盗む *nusumu*	盗みます *nusumimasu*	盗んで *nusunde*	盗まない *nusumanai*	盗んだ *nusunda*
stop (*intransitive verb*)	止まる *tomaru*	止まります *tomarimasu*	止まって *tomatte*	止まらない *tomaranai*	止まった *tomatta*
stop (of rain) (*intransitive verb*)	止む *yamu*	止みます *yamimasu*	止んで *yande*	止まない *yamanai*	止んだ *yanda*
support	養う *yashinau*	養います *yashinaimasu*	養って *yashinatte*	養わない *yashinawanai*	養った *yashinatta*
swim	泳ぐ *oyogu*	泳ぎます *oyogimasu*	泳いで *oyoide*	泳がない *oyoganai*	泳いだ *oyoida*
take	とる *toru*	とります *torimasu*	とって *totte*	とらない *toranai*	とった *totta*
take (time)	かかる *kakaru*	かかります *kakarimasu*	かかって *kakatte*	かからない *kakaranai*	かかった *kakatta*
take off	脱ぐ *nugu*	脱ぎます *nugimasu*	脱いで *nuide*	脱がない *nuganai*	脱いだ *nuida*
turn off/erase	消す *kesu*	消します *keshimasu*	消して *keshite*	消さない *kesanai*	消した *keshita*

BA FORM	*TARA* FORM	POTENTIAL FORM	VOLITIONAL FORM	PASSIVE FORM	CAUSATIVE FORM
過ごせば sugoseba	過ごしたら sugoshitara	過ごせる sugoseru	過ごそう sugosō	過ごされる sugosareru	過ごさせる sugosaseru
話せば hanaseba	話したら hanashitara	話せる hanaseru	話そう hanasō	話される hanasareru	話させる hanasaseru
立てば tateba	立ったら tattara	立てる tateru	立とう tatō	立たれる tatareru	立たせる tataseru
残れば nokoreba	残ったら nokottara	残れる nokoreru	残ろう nokorō	残られる nokorareru	残らせる nokoraseru
泊まれば tomareba	泊まったら tomattara	泊まれる tomareru	泊まろう tomarō	泊まられる tomarareru	泊まらせる tomaraseru
盗めば nusumeba	盗んだら nusundara	盗める nusumeru	盗もう nusumō	盗まれる nusumareru	盗ませる nusumaseru
止まれば tomareba	止まったら tomattara	止まれる tomareru	止まろう tomarō	止まられる tomarareru	止まらせる tomaraseru
止めば yameba	止んだら yandara	——	——	——	——
養えば yashinaeba	養ったら yashinattara	養える yashinaeru	養おう yashinaō	養われる yashinawareru	養わせる yashinawaseru
泳げば oyogeba	泳いだら oyoidara	泳げる oyogeru	泳ごう oyogō	泳がれる oyogareru	泳がせる oyogaseru
とれば toreba	とったら tottara	とれる toreru	とろう torō	とられる torareru	とらせる toraseru
かかれば kakareba	かかったら kakattara	——	——	——	——
脱げば nugeba	脱いだら nuidara	脱げる nugeru	脱ごう nugō	脱がれる nugareru	脱がせる nugaseru
消せば keseba	消したら keshitara	消せる keseru	消そう kesō	消される kesareru	消させる kesaseru

	PLAIN FORM	MASU FORM	TE FORM	NAI FORM	TA FORM
translate	訳す *yakusu*	訳します *yakushimasu*	訳して *yakushite*	訳さない *yakusanai*	訳した *yakushita*
tear up	破る *yaburu*	破ります *yaburimasu*	破って *yabutte*	破らない *yaburanai*	破った *yabutta*
think	思う *omou*	思います *omoimasu*	思って *omotte*	思わない *omowanai*	思った *omotta*
understand	分かる *wakaru*	分かります *wakarimasu*	分かって *wakatte*	分からない *wakaranai*	分かった *wakatta*
use	使う *tsukau*	使います *tsukaimasu*	使って *tsukatte*	使わない *tsukawanai*	使った *tsukatta*
wait	待つ *matsu*	待ちます *machimasu*	待って *matte*	待たない *matanai*	待った *matta*
walk	歩く *aruku*	歩きます *arukimasu*	歩いて *aruite*	歩かない *arukanai*	歩いた *aruita*
wash	洗う *arau*	洗います *araimasu*	洗って *aratte*	洗わない *arawanai*	洗った *aratta*
wear (shoes)	はく *haku*	はきます *hakimasu*	はいて *haite*	はかない *hakanai*	はいた *haita*
work	働く *hataraku*	働きます *hatarakimasu*	働いて *hataraite*	働かない *hatarakanai*	働いた *hataraita*
write	書く *kaku*	書きます *kakimasu*	書いて *kaite*	書かない *kakanai*	書いた *kaita*

BA FORM	TARA FORM	POTENTIAL FORM	VOLITIONAL FORM	PASSIVE FORM	CAUSATIVE FORM
訳せば *yakuseba*	訳したら *yakushitara*	訳せる *yakuseru*	訳そう *yakusō*	訳される *yakusareru*	訳させる *yakusaseru*
破れば *yabureba*	破ったら *yabuttara*	破れる *yabureru*	破ろう *yaburō*	破られる *yaburareru*	破らせる *yaburaseru*
思えば *omoeba*	思ったら *omottara*	思える *omoeru*	思おう *omoō*	思われる *omowareru*	思わせる *omowaseru*
分かれば *wakareba*	分かったら *wakattara*	———	分かろう *wakarō*	———	分からせる *wakaraseru*
使えば *tsukaeba*	使ったら *tsukattara*	使える *tsukaeru*	使おう *tsukaō*	使われる *tsukawareru*	使わせる *tsukawaseru*
待てば *mateba*	待ったら *mattara*	待てる *materu*	待とう *matō*	待たれる *matareru*	待たせる *mataseru*
歩けば *arukeba*	歩いたら *aruitara*	歩ける *arukeru*	歩こう *arukō*	歩かれる *arukareru*	歩かせる *arukaseru*
洗えば *araeba*	洗ったら *arattara*	洗える *araeru*	洗おう *araō*	洗われる *arawareru*	洗わせる *arawaseru*
はけば *hakeba*	はいたら *haitara*	はける *hakeru*	はこう *hakō*	はかれる *hakareru*	はかせる *hakaseru*
働けば *hatarakeba*	働いたら *hataraitara*	働ける *hatarakeru*	働こう *hatarakō*	働かれる *hatarakareru*	働かせる *hatarakaseru*
書けば *kakeba*	書いたら *kaitara*	書ける *kakeru*	書こう *kakō*	書かれる *kakareru*	書かせる *kakaseru*

Regular II Verbs

	PLAIN FORM	MASU FORM	TE FORM	NAI FORM	TA FORM
be/exist	いる *iru*	います *imasu*	いて *ite*	いない *inai*	いた *ita*
born, be	生まれる *umareru*	生まれます *umaremasu*	生まれて *umarete*	生まれない *umarenai*	生まれた *umareta*
broken, be	壊れる *kowareru*	壊れます *kowaremasu*	壊れて *kowarete*	壊れない *kowarenai*	壊れた *kowareta*
believe	信じる *shinjiru*	信じます *shinjimasu*	信じて *shinjite*	信じない *shinjinai*	信じた *shinjita*
borrow	借りる *kariru*	借ります *karimasu*	借りて *karite*	借りない *karinai*	借りた *karita*
build	建てる *tateru*	建てます *tatemasu*	建てて *tatete*	建てない *tatenai*	建てた *tateta*
can/be able to	出来る *dekiru*	出来ます *dekimasu*	出来て *dekite*	出来ない *dekinai*	出来た *dekita*
change	変える *kaeru*	変えます *kaemasu*	変えて *kaete*	変えない *kaenai*	変えた *kaeta*
collect	集める *atsumeru*	集めます *atsumemasu*	集めて *atsumete*	集めない *atsumenai*	集めた *atsumeta*
close (*transitive verb*)	閉める *shimeru*	閉めます *shimemasu*	閉めて *shimete*	閉めない *shimenai*	閉めた *shimeta*
complete	仕上げる *shiageru*	仕上げます *shiagemasu*	仕上げて *shiagete*	仕上げない *shiagenai*	仕上げた *shiageta*
continue	続ける *tsuzukeru*	続けます *tsuzukemasu*	続けて *tsuzukete*	続けない *tsuzukenai*	続けた *tsuzuketa*
decide (on)	決める *kimeru*	決めます *kimemasu*	決めて *kimete*	決めない *kimenai*	決めた *kimeta*

BA FORM	*TARA* FORM	POTENTIAL FORM	VOLITIONAL FORM	PASSIVE FORM	CAUSATIVE FORM
いれば *ireba*	いたら *itara*	いられる *irareru*	いよう *iyō*	——	いさせる *isaseru*
生まれれば *umarereba*	生まれたら *umaretara*	——	生まれよう *umareyō*	——	生まれさせる *umaresaseru*
壊れれば *kowarereba*	壊れたら *kowaretara*	——	——	——	——
信じれば *shinjireba*	信じたら *shinjitara*	信じられる *shinjirareru*	信じよう *shinjiyō*	——	信じさせる *shinjisaseru*
借りれば *karireba*	借りたら *karitara*	借りられる *karirareru*	借りよう *kariyō*	借りられる *karirareru*	借りさせる *karisaseru*
建てれば *tatereba*	建てたら *tatetara*	建てられる *taterareru*	建てよう *tateyō*	建てられる *taterareru*	建てさせる *tatesaseru*
出来れば *dekireba*	出来たら *dekitara*	——	——	——	——
変えれば *kaereba*	変えたら *kaetara*	変えられる *kaerareru*	変えよう *kaeyō*	変えられる *kaerareru*	変えさせる *kaesaseru*
集めれば *atsumereba*	集めたら *atsumetara*	集められる *atsumerareru*	集めよう *atsumeyō*	集められる *atsumerareru*	集めさせる *atsumesaseru*
閉めれば *shimereba*	閉めたら *shimetara*	閉められる *shimerareru*	閉めよう *shimeyō*	閉められる *shimerareru*	閉めさせる *shimesaseru*
仕上げれば *shiagereba*	仕上げたら *shiagetara*	仕上げられる *shiagerareru*	仕上げよう *shiageyō*	仕上げられる *shiagerareru*	仕上げさせる *shiagesaseru*
続ければ *tsuzukereba*	続けたら *tsuzuketara*	続けられる *tsuzukerareru*	続けよう *tsuzukeyō*	続けられる *tsuzukerareru*	続けさせる *tsuzukesaseru*
決めれば *kimereba*	決めたら *kimetara*	決められる *kimerareru*	決めよう *kimeyō*	決められる *kimerareru*	決めさせる *kimesaseru*

	PLAIN FORM	MASU FORM	TE FORM	NAI FORM	TA FORM
eat	食べる *taberu*	食べます *tabemasu*	食べて *tabete*	食べない *tabenai*	食べた *tabeta*
fall down	倒れる *taoreru*	倒れます *taoremasu*	倒れて *taorete*	倒れない *taorenai*	倒れた *taoreta*
find	見つける *mitsukeru*	見つけます *mitsukemasu*	見つけて *mitsukete*	見つけない *mitsukenai*	見つけた *mitsuketa*
finish	済ませる *sumaseru*	済ませます *sumasemasu*	済ませて *sumasete*	済まさない *sumasanai*	済ませた *sumaseta*
forget	忘れる *wasureru*	忘れます *wasuremasu*	忘れて *wasurete*	忘れない *wasurenai*	忘れた *wasureta*
get off (bus)	降りる *oriru*	降ります *orimasu*	降りて *orite*	降りない *orinai*	降りた *orita*
get thin	やせる *yaseru*	やせます *yasemasu*	やせて *yasete*	やせない *yasenai*	やせた *yaseta*
get up	起きる *okiru*	起きます *okimasu*	起きて *okite*	起きない *okinai*	起きた *okita*
give	あげる *ageru*	あげます *agemasu*	あげて *agete*	あげない *agenai*	あげた *ageta*
give (me)	くれる *kureru*	くれます *kuremasu*	くれて *kurete*	くれない *kurenai*	くれた *kureta*
heard, can be	聞こえる *kikoeru*	聞こえます *kikoemasu*	聞こえて *kikoete*	聞こえない *kikoenai*	聞こえた *kikoeta*
increase (*intransitive verb*)	増える *fueru*	増えます *fuemasu*	増えて *fuete*	増えない *fuenai*	増えた *fueta*
investigate	調べる *shiraberu*	調べます *shirabemasu*	調べて *shirabete*	調べない *shirabenai*	調べた *shirabeta*
late, be	遅れる *okureru*	遅れます *okuremasu*	遅れて *okurete*	遅れない *okurenai*	遅れた *okureta*

BA FORM	*TARA* FORM	POTENTIAL FORM	VOLITIONAL FORM	PASSIVE FORM	CAUSATIVE FORM
食べれば *tabereba*	食べたら *tabetara*	食べられる *taberareru*	食べよう *tabeyō*	食べられる *taberareru*	食べさせる *tabesaseru*
倒れれば *taorereba*	倒れたら *taoretara*	倒れられる *taorerareru*	倒れよう *taoreyō*	倒れられる *taorerareru*	倒れさせる *taoresaseru*
見つければ *mitsukereba*	見つけたら *mitsuketara*	見つけられる *mitsukerareru*	見つけよう *mitsukeyō*	見つけられる *mitsukerareru*	見つけさせる *mitsukesaseru*
済ませれば *sumasereba*	済ませたら *sumasetara*	済ませられる *sumaserareru*	済ませよう *sumaseyō*	済ませられる *sumaserareru*	済ませさせる *sumasesaseru*
忘れれば *wasurereba*	忘れたら *wasuretara*	忘れられる *wasurerareru*	忘れよう *wasureyō*	忘れられる *wasurerareru*	忘れさせる *wasuresaseru*
降りれば *orireba*	降りたら *oritara*	降りられる *orirareru*	降りよう *oriyō*	降りられる *orirareru*	降りさせる *orisaseru*
やせれば *yasereba*	やせたら *yasetara*	やせられる *yaserareru*	やせよう *yaseyō*	——	やせさせる *yasesaseru*
起きれば *okireba*	起きたら *okitara*	起きられる *okirareru*	起きよう *okiyō*	——	起きさせる *okisaseru*
あげれば *agereba*	あげたら *agetara*	あげられる *agerareru*	あげよう *ageyō*	——	あげさせる *agesaseru*
くれれば *kurereba*	くれたら *kuretara*	——	——	——	——
聞こえれば *kikoereba*	聞こえたら *kikoetara*	——	——	——	——
増えれば *fuereba*	増えたら *fuetara*	——	——	——	増えさせる *fuesaseru*
調べれば *shirabereba*	調べたら *shirabetara*	調べられる *shiraberareru*	調べよう *shirabeyō*	調べられる *shiraberareru*	調べさせる *shirabesaseru*
遅れれば *okurereba*	遅れたら *okuretara*	——	遅れよう *okureyō*	遅れられる *okurerareru*	遅れさせる *okuresaseru*

	PLAIN FORM	*MASU* FORM	*TE* FORM	*NAI* FORM	*TA* FORM
leave	出る *deru*	出ます *demasu*	出て *dete*	出ない *denai*	出た *deta*
memorize	覚える *oboeru*	覚えます *oboemasu*	覚えて *oboete*	覚えない *oboenai*	覚えた *oboeta*
open (*transitive verb*)	開ける *akeru*	開けます *akemasu*	開けて *akete*	開けない *akenai*	開けた *aketa*
praise	ほめる *homeru*	ほめます *homemasu*	ほめて *homete*	ほめない *homenai*	ほめた *hometa*
quit	辞める *yameru*	辞めます *yamemasu*	辞めて *yamete*	辞めない *yamenai*	辞めた *yameta*
rent	借りる *kariru*	借ります *karimasu*	借りて *karite*	借りない *karinai*	借りた *karita*
see/look/watch	見る *miru*	見ます *mimasu*	見て *mite*	見ない *minai*	見た *mita*
seen, can be	見える *mieru*	見えます *miemasu*	見えて *miete*	見えない *mienai*	見えた *mieta*
show	見せる *miseru*	見せます *misemasu*	見せて *misete*	見せない *misenai*	見せた *miseta*
sleep	寝る *neru*	寝ます *nemasu*	寝て *nete*	寝ない *nenai*	寝た *neta*
start/begin (*transitive verb*)	始める *hajimeru*	始めます *hajimemasu*	始めて *hajimete*	始めない *hajimenai*	始めた *hajimeta*
teach	教える *oshieru*	教えます *oshiemasu*	教えて *oshiete*	教えない *oshienai*	教えた *oshieta*
throw away	捨てる *suteru*	捨てます *sutemasu*	捨てて *sutete*	捨てない *sutenai*	捨てた *suteta*
turn on (lights)	つける *tsukeru*	つけます *tsukemasu*	つけて *tsukete*	つけない *tsukenai*	つけた *tsuketa*

BA FORM	*TARA* FORM	POTENTIAL FORM	VOLITIONAL FORM	PASSIVE FORM	CAUSATIVE FORM
出れば *dereba*	出たら *detara*	出られる *derareru*	出よう *deyō*	出られる *derareru*	出させる *desaseru*
覚えれば *oboereba*	覚えたら *oboetara*	覚えられる *oboerareru*	覚えよう *oboeyō*	覚えられる *oboerareru*	覚えさせる *oboesaseru*
開ければ *akereba*	開けたら *akerara*	開けられる *akerareru*	開けよう *akeyō*	開けられる *akerareru*	開けさせる *akesaseru*
ほめれば *homereba*	ほめたら *hometara*	ほめられる *homerareru*	ほめよう *homeyō*	ほめられる *homerareru*	ほめさせる *homesaseru*
辞めれば *yamereba*	辞めたら *yametara*	辞められる *yamerareru*	辞めよう *yameyō*	辞められる *yamerareru*	辞めさせる *yamesaseru*
借りれば *karireba*	借りたら *karitara*	借りられる *karirareru*	借りよう *kariyō*	借りられる *karirareru*	借りさせる *karisaseru*
見れば *mireba*	見たら *mitara*	見られる *mirareru*	見よう *miyō*	見られる *mirareru*	見させる *misaseru*
見えれば *miereba*	見えたら *mietara*	——			——
見せれば *misereba*	見せたら *misetara*	見せられる *miserareru*	見せよう *miseyō*	見せられる *miserareru*	見せさせる *misesaseru*
寝れば *nereba*	寝たら *netara*	寝られる *nerareru*	寝よう *neyō*	寝られる *nerareru*	寝させる *nesaseru*
始めれば *hajimereba*	始めたら *hajimetara*	始められる *hajimerareru*	始めよう *hajimeyō*	始められる *hajimerareru*	始めさせる *hajimesaseru*
教えれば *oshiereba*	教えたら *oshietara*	教えられる *oshierareru*	教えよう *oshieyō*	教えられる *oshierareru*	教えさせる *oshiesaseru*
捨てれば *sutereba*	捨てたら *sutetara*	捨てられる *suterareru*	捨てよう *suteyō*	捨てられる *suterareru*	捨てさせる *sutesaseru*
つければ *tsukereba*	つけたら *tsuketara*	つけられる *tsukerareru*	つけよう *tsukeyō*	つけられる *tsukerareru*	つけさせる *tsukesaseru*

	PLAIN FORM	_MASU_ FORM	_TE_ FORM	_NAI_ FORM	_TA_ FORM
visit	訪ねる _tazuneru_	訪ねます _tazunemasu_	訪ねて _tazunete_	訪ねない _tazunenai_	訪ねた _tazuneta_
wear	着る _kiru_	着ます _kimasu_	着て _kite_	着ない _kinai_	着た _kita_
work for	勤める _tsutomeru_	勤めます _tsutomemasu_	勤めて _tsutomete_	勤めない _tsutomenai_	勤めた _tsutometa_

Irregular Verbs

	PLAIN FORM	_MASU_ FORM	_TE_ FORM	_NAI_ FORM	_TA_ FORM
come	来る _kuru_	来ます _kimasu_	来て _kite_	来ない _konai_	来た _kita_
do	する _suru_	します _shimasu_	して _shite_	しない _shinai_	した _shita_

* _Dekiru_ belongs to the Regular I verbs.

BA FORM	*TARA* FORM	POTENTIAL FORM	VOLITIONAL FORM	PASSIVE FORM	CAUSATIVE FORM
訪ねれば	訪ねたら	訪ねられる	訪ねよう	訪ねられる	訪ねさせる
tazunereba	*tazunetara*	*tazunerareru*	*tazuneyō*	*tazunerareru*	*tazunesaseru*
着れば	着たら	着られる	着よう	着られる	着させる
kireba	*kitara*	*kirareru*	*kiyō*	*kirareru*	*kisaseru*
勤めれば	勤めたら	勤められる	勤めよう	勤められる	勤めさせる
tsutomereba	*tsutometara*	*tsutomerareru*	*tsutomeyō*	*tsutomerareru*	*tsutomesaseru*

BA FORM	*TARA* FORM	POTENTIAL FORM	VOLITIONAL FORM	PASSIVE FORM	CAUSATIVE FORM
来れば	来たら	来られる	来よう	来られる	来させる
kureba	*kitara*	*korareru*	*koyō*	*korareru*	*kosaseru*
すれば	したら	出来る	しよう	される	させる
sureba	*shitara*	*dekiru**	*shiyō*	*sareru*	*saseru*

Index

An all-new edition of the all-time best-selling textbook

JAPANESE FOR BUSY PEOPLE:
Revised 3rd Edition

Association for Japanese-Language Teaching (AJALT)

The leading textbook series for conversational Japanese has been redesigned, updated, and consolidated to meet the needs of today's students and businesspeople.

- Free CD with each text and workbook
- Edited for smoother transition between levels
- Hundreds of charming illustrations make learning Japanese easy
- Clear explanations of fundamental grammar

VOLUME 1
Teaches survival Japanese, or about one-third of the vocabulary and grammar typically introduced in beginner courses.

- **Japanese for Busy People I: Revised 3rd Edition, Romanized Version**
  Paperback, 296 pages, CD included   ISBN: 978-1-56836-384-4

- **Japanese for Busy People I: Revised 3rd Edition, Kana Version**
  Paperback, 296 pages, CD included   ISBN: 978-1-56836-385-1

- **Japanese for Busy People I: The Workbook for the Revised 3rd Edition**
  Paperback, 128 pages, CD included   ISBN: 978-1-56836-399-8

- **Japanese for Busy People I: Teacher's Manual for the Revised 3rd Edition**
  Paperback, 152 pages, all in Japanese   ISBN: 978-1-56836-4001

- **Japanese for Busy People: Kana Workbook for the Revised 3rd Edition**
  Paperback, 104 pages, CD included   ISBN: 978-1-56836-401-8

- **Japanese for Busy People I—App**
  Skill Practice on the Go app based on Volume I for iPhone, iPad, and iPod

VOLUME 2
Brings learners to the intermediate level, enabling them to carry on basic conversations in everyday situations.

- **Japanese for Busy People II: Revised 3rd Edition**
  Paperback, 328 pages, CD included   ISBN: 978-1-56836-386-8

- **Japanese for Busy People II: The Workbook for the Revised 3rd Edition**
  Paperback, 176 pages, CD included   ISBN: 978-1-56836-402-5

VOLUME 3
Covers intermediate-level Japanese.

- **Japanese for Busy People III: Revised 3rd Edition**
  Paperback, 328 pages, CD included   ISBN: 978-1-56836-403-2

- **Japanese for Busy People III: The Workbook for the Revised 3rd Edition**
  Paperback, 144 pages, CD included   ISBN: 978-1-56836-404-9

- **Japanese for Busy People II & III: Teacher's Manual for the Revised 3rd Edition**
  Paperback, 256 pages, all in Japanese   ISBN: 978-1-56836-405-6

JAPANESE LANGUAGE GUIDES

Easy-to-use Guides to Essential Language Skills

13 SECRETS FOR SPEAKING FLUENT JAPANESE   *Giles Murray*

The most fun, rewarding, and universal techniques of successful learners of Japanese that anyone can put immediately to use. A unique and exciting alternative, full of lively commentaries, comical illustrations, and brain-teasing puzzles.

Paperback, 184 pages, ISBN 978-1-56836-426-1

BREAKING INTO JAPANESE LITERATURE: Seven Modern Classics in Parallel Text

Giles Murray

Read classics of modern Japanese fiction in the original with the aid of a built-in, customized dictionary, free MP3 sound files of professional Japanese narrators reading the stories, and literal English translations. Features Ryunosuke Akutagawa's "Rashomon" and other stories.

Paperback, 240 pages, ISBN 978-1-56836-415-5

EXPLORING JAPANESE LITERATURE: Read Mishima, Tanizaki and Kawabata in the Original

Giles Murray

Provides all the backup you need to enjoy three works of modern Japanese fiction in the original language: Yukio Mishima's "Patriotism," Jun'ichiro Tanizaki's "The Secret," and Yasunari Kawabata's "Snow Country Miniature."

Paperback, 352 pages, ISBN 978-1-56836-541-1

READ REAL JAPANESE FICTION: Short Stories by Contemporary Writers

Edited by Michael Emmerich

Short stories by cutting-edge writers, from Otsuichi to Tawada Yoko. Set in vertical text with translations, notes, and an audio CD containing narrations of the works.

Paperback, 256 pages, ISBN 978-1-56836-529-9

READ REAL JAPANESE ESSAYS: Contemporary Writings by Popular Authors

Edited by Janet Ashby

Essays by Japan's leading writers. Set in vertical text with translations, notes, and an audio CD containing narrations of the works.

Paperback, 240 pages, ISBN 978-1-56836-414-8

BASIC CONNECTIONS: Making Your Japanese Flow   *Kakuko Shoji*

Explains how words and phrases dovetail, how clauses pair up with other clauses, how sentences come together to create harmonious paragraphs. The goal is to enable the student to speak both coherently and smoothly.

Paperback, 160 pages, ISBN 978-1-56836-421-6

JAPANESE CORE WORDS AND PHRASES: Things You Can't Find in a Dictionary

Kakuko Shoji

Some Japanese words and phrases, even though they lie at the core of the language, forever elude the student's grasp. This book brings these recalcitrants to bay.

Paperback, 144 pages, ISBN 978-1-56836-488-9

JAPANESE SPIRITUALITY

BUSHIDO The Soul of Japan *Inazo Nitobe*
Written specifically for a Western audience in 1900 by Japan's under-secretary general to the League of Nations, *Bushido* explains concepts such as honor and loyalty within traditional Japanese ethics. The book is a classic, and as such throws a great deal of light on Japanese thinking and behavior, both past and present.
Hardcover, 160 pages, ISBN 978-1-56836-440-7

MUSASHI An Epic Novel of the Samurai Era *Eiji Yoshikawa*
This classic work tells of the legendary samurai who was the greatest swordsman of all time. "... a stirring saga... one that will prove popular not only for readers interested in Japan but also for those who simply want a rousing read."—*The Washington Post*
Hardcover, 978 pages, ISBN 978-1-56836-427-8

SEPPUKU A History of Samurai Suicide *Andrew Rankin*
A collection of thrilling samurai tales tracing the history of seppuku from ancient times to the twentieth century.
Hardcover, 256 pages, ISBN 978-4-7700-3142-6

EAT SLEEP SIT My Year at Japan's Most Rigorous Zen Temple *Kaoru Nonomura*
The true story of one ordinary man's search for meaning to life at Japan's strictest Zen Temple.
Hardcover, 328 pages, ISBN 978-4-7700-3075-7

THE ESSENCE OF SHINTO Japan's Spiritual Heart *Motohisa Yamakage*
The author explains the core values of Shinto, as well as exploring the very profound aspects of the original Shinto of ancient times. He also carefully analyzes the relationships of the spirit and soul, which will provide readers with informed and invaluable insight into how spirituality affects our daily existence.
Hardcover, 232 pages, ISBN 978-1-56836-437-7

THE TWENTY GUIDING PRINCIPLES OF KARATE
The Spiritual Legacy of the Master *Gichin Funakoshi*
Gichin Funakoshi, "the father of karate," penned his now legendary twenty principles more than 60 years ago. While the principles have circulated for years, a translation of the accompanying commentary has never found its way into publication—until now.
Hardcover, 128 pages, ISBN 978-1-56836-496-4

MIND OVER MUSCLE Writings from the Founder of Judo *Jigoro Kano*
In 1882 Jigoro Kano founded Kodokan Judo in Tokyo. This book is a collection of the essential teachings by the founder, selected and compiled from his wealth of writings and lectures spanning a period of fifty-one years. Throughout his life, Kano repeatedly emphasized grasping the correct meaning of judo and putting it into practice.
Hardcover, 160 pages, ISBN 978-1-56836-497-1